EVADER

EVADER

The original *true* story of escape and evasion behind enemy lines

Denys Teare

Air Data Publications

EVADER

First published in 1954

This edition published in 1996
by Air Data Publications Limited

© Denys Teare 1996

Denys Teare is hereby identified as author of this work in accordance with
Section 77 of the Copyright, Designs and Patents Act 1988.

A CIP record for this book is available from the British Library

ISBN 0 85979 096 7

Air Data Publications Limited
Southside, Manchester Airport,
Wilmslow, Cheshire. SK9 4LL

CONTENTS

Prelude

Have you seen children running around, arms widely stretched, purring their own vocal imitations of aeroplane engines? Such a childhood fantasy developed into a rather serious ambition for me as I grew up in the 1930s. As soon as I was 15 years old, and completely against my parents' wishes, I left grammar school and signed away the next fifteen years of my life in service to the Royal Air Force.

Of course, dreams of flight are one thing, but the regimentation of RAF Halton in Buckinghamshire in 1937, with its incessant spit and polish and parade-ground inspections, made the probability of ever swooping around the sky in the cockpit of an aircraft seem extremely remote. Proceedings were enlivened by the official one-day visit of an important delegation from the Third Reich – a diplomatic indiscretion which incurred the full and well-recorded wrath of Winston Churchill – but otherwise it was three months of repetitive drill instruction and tackling the rudiments of becoming an apprentice aero-engine fitter.

Home leave, 1937

At the end of the third month, a letter arrived from my father. Apparently I was being sadly missed in the family home, and was causing considerable distress to my dear Mother. Furthermore, he pointed out, it was still possible to purchase my discharge from the service. Enclosed was the sum of £20 – probably the entire month's salary for a village headmaster. Here, then, was the final opportunity to leave the spartan barrack block and return to the comfort of the bedroom I shared with my younger brother, where my model aircraft still hung from the ceiling: it was a chance I could not turn down.

From now on my career came under the total supervision of my parents. First there was a short course at Liverpool Commercial College, and then an interview with the Trustee Savings Bank. A clean white shirt, well-scrubbed finger nails and a natural aptitude for mental arithmetic secured me the appointment of Junior Bank Clerk at Runcorn branch, just a few miles from home, paying the princely sum of £50 per annum.

The remains of the family home after the attentions of the Luftwaffe (Liverpool Blitz, 1941)

Within a few short years the unrest in Europe had erupted into warfare and the towns and cities of Britain were enduring the fury of the Nazi Blitzkrieg, the port of Liverpool being no exception. In the business of aerial bombing there is a technical term called 'creep-back', whereby the bombers begin to let their loads fall short of the target. In May 1941, during a raid on Liverpool docks, just such a thing occurred, bringing bombs down into the (then) rural area of Halewood. Crawling out of the devastated wreckage of my parents' home I made a decision. Within 12 months of that day I had not only re-entered the RAF and flown the Tiger Moth trainer, I had also crossed the Atlantic in a cargo boat and soloed an American PT27 Stearman. Climbing, diving, turning and side-slipping in the clear blue sky above the Canadian prairie brought the pure delight of fulfilling my childhood dreams.

Pilot training in Canada, 1942

The final stages of training took place at North Battleford, Saskatchewan, but I was not at ease with the twin-engined Airspeed Oxford. After spending a few days in the sick bay with temporary deafness, I was taken off the course. The sheer wretchedness of failure was partially eased by the inauguration of an entirely new flying trade – the 'Air Bomber', a post brought about by the advent of the new four-engined bombers coming into service with the RAF. After further courses at the Picton Bombing and

Gunnery School and the Mount Hope Air Navigation School, flying in Avro Ansons and Fairey Battles, I returned to Britain via New York and the liner *Queen Elizabeth*. I was now qualified as a Bomber Command 'jack of all trades', available for any emergency. The pay was the same as a pilot's, but there was not the prestige nor the responsibility.

In Staffordshire, pilots, air bombers, navigators, wireless operators and rear-gunners were all thrown together. Whilst attending lectures and living, eating and drinking together, this human assortment were expected to arrange themselves into crews of five to fly the twin-engined Vickers Wellington. This done, a conversion course on to the four-engined Handley Page Halifax followed, with the addition of a mid-upper gunner and a flight engineer. Finally came a series of cross-country flights and gunnery practices in the Avro Lancaster.

After two years of continuous training, the seven-man crew made its way North, to the Humberside bomber base of Elsham Wolds and the uncertain future beyond.

A Lancaster of 103 squadron at RAF Elsham Wolds, 1943

CHAPTER ONE

Drop into Darkness

"**B**ale out! Bale out!" came the urgent order over the intercom, and I knew that a moment far more dangerous and exciting than anything I had yet experienced was close at hand. The crippled bomber was plunging down towards the inky blackness of enemy territory below.

At dusk on 5 September 1943 we had crossed the North Sea at 20,000ft, but after making our way through the reception thrown up by the coastal defences, we had only three engines left intact. Although losing height, we reached our target – Mannheim – and found that the Pathfinders had already dropped their green flares to indicate the target area. While making our run with bomb doors open, I could see the familiar pattern made by tons of explosives dropping all over the town. There were clusters of tiny white lights which kept appearing as the incendiaries landed, and amongst them the huge orange flashes made by the 4,000lb 'cookies'. As the centre of the blazing inferno slid below my bomb sight, I pressed the release button, and the slight upward lift of the aircraft told me that my own deadly load was on its way.

Closing the bomb doors, we altered course for home. But as fast as missiles descended from the five hundred or so aircraft in the darkness around us, so also were hundreds of shells coming up from the ground and bursting dangerously near. We were by now a mile below the rest of our compatriots, and we soon began to receive far more than our share of hot shrapnel.

Suddenly the remaining starboard engine, which had been pulling so well on its own, was hit, coughed, and died out. The situation was now grim; we plunged about the sky while Bob, the pilot, wrestled with the controls to stop the wounded monster from rolling on its back. We gamely struggled along through flak and fields of waving searchlights, losing height all the time. For a time we thought that perhaps we would just reach the Channel; then one of the remaining two engines began to misfire.

A microphone switched on with a click and a voice came over the crackling intercom: "Whereabouts are we, Tommy?"

"About thirty miles from Luxembourg, I think," replied the navigator. Tommy was a born gambler, but I could tell by the tone of his voice that he did not like the heavy odds against him.

"Is everyone OK?" asked the pilot. Each man in turn switched on and answered – rear gunner, mid-upper gunner, wireless operator, engineer, navigator, and myself. At least no one had been wounded, which was something to be thankful for.

"She won't maintain height," Bob continued. "We'll probably have to jump soon, chaps."

No one had the chance to reply, for just then the spluttering engine caught fire and the aircraft lurched dangerously and hurtled downwards. With a last gallant effort Bob straightened her out once more, but she was still sinking. He pressed the button operating the fire extinguishers in the port inner engine without effect; in a few seconds the whole wing would be ablaze.

We had practised the 'abandon aircraft' routine dozens of times on the ground, so when the order was given each man knew exactly what to do. I had often wondered what my reactions would be on an occasion of extreme emergency such as this. As soon as Bob's words reached me, both hands started to work mechanically. First I snatched off my flying helmet with its electrical leads and oxygen pipe attached, lest they foul the silken cords upon which my life was about to depend. Then I jumped to my feet astride the rubber pads I had been lying on behind the bomb sights and bent down to tug at the release handle. Up came the hatch itself, helped by the pressure outside. Wind rushed into the aircraft and I felt maps swirling round my legs. My parachute was already clipped in position on my chest; all that remained was to dive head-first through the square opening in the floor.

I felt the cold rush of night air as I somersaulted through the slipstream. On the first revolution I got a glimpse of the underside and tail of the aircraft silhouetted against the moon, but on the second I saw the moon alone.

In the course of various lectures during training, I had learned the number of strands of wire used in the manufacture of a parachute rip cord, the strength of each strand, and the tests to which the completed object was subjected before coming into use. This instruction certainly increased the confidence of the pupil, but in my case I was left with the impression that the wire was made so strong in order to withstand the heavy tug required to release the parachute. In consequence, a few seconds after leaving the aircraft, I gave a terrific wrench on the chromium handle, knowing my life depended on it, and was horrified to feel it come away with no noticeable resistance whatsoever. For a ghastly split-second nothing happened, and I continued to drop like a stone. Then something flashed past my face and a mighty jolt on the harness shook every bone in my body.

I had stopped falling and seemed to be standing still in mid-air. I gathered my senses together and began to take stock of my surroundings. I was alive, my parachute was above my head forming a big round dome lowering me to Mother Earth. I looked down past my dangling legs, saw that there was still a long way to drop and felt very sick.

During the previous four hours I had heard the incessant roar of engines in my ears, but now there was a peaceful quietness, broken only by the sound of one single aircraft going away in the distance. Just then another thought flashed into my mind. Had the rest of the crew baled out, or had I misunderstood the words spoken over the intercom? Perhaps the boys would be back in England at dawn; similar instances had happened in Bomber Command. But then a huge sheet of flame lit up the countryside a couple of miles away, and the sound of a sickening crash and explosion reached me. The silence was now unbroken, and I knew that old 'S for Sugar' would definitely not see England in the morning.

Although I was slightly relieved to think I had not made a *faux pas*, I wondered if all seven of us were now drifting to earth, or whether the others were dying in the wreckage below. I peered in all directions but saw nobody.

My descent probably lasted only two or three minutes, but during the time I hung in mid-air it seemed very much longer. The ground below still looked black and threatening. Gradually, the landscape became clearer and in the moonlight I could see a wood directly beneath me and a small town at one side. The aircraft seemed to have crashed into a hillside. Quite suddenly, everything became much clearer. I could see the little houses in the town, and the church, and then the trees seemed to rush towards me. I closed my eyes, covered my face with my arms, and curled up into a ball.

Crash! Branches rushed past me, then came another jerk on my harness as my parachute got caught in the tree tops and I found myself still suspended in mid-air. After swinging about in all directions for several minutes, I finally wrapped my arms and legs tightly round nearby branches. Assuring myself that they were strong enough to take my weight, I gingerly released the buckle of the parachute harness and cautiously climbed down. With immense relief, I felt my feet touch solid earth. One fist was clenched tightly, and, looking down, I saw that my shaking hand still gripped the rip-cord handle.

I did not know whether I was in Germany, Nazi-occupied France or Luxembourg. Wherever I was, the procedure was the same. I tried to dislodge my parachute in order to bury it, together with my flying kit, but struggling in the pitch darkness of the forest I found this task far easier said than done. After wasting a quarter of an hour in a vain attempt to cut it away or shake it down, I abandoned the job. The few hours before daylight were too precious to be lost. Emptying the pockets, I regretfully threw my flying kit and Mae West in a heap on the ground. The trees were very dense, and there was a chance, unless a thorough search were made, that even the parachute might remain unseen indefinitely. Forcing my way in the darkness through the bushes, I kept in a straight line, aided by glimpses of the moon through the thick foliage, and eventually reached open fields.

In the clear moonlight, I took stock of my possessions. My celluloid escape pack was still inside my battledress, but when I opened it I found that the tube of condensed milk had split, turning the Horlicks tablets, miniature compasses, matches, and energy tablets into one sticky mess. Licking the compass clean, I tried to read the tiny dial, but it was impossible in the moonlight. So I stepped back into the wood in order to use the light from a match, but not one of the whole box would strike. I knew I would have to rely on the stars until the dawn.

I carried a sheath knife on operational flights, and used it now to cut off the tops of my sheepskin flying boots and remove my brevet and sergeant's stripes. At the squadron I had been issued with a revolver, but had left it in the billet before taking off. My only other possessions were maps and Continental money in a waterproof packet which I would open in daylight. From now on I was an evader.

I knew that my best direction lay to the south-west – perhaps a few weeks' cross-country running would bring me to the Spanish border, and eventually to the British Embassy in Madrid. Setting off at a jog-trot along the rough track by the edge of the trees, I pulled up suddenly as I heard a church clock strike one. Remembering the small town I had seen from above, I realised that it lay directly in my path. Leaving the track, I circled to the left across the fields, avoiding the town.

Half an hour of hard running over potato drills, across fields, through hedges and barbed wire brought me to a wood even denser than the one I had left. Finding it impossible to make any headway, I retraced my steps and tried to get round to the other side of the town. Here again, I found more dense woodland and also a kind of cliff which appeared to form the edge of the town.

The streets were dark and deserted, so I cautiously made my way directly across the town. Reaching the first of the buildings, I was surprised to find them derelict; tip-toeing silently along, I found two streets of shattered houses with no windows, doors or roofs. I learned later that this town had been almost completely destroyed during the 1914-18 war and a new one erected at its side. Of course, I had entered the ruined town first.

Leaving the scene of destruction behind me, I slid stealthily through the inhabited streets, keeping to the shadows. In what appeared to be the main street, I came across a route indicator, on which I read in the moonlight the distances to Metz, Strasbourg and Nancy. I was thus able to establish my position fairly accurately, and was relieved to find that I was actually over the border in Occupied France.

While I was looking at the indicator, I heard a motor approaching, and just had time to dive behind a pile of wood before it swung round the bend. Peeping out after it had passed, I got my first glimpse of enemy troops; the two uniformed occupants had probably been aroused to investigate the burning aircraft nearby.

Gliding silently along the walls, I continued my journey, passing little cafés and shops with their various advertisements. Throughout the town I did not see a single window without shutters across it. The French people seemed to have a distinct dislike for fresh air, but this was perhaps an advantage to me – otherwise some sleepless person might have heard a slight footfall, seen a dark figure flitting from shadow to shadow and given the alarm. The dogs knew something unusual was happening, however, and I could hear them howling from miles around.

Reaching open country once more, I heard the clock behind me strike three times, and realised that it would soon be daylight. I was still not far from the aircraft, and the German troops would be searching for her crew, so I went into a steady trot which I hoped to keep up without tiring too quickly. I plodded along for two hours, but my feet had become so sore that I went into a wood, crawled under a bush and rested. The soles of my feet were like pieces of raw meat, for I had left off an extra pair of socks thinking I might be too warm and my feet had been slipping up and down in the big flying boots. This had caused blisters, which had burst and re-formed. After bathing my feet in a stream, washing my hands and face and filling my rubber water bag, I lay down to sleep.

CHAPTER TWO

Pierrot

I awoke at about six o'clock and felt very refreshed. It was a beautiful September morning and one which reminded me of pre-war camping days – I would have thoroughly enjoyed a breakfast of bacon and eggs cooked over a wood fire.

My dreams stopped abruptly when I heard the sound of snapping twigs. Someone else was in the wood only a few yards away. I did not wait to see who it was, but I could vividly imagine a German soldier prodding his bayonet in the bushes, looking for the late occupants of the burnt-out Lancaster (I learned afterwards that it was Bill Milburn, another member of our crew). I squirmed along on my elbows for a hundred yards, then ran in a crouched position, keeping under cover as much as possible.

With the aid of my compass, I kept in the same direction through the woods, seeing evidence of the 1914-18 war in the overgrown trenches I jumped over, which were still littered with rusty remains of barbed wire and steel helmets. A mile farther on, I came across some more recently laid barbed-wire entanglements and a notice board with large red printing on it in French and German. I could not make out what it meant, my knowledge of both languages being slight, and thought it probably referred to the property being private, so I crawled under the wire. I went at a jog-trot among the undergrowth until I came to where the ground was dotted with holes. I then realised what the notice was – I was running over a German artillery range! Luckily, no firing was taking place that morning, but when I reached the other side safely I promised myself to walk round all red notices in future.

I was now into open country and running along the hedges, heading in the direction of a smaller wood. Reaching this, I penetrated a few yards and then came upon a sheer drop of about fifty feet covered densely with brambles and bushes. From where I stood, I could see the River Meuse twisting its way through the fields. At the foot of the cliff ran a road which made an 'S' bend, then crossed the river by a concrete bridge. It was evident that in order to continue in a straight line, I would have to cross the bridge or swim the river. I could just faintly see two figures on the bridge, so I decided to descend the cliff and get as near as possible to see whether they were guards or road workers.

A narrow footpath zigzagged steeply downwards through the bushes. I took this, but soon the steepness and loose shingle turned my cautious walk into an uncontrollable slide. Halfway down, on rounding a bush, I crashed right into a man trying to half-carry, half-push a bicycle up the pathway. I don't know which of us was more surprised. I helped him to his feet, and judged from his clothes that he was a woodcutter on his way to work. Letting my handkerchief fall to earth several times, I indicated that I had descended by parachute. He understood, looked anxiously in all directions and was obviously scared lest anyone saw him talking to me. He glanced down once or twice, probably realising he would perhaps be thrown down the rest of the cliff if I thought he would betray me. Hurriedly going through his pockets, he offered me some money, which I refused, showing him the French notes in my RAF emergency kit. I looked at his shoes but they were not worth exchanging; they should have been in the dustbin long ago. So, with a handshake and a smile, we separated.

Reaching the foot of the cliff, I left the bushes to walk along the road. My feet had become worse, and walking on the smooth roadway after the shingle gave me unimaginable relief. Hardly had I enjoyed this pleasure for ten yards when I heard the sound of motors approaching, and round the bend of the road came an army lorry full of German soldiers. Across the bridge came a second one. In a flash, I dived back into the bushes and lay there perfectly still, only a few feet from the road.

In each lorry were about twenty fully armed men dressed in green uniform, half of them armed with rifles and bayonets and the other half with sub-machine guns. I realised that they were part of the search party turned out to look for the crew of the Lancaster. When they had disappeared in the distance, I crept out and went towards the bridge to get a closer look at the two men. They were both in civilian clothes, so I walked past them with my hands in my pockets, whistling 'Alouette' and trying to look unconcerned, as if I had lived there all my life. Even though my clothes looked a bit odd, I could hardly be described as having a military appearance. I wore no hat, no brass buttons, no badges and no chevrons. I needed a shave and a haircut and did not expect anyone to recognise the colour of my battledress. However, these two men – as I found out later – had lived there all their lives and regarded me with suspicion while I was still a hundred yards away. Drawing level, I nodded my head and gave a slight grunt as if in greeting, but they just gaped at me in amazement. Walking right past them and over the bridge, I did not turn until I was two hundred yards on the other side. They were both still peering in my direction; apparently I looked like anything but a local inhabitant!

On either side of the road stretched potato and turnip fields, and instead of the hedges one sees in England there were apple and pear trees every fifty yards or so. These were laden with fruit, and needless to say I helped myself. I hoped to sight an isolated farm which I might approach without being seen. Then I would explain with signs and drawings who I was, and hope that the occupants would be patriotic and give me assistance. After trudging along the dusty road for a couple of miles, I saw a car approaching. There was no cover at hand so I ran quickly into the turnip field and knelt there, pulling up weeds as though I were a farm worker. The vehicle passed by unheeding, so I continued on my way. For three more miles I walked wearily along without seeing a single house, but I was obliged to resort to pulling weeds on two other occasions – first for a cyclist, and next for a motorcyclist. On my right were a railway line and a canal, both gradually converging on to the road. Eventually, I reached the point where they crossed; there I sat down and bathed my feet in the canal. It was there that I met Pierrot and M.Pierre, who were guarding the bridge.

In Occupied France, every bridge of even the slightest importance was guarded; the main ones by German troops, those of lesser importance by local Frenchmen conscripted for the work. At certain times during the day and night, each bridge was visited by German patrols, and if they found a Frenchman absent or not alert, he was punished. Although these men were unarmed, they were expected to resist attempts by saboteurs or paratroops, and if the bridge was wrecked they were held responsible. In some cases their families had been taken as hostages. The two men I had passed on the first bridge must have been on duty.

Pierrot was a very different person from the labourer I had met earlier in the morning. I will never forget the excitement in his dark eyes when he realised who I was. He danced round shaking my hand again and again, hardly believing that here was a real live *aviateur anglais.* He was crazy about aeroplanes; night after night he listened to the deep roar of our heavy bombers and in the daylight strained his eyes into the sky searching for the American Fortresses, usually flying so high that they were almost out of sight. He had wished time and time again that he could see a parachutist come down and help him to escape. And now before him stood an Englishman. At eight o'clock that morning he had been along to see the smoking ruins of my aircraft before mounting guard on the bridge. Pierrot's companion was a small middle-aged man, very shabbily dressed, with an unlit cigarette drooping from his lips. He badly needed a shave, and the bottom row of his dirty, tobacco-stained teeth overlapped the top.

Alongside the bridge was a stone cabin, into which they motioned me. This was used as a guardroom-cum-sentry box, and in one corner a wood fire was burning – the smoke going out through a hole in the roof. The only furniture was a wooden bench, and on the floor was a straw-filled palliasse. An earnest discussion took place between the two men. There was obviously a difference of opinion, and it looked as though the elder wanted to give me some food and let me wander off while Pierrot wished to take me to his home. At length, a decision seemed to have been reached. Pierrot thrust a couple of apples in my hand, then dashed off on his bicycle down the towpath.

When I was alone with M.Pierre, he seemed uneasy in case anyone approached, but he produced a piece of dark bread and a small slice of raw bacon. As he handed them to me his fingers trembled and the bacon fell on to the earth floor. Cursing, he picked it up, scraped it with his penknife and rebalanced it on the bread. This was my first taste of black bread, and although the bacon was now rather dirty and smaller than a

'Pierrot' Patural (on the right) with the author

matchbox, I was hungry enough to be grateful for it. From another pocket my host took out half a bottle of wine, from which he filled a small glass and handed it to me. It tasted rather sour, but I found it quite refreshing; twice I emptied the glass and twice M.Pierre offered me more, trying to tell me it was good stuff.

Unfolding my small escape maps and, using signs, I asked M.Pierre to indicate where I was, pointing in the direction by which I had arrived. He repeated "St. Mihiel" several times, until I gathered that this was the name of the town through which I had passed in the darkness. I had found two handkerchiefs in my waterproof escape packet, one printed with the map of Germany on one side and Northern France on the reverse side, the other one with maps of Italy and Southern France. Searching through the German towns, my companion put his finger on Berlin; making whistling noises and indicating with his hands the dropping of bombs, he looked questioningly into my face. I nodded my head and he shook my hand with great approval. I pointed out other German towns I had bombed, and managed to make him understand that I had never dropped a single bomb on any target in France. He grinned approval, spat on the floor and babbled some incomprehensible phrase which ended in the word "Hitler".

Fingering the map of Italy, he repeated his sign-language question. Pointing first to Turin and then Milan, with the accompanying sound effects, I gave my answer. He appeared slightly perturbed and said a lot more in French that I did not understand. Then he tried German, to which I shook my head and said "nix", whereupon he changed to a third language which I believed was either Italian or Spanish – but still I could not understand him.

At that moment young Pierrot returned on his bicycle with a sack over his shoulder. He spoke to the older man, then turning to me and using the words *'Mama', 'Papa',* and *'Babba',* gave me to understand that M.Pierre was an Italian, born in Turin, and that the rest of his family still lived there. Noticing my worried expression, M.Pierre indicated his attitude towards the war by spitting on the floor, banging his fist on the bench, and disgustedly muttering *"Boches"* and *"C'est la guerre."* I learned later that he had never declared his true nationality when the Germans overran France but had continued to live as a Frenchman, proprietor of a little café in a village nearby, where he lived with his wife and twenty-two year old daughter.

Opening the sack, Pierrot produced some civilian clothes and a note written in English which read: 'Follow the boy, he will lead you to friends.' This was luck, I thought, and proceeded to change out of my uniform.

Had the Nazi search parties seen the figure which walked alongside the canal ten minutes later, I doubt if their suspicions would have been aroused. With a fishing-rod under my arm, a black beret on my head, an old sports jacket which was too tight across the back and too short in the sleeves, and a pair of trousers with several inches tucked up at the bottom, I was a typical country yokel looking for somewhere to sit and fish.

On the opposite bank, Pierrot wheeled his bicycle and carried the sack – which of course now contained my RAF uniform. He remained on the other side so that if I were stopped and questioned he could get away without being associated with me. In this manner we walked along for about a mile, turning and grinning at each other from time to time.

Farther along, a bridge crossed the canal, and making signs that I should continue walking, Pierrot jumped on his bicycle and rode ahead. A few minutes later I saw him coming towards me on my side of the canal. As we walked along side-by-side he produced photographs, and wheeling his bicycle with one hand and making signs with the other he described his family. I learned that he was eighteen years of age, lived with his parents, had a sister, Jeannette, aged 21 and another, Annie, a year older.

Eventually, we reached another bridge, beside which stood a few wooden shacks. In the doorway of one stood a short, plump, dark-haired Frenchwoman whose sun-tanned arms and face were evidence of the hard-working outdoor life she led. When I entered, the door was locked and the lace curtains drawn across the windows.

Glancing round the room, I saw it contained four plain wooden chairs, a table covered with oilcloth, a huge old-fashioned dresser, which looked as if it had been handed down from generation to generation, a pile of firewood, a stove with a pipe leading through the ceiling, and a shallow stone sink with a water pump beside it. On a shelf in a corner stood what appeared to be the only link with twentieth-century England – a small radio set.

An attractive-looking girl leaned against the table; I recognised her from the photographs as Jeannette. As she came forward to shake hands I saw she was a cripple, unable to walk without the aid of two sticks. The small dark lady, Pierrot's mother, motioned towards the sink, indicating that I could have a wash. Pierrot pumped some ice-cold water which was very refreshing as I swilled my sweaty face and arms. The piece of soap I had been given was very gritty, almost like pumice stone, and made no lather. Seeing that I was unaccustomed to such soap, the mother explained that the Germans took all the fats required for soap manufacture and that even the gritty clay-like substance could only be purchased on coupons. My uniform was produced from the sack and thoroughly examined. I put the battledress on Pierrot and he walked about the room in it, highly delighted. In my pockets were a few odds and ends – pennies, a match box, chewing gum, and the usual oddments – which aroused considerable interest.

A knock came on the door and I was ushered into the bedroom until the visitor had been identified. It was the father of the household. He also was very dark and had a sunburned complexion, partly hidden by a black, walrus moustache. I was introduced and we shook hands. He apparently made no objection to my presence and simply agreed with his wife's decision to help me all she could, much to my relief (I later learnt that my own navigator walked one hundred and fifty miles before he found a family willing to accept him into their household in this way).

It was now noon, and the table was set for dinner. A thick soup was served containing potatoes and haricot beans, mashed and sieved to a thick paste in which the spoon would almost stand upright. I was hungry and it tasted good. The second course was mashed potatoes and meat of a dark colour and strong taste – my first piece of horse-flesh. Black bread was put on the table in the form of a long, thin loaf; it was actually dark brown and coarse. Each person, as he wanted a piece, took the loaf, hugged it to his chest, and hacked away a slice with a penknife. The last slice would be rather grubby – especially as, before being delivered, the bread would be carried tied to the handlebars of a bicycle, or over the shoulder of a school child, or brought in the cart by a farm labourer who would use it as a whip! Very weak beer was drunk out of small quarter-pint glasses.

After dinner all the family, with the exception of the little cripple, shook hands with me and left to return to their work. Madame worked in the fields for a local farmer. Monsieur was a canal labourer, his job being to keep the sides of the canal free from weeds and rushes. Pierrot was an apprentice blacksmith in a nearby village.

The door was re-locked as they went out and I helped Jeanette to wash the dishes. After that, with pencil and paper and sign language, we carried on an interesting 'conversation'. With a sad expression on her face, she wrote down the name of President Roosevelt, and told me with resentful gestures towards her deformed legs that she had suffered from infantile paralysis since she was six.

I wondered who had written the note in English. Jeanette told me that that it was from a lady who lived nearby and would be visiting the house after dark. There was a map pinned on the wall beside the radio and I pointed out Liverpool, my home town, whereupon she showed me exactly where I was in France. We measured the distance, and when I said "It's a hell of a long way to walk," she seemed to understand and agree with me.

Hearing a railway engine nearby, Jeanette ushered me through a door leading to her bedroom. Looking through the lace curtains at the window I saw a train standing in the little village station less than a hundred yards away. Laughingly, Jeanette pointed to some German soldiers who were leaning out of the carriage windows. Screwing up her face in disgust, she said *"Soldats allemands,"* and, patting me on the back, *"Aviateur anglais"*.

Seeing how tired I was, she pointed to the bed and indicated that I should rest. Then she hobbled out of the room, shutting the door behind her. Taking off my shoes, I lay down and thought how fortunate I was still to be alive and in the hands of such good-hearted, patriotic French people. But before dropping off to sleep my thoughts wandered back to England, to my home, where a telegram would by now have been received saying that I had failed to return from the night's air operations.

I slept for several hours, then awoke to find Jeanette preparing the evening meal. Pierrot was the first to return. Although he had guarded the bridge in the morning, he was still required to continue his normal work for the rest of the day. His next turn of duty would probably fall due in a fortnight's time, as each man in the village between the ages of sixteen and sixty had to take his turn. The father and mother came home at seven o'clock and we all sat down to supper. The meal was almost identical with the midday one, except that Jeanette had baked a special plum tart for the occasion. When the supper dishes had been washed, we all sat round the table, and Pierrot bombarded me with questions about flying, bombing and baling out.

CHAPTER THREE

Madame Barbierri

After dark, there was a tap on the door. I stepped quickly into the bedroom and waited behind the door until Jeanette called me. The visitor was a tall, thin, white-haired old lady. Stepping forward she shook my hand and bade me "Good evening" in a quaint French-American accent. Despite her seventy years, Madame Barbierri stood very erect and I learned later that she was far more capable of doing a hard day's work than most of the women I knew who were half her age.

Speaking quietly in her curious accent, she told me she had written the note and asked if I had destroyed it. Apologising for her speech, she explained that after living four years in America, she had hardly spoken a word of English for twenty-five years. She and the others in the room hated the Germans, and she gave me instances of their barbaric behaviour towards the French population. They wished to help me as much as possible, but would have to take great care; any person arrested for giving assistance to Allied airmen was liable to be tortured and eventually executed. I felt very uncomfortable at the thought that these people were risking their lives for me, and asked the old lady to express my deepest thanks for everything they had done so far.

Next we discussed my immediate future. I told Mme Barbierri that I intended setting off on foot in the direction of Spain, dressed in civilian clothes. This, she said, was an impossibility; I should be caught and shot within a few hours. I reminded her that if I retained some item of military clothing – for example, my RAF shirt or trousers – no matter what the rest of my clothing was, I was fully entitled by international law to receive the respect and treatment due to a prisoner of war. Turning to the French family, Mme Barbierri babbled in her native tongue, repeating my words, at which everyone laughed, making a rather grim joke of my ideas. "Perhaps people in England believe that international laws are kept," she said, "but we French people have been under the Germans for over three years now, and know their cruel and dishonourable methods."

I was persuaded to stay with the family for three days, until the hue and cry in the district had died down, before venturing farther afield. The house was small, with very little room to spare, so Mme Barbierri had prepared a bed for me in her own home nearby. Looking at the clock, she saw it was almost ten and told me that a curfew was in operation throughout France, and that German soldiers had orders to shoot anyone found in the streets after that hour. Putting on the black beret and the jacket, I bade "*Bonsoir*" to Jeanette and her father. Pierrot went outside to make sure the coast was clear and then, with the two ladies linking arms with me, I stepped out into the darkness. I was hustled along in silence for about two hundred yards, then gently guided through a doorway. A match was struck and a candle lit, and in the dim light I saw we were in a kitchen similar to the one we had left, except that everything was on a smaller scale. Whispering goodbye and taking my hand in hers, rough as sandpaper through years of potato picking, Pierrot's mother slipped back into the darkness. The old lady led the way through the cottage, holding the candle aloft, to a small bedroom. Pointing to the bed, she said in English, "Sleep well," then went out, quietly shutting the door behind her. I lost no time in undressing and sliding between the snow-white sheets, blew out the candle, and fell fast asleep.

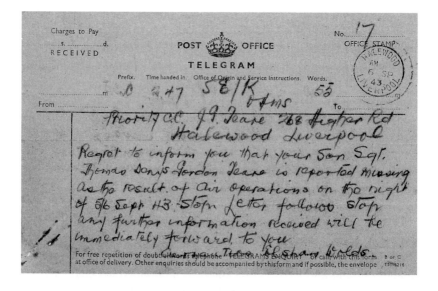

I awoke to see the sun streaming through the window. As I lay in bed thinking, the village clock struck eight. Sitting up, I examined my surroundings. Through the window I could see the railway and the station. Then I was surprised to hear the church clock again strike eight. Apparently, this was a custom in many French country villages; when the workers in the field are uncertain how many times the village clock has struck, they need only wait a further two minutes to hear the hour chime again.

I dressed and made my way to the kitchen. The cottage was little more than a wooden shed sectioned off into four rooms, but it was so homely that I felt it unfair to use the word 'shack' to describe it. Mme Barbierri greeted me with *"Bonjour,"* then asked me in English if I had slept well. She poured out a bowl of hot coffee and dropped in a lump of sugar. This, together with a piece of bread and butter, was my breakfast. I ate it slowly, realising there was nothing to follow – but I noticed that when the old lady took her own breakfast, no sugar went in the coffee and no butter on the bread. Shortly afterwards, M. Barbierri came back from Mass. He was the kindest old gentleman I have ever known. Most of his life had been spent in the building trade, but now he was a watchman at the remains of a factory nearby. He had travelled round China and the Pacific about fifty years previously, and served with distinction with the French Army in the First World War. In his buttonhole were miniature medal ribbons for the *Croix de Guerre* and *Médaille Militaire*. Twice he had been wounded in the trenches, leaving him handicapped with a distorted arm. M.Barbierri brought news from the village that the Germans were searching the district for parachutists, but luckily a house-to-house search was unlikely here.

The rest of the day I spent wandering round the rooms, playing with the two cats and gazing through the windows, always ducking out of sight if anyone approached. We had two meals during the day, one at midday and the other about seven in the evening; potatoes were the main ingredient of both. I passed the time helping Mme Barbierri with the housework, peeling potatoes, washing dishes and dusting.

Pierrot called at the house at eight o'clock, and, after carrying out a careful reconnaissance, he and the old lady escorted me to his home. Here we had a council of war. I emphasised that I wished to move on within the next couple of days, but everyone was against me; they advised me to hide in the village until the Allies had driven away the Germans. I persisted in my views until I saw an unhappy expression come into their faces. Mme Barbierri suggested that perhaps I did not wish to stay with them because they could only offer the meagre rations and humble home of peasant folk. Immediately I told Mme Barbierri to translate a violent denial of this; I was sure I could not find a better home throughout the whole of France.

Monsieur and Madame Barbierri with Jeanette Patural and their recently arrived visitor, still sporting a white aircrew sweater

The eldest daughter, Annie, was married and lived in Paris; she was expected home in a fortnight with her husband Henri, and baby daughter. Henri Moratille, who worked on the railway, was in daily contact with a number of people, and perhaps he would know of someone in the Resistance Movement. Eventually, I was persuaded to wait until he came. The fourteen days passed very slowly. I paced up and down the kitchen of Mme Barbierri's little cottage hour after hour waiting for nightfall, when Pierrot would call and take me to his home for the evening. I was picking up the language very quickly and could now make myself understood without Mme Barbierri's assistance. Each night Pierrot asked me more and more questions about flying, football and life in England. He was very interested in the possibility of my parachute and flying kit being still in the wood, and I drew sketches to the best of my ability showing where it was located. One evening he went along on his bicycle, but after an hour's search he returned empty-handed. The thought of the full flying kit and the yards and yards of silk in the parachute rotting away in the woods eventually became too much for him, and it was agreed that Pierrot should show me a route by which I could cycle to the edge of the town without danger of meeting anyone. From there I would be able to retrace my journey of the week before.

It was a glorious Sunday morning when we set off. I was riding the father's bicycle and had the necessary tax card in my pocket. The route took us along narrow lanes and footpaths, and Pierrot pointed out a black scar on the hillside – all that remained of my aircraft. We did not linger beside it in case we aroused suspicion. Although Pierrot assured me there had been no smell of burning flesh or charred human remains, I still wondered and worried about the rest of the crew.

Pushing our cycles along narrow pathways in the woods, I saw more remains of the 1914–18 war: overgrown trenches, twisted metal and rusty barbed wire. Reaching the outskirts of the town, I recognised a few landmarks and knew my position. Remembering to ride on the right-hand side of the road, I led the way through the streets. Everything looked very different now, but I continued to turn left and right as my memory guided me. There were several people about, children playing, and a few German soldiers whom I rode straight past with little more than a sideways glance. Without mishap we reached the cart-track leading to the woods and were soon standing on what I believed to be the exact spot where I first examined my compass in the moonlight.

I hoped to be able to walk a hundred yards through the bushes and find my parachute without much difficulty. But after the first few paces, I found the wood so thick that it was like looking for the proverbial needle in a haystack. Peering up into the tree tops for a glimpse of white silk, we wandered round in circles until we had to admit defeat. We arrived back tired and disappointed, but I was glad of the exercise.

The following weekend, the young family arrived from Paris. Henri was a smart-looking young fellow about my own age. With the assistance of Mme Barbierri he told me that he would contact a person who had already helped several Allied aircrew to return home via Spain. At first I found it difficult to understand his French, having become acquainted by now with the rough country speech of my hosts. After listening earnestly for half an hour, however, I began to pick up his words more clearly. He advised me to put completely out of my head all ideas of walking off on my own as being both unsafe and impractical. Although I was comparatively secure in this little village, I could not possibly travel far without being asked to produce my identity card. He asked me to be patient, and wait until his next visit a fortnight hence, when he assured me he would bring good news.

CHAPTER FOUR

Waiting for News

The following two weeks passed even more slowly than the first, for by now the routine was no longer new to me. I would rise, have my piece of bread and bowl of coffee, wash the bowls and put them in the cupboard, then grind some corn. This was a long and tedious job. Mme Barbierri had 'gleaned' the ears of wheat, going on her hands and knees after the harvest had been gathered. Taking a handful of the precious grain, I would put it in the coffee grinder, then turn the handle round and round until I had made sufficient flour for the pastry of a blackcurrant tart to eat at midday. The grinding and sifting of one pound of flour employed me continuously for three hours. Several times a day, I would watch M.Barbierri toddle off to Mass. This was his only pleasure in life, for I could see that everything was not always peaceful in the 'Home Sweet Home'. The old lady would regularly unleash a terrific temper, giving the poor old chap a dog's life. She herself was an atheist and at the least opportunity she would cruelly ridicule his religion, making fun of the Virgin Mary. This made the old man clench his fists and dash off to church to pray for forgiveness for her.

When her temper had subsided, M. Barbierri would return to the house and spend the rest of the day with the rabbits, which he bred in a lean-to at the rear. Everyone in France kept rabbits to augment the rations, which I found were much less than we had at home. A single week's ration of most foodstuffs in England would be expected to last a month or more in France under Nazi occupation.

Pierrot called for me each evening, and I easily picked up the card games we played. My vocabulary was increasing, and gradually I learned to understand the language at the speed it came over the radio. The most important moment each evening was when we crowded round the receiver, tuned to a whisper, and listened to the news from the BBC in London. In between news items, popular patriotic songs – which of course were forbidden by the Germans – were played. As I listened, they began to affect me as they did the rest of the household. I got a strange feeling inside as though I must march down the street shouting the *Marseillaise*. Then would come a sadder tune, and news of the poor French prisoners, the slave workers and the heroes dying in concentration camps. Someone would say quietly *"Pauvre France",* and, glancing round the room at the tear-filled eyes, I began to realise what the years of occupation had meant to these people.

The humble wooden dwelling that became my first sanctuary under Nazi occupation
(Sampigny, Meuse)

One afternoon, a letter bearing the Paris postmark came under the door. It was from Henri. Jeanette opened it and came hurrying across as fast as her crippled legs and two sticks would carry her to tell me the news. Henri had asked for a photograph and my size in shoes. The first item was wanted to put on a false identity card, the size of shoes because I would be supplied with a pair of rope-soled plimsolls to travel in silence. The reason was that this particular escape method involved passing through coastal defences, leaving France by rowing boat, and being picked up offshore by British submarine. The letter itself gave no details, and, apart from the two requests, appeared to be just an ordinary letter of a young man to his sister-in-law. Jeanette dispatched one of the small photos of me in civilian clothes which had been specially taken in England for use in occupied countries, and I waited eagerly until the next weekend.

Saturday morning seemed unbearably long as I watched by the window for Henri to appear. At last I saw him in the distance, with little Françoise in his arms and Annie at his side, walking towards the house where I knew Jeanette and Pierrot awaited the news almost as eagerly as I did. As soon as it was dusk, I slipped on my coat and beret. Without waiting for Pierrot to call for me, I stepped quickly and silently along the canal bank to his home. Tip-toeing to the windows, I peered through the cracks in the shutters, listening to the conversation going on inside to make certain that the family was alone. Pierrot answered my knock. Inside, I listened eagerly to Henri's good news. An agent – possibly a woman who could speak English – was coming to the village in seven days' time and would bring a French identity card bearing my photograph. She would then hand me over to another agent who would escort me to the coast.

I danced round the kitchen table with joy at the thought of being back in England within a few days; the weeks in France living on black bread and potatoes would seem like a nightmare. But I knew I would never forget the wonderful hospitality given to me by these humble folk at such a great risk.

The visitor would probably arrive by train at Leroville, a railway junction three miles away, and walk to the village. Only two trains a day arrived from Paris, and after allowing an hour for the walk, I knew my unknown friend would arrive in the village either at nine o'clock in the morning or five in the afternoon.

Each day I waited, first listening for the express whistle in the far distance. Then I counted the minutes until I could expect someone to walk up the path towards the house. This went on for a fortnight, during which my eyes hardly left the windows. Every time an unfamiliar figure approached the cottage my heart missed a beat – but my hopes always ended in disappointment.

The next time I saw Henri, he explained that several members of the organisation which had planned to repatriate me had been arrested. The man with whom Henri had made the necessary contacts, together with several others, had disappeared from Paris for safety. This was very sad news to me, for I had banked on being home within a few days, and it was now six weeks since I had gone into hiding.

Once more I told my friends that I had better set off on foot to the Spanish frontier. I knew the winter would soon be here. Food would be more scarce then – especially at Mme Barbierri's, where the little supply of corn was almost gone. With an extra mouth to feed, the store of bottled fruit, which would have lasted the old couple until the spring, was nearly finished. However, when I had spoken of this to M.Barbierri a few days before, he had insisted that I was welcome to stay with them as long as I wished. When they came to eat the last potato it would be cut in three, the same as everything else had been.

Henri begged me to have patience. He knew several other patriotic Parisians through whom he thought he could contact another group of the Resistance Movement. He returned to Paris as usual on the Sunday evening, taking with him the second of my passport-size photos. The previous one was believed to have fallen into enemy hands when the arrests were made.

Half-way through the following week, Jeanette received a letter. Again it was mainly on ordinary everyday topics, such as the weather, the health of the family and so forth. But glancing through quickly, we came to the vital sentence: 'Denise will receive a visitor next week; it will be a big surprise.' My name had been put in the feminine form to allay suspicion.

During the evening, we read that sentence over and over, mystified by the words 'big surprise'. Could it mean that one of my crew was in hiding nearby and we were being brought together? Could the visit be a British Secret Service agent? Would we be surprised by the visitor arriving in the disguise of a German soldier?

The monotony of the rest of the week was relieved during a couple of afternoons when I went potato-picking with the two ladies and Pierrot. Almost all the crops in France were commandeered for transportation to Germany, each farmer being allowed only a small piece of land for local use. The farmer for whom Pierrot's mother worked had sown a field with potatoes, then sold it in drills to the villagers before the crop had actually grown. M. and Mme Barbierri had been allowed one complete drill to last them throughout the year. Larger families were allowed as many as five or six drills, but since the crops were likely to be better in some parts of the field than others, all the names and numbers of the drills were drawn from a hat. Now that the crop was ready, the farmer had been along the drills with a horse-drawn digger and each family was left to pick its own potatoes.

The next week came round and both families awaited the mysterious visitor with an air of tense excitement. I continued to turn the coffee grinder for several hours each morning, but always kept a sharp look-out through the windows. During the week there were several visitors to see M.Barbierri in connection with the church, where he was churchwarden, bell-ringer and general handyman. Each time anyone entered the garden gate I would dash quickly out of the kitchen into the adjoining room, listening with my ear against the keyhole to the village gossip until the visitors had left, when Mme Barbierri would call in her quaint English accent, "Come in".

Day after day went by until the end of the week when, peering through the net curtains one morning, I saw two Germans approaching. My heart thumped wildly, and I caught the old lady by the arm and took her to the window. "This looks like our long-awaited visitors, Denys; you will soon be going home" she whispered. I watched until they entered the garden gate, then stepped into the other room and listened breathlessly. They knocked on the door, Mme Barbierri opened it, and they entered into conversation. I could not understand what they were saying, but I heard Madame's high-pitched voice say, "Come in, come in". Putting my hand on the door knob, I half turned it, then hesitated, for I could hear the heavily studded boots on the concrete floor, and the two men were talking to each other – in German!

Mme Barbierri had been born in Alsace, and was now trying to muster her long-disused German, but in her excitement she was babbling forth a mixture of French, German and even English. The "Come in" I had heard was intended for the Germans and definitely not for me; the phrase sounds similar in both languages. They had come to borrow the keys of the disused cement works, of which M.Barbierri was the watchman. Apparently the Germans were considering making use of the building for their own purposes. The old lady handed over the keys, and bade them good-bye, and as they went out of the garden gate she opened the door behind which I was hiding and we watched them march away. Opening a cupboard, the old lady produced two wine glasses and filled them from a bottle of her precious home-made whisky with a trembling hand. *"Vive la France, Vive l'Angleterre"* we toasted, both realising how near we had been to disaster.

Two more weeks passed in anxious anticipation, waiting for the person who was to lead me to England and home. Ultimately I learnt through Henri of further arrests and executions in Paris, and that all communications were cut once more. To make matters worse, a coldness was developing between the women of the two houses. It had originated, I believe, in a statement of Henri's that the British Government would pay thousands of francs to anyone who sheltered parachutists or escaped prisoners of war. The thought of what was to these poor country folk such a large sum of money made them wonder whose name I would give when I returned to England as having helped me throughout these weeks of hiding. Jeanette, her mother, and Mme Barbierri split into two parties, each trying to outdo the other in kindness towards me. I realised that an old deep-seated wound was being reopened and learnt that, until I had arrived in the village, the two families had not been on speaking terms.

Mme Barbierri no longer accompanied me each evening to listen to the radio in the other house. Instead, she would interrogate me when I returned, asking what I had eaten, and whether I had enjoyed the supper better than the dinner she had cooked. Realising how the land lay, I took a strictly neutral attitude. Each family began to tell me of the faults of the other, but no one knew better than myself that they had one thing very much in common between them – enough bravery to risk everything, even death, to help an Englishman. This was a thought that never left my mind for a moment.

The atmosphere became more and more tense. I wanted to get away but it was now November, winter was setting in, and there was frost on the ground each morning. The idea of crossing France on foot with an empty stomach and a hedge for shelter at night was not exactly inviting. I had promised Henri that I would wait a little longer to give him time to make further contacts in Paris when the hue and cry of local arrests had died down.

One day, M.Barbierri had the good fortune to hear a rumour in the village that a certain curate in a parish fifteen kilometres away was known to have helped to repatriate some parachutists who had passed that way. Unknown to me, he set off to walk there and back – a distance of thirty kilometres – to make inquiries. The poor old fellow returned at dusk very hungry, and weary, for he was 69 years old and had the further discomfort of being doubly ruptured. He had not seen the curate but had spoken to the servant. At first she had denied all knowledge of Resistance activities, but after a while the old man had gained her confidence. She had promised to tell the curate about me, saying he would probably come round on his bicycle during the week.

It was about this time that the Americans carried out their first daylight raid on Germany. Hearing the heavy drone of aircraft flying several miles above, I stepped into the garden at the back of the house; peering upwards, I could see the tightly-packed formations heading for Germany. Their target was Schweinfurt. The thrill of seeing the sun glinting on their silver-painted wings and the feel of the air vibrating with the power of their engines made my spine tingle. As I watched the formations disappear, another sound reached my ears – the hesitant spluttering of an aircraft in trouble. Searching the sky, I spotted a crippled Flying Fortress. She was down to about 15,000ft with no chance of catching up with the rest of the formation, and losing height. I heard the high-pitched scream of a fighter aircraft diving to attack, but could only see a glint in the sun. The fighter opened fire, and I heard the distant roar as perhaps a dozen or more machine guns poured bullets into the stricken bomber. Then came the heavier thumping as gunners replied from the Flying Fortress with their 0·5 inch Brownings. She was going down fighting!

The aircraft was now passing directly overhead. I made out three, four, five, six, dots in the sky above her, and the first attacker was now climbing back into position to try again; the lone bomber was hopelessly outnumbered by seven fighters. Shouts and cheers were coming from all over the village as people called one another out of their houses to watch the grim struggle. They were cheering for the Fortress, but I knew only too well that a massacre was about to take place. One fighter dived, then another and another, all with guns hammering. She was still firing back, but now the fighters were coming in on all sides and the bomber became a mass of flames. The firing ceased, and the blazing giant spiralled downwards. It was then that I noticed little white balls high in the sky; at first I thought they were puffs from anti-aircraft shells, but suddenly realised they were parachutists. There were more cheers from the villagers as they saw that five of the Americans who had put up such a good fight had managed to get out of the aircraft and were still alive.

While the parachutes slowly floated down, the Nazi fighters circled triumphantly round and round. Standing on tip-toe, I watched them disappear behind the buildings in the village, two or three miles away. As they passed out of sight I was puzzled at the sound of more bursts of machine-gun fire. The chilling explanation of these came later in the day. After circling round, the fighters had decided to machine-gun the parachutists, one of whom had dropped like a stone. Witnesses told how the Germans had raced to the spot on various vehicles and, on reaching the dead airman, had emptied his pockets, put a rope round his ankles and dragged him round and round the field behind a motor-cycle.

On 22 November the curate arrived. He turned out to be a cheerful, middle aged, red-faced gentlemen who was very much surprised to learn that I had been in France eleven weeks. He assured me I would be back in England as soon as possible, probably within a fortnight but most certainly before my birthday on 22 December. Several aircrew had passed through his hands, but the names of my crew were not familiar to him. Before he departed, he told Mme Barbierri to expect through the post within the next few days a letter which would refer to a parcel of vegetables and give the date of their delivery. The parcel of vegetables, of course, was to be myself, and on the date fixed M.Barbierri was to take me several kilometres outside the village. He would then turn back while I continued alone for a short distance. I would then be met by a member of the Resistance Movement.

During the eleven weeks of semi-captivity I had become very much out of condition. As darkness fell so early nowadays, it was arranged that I should take a brisk walk or run in a field each evening with Pierrot. The first night we jogged along together I became sadly out of breath after a hundred yards, but as the week went by I improved considerably. During the day I did keep-fit exercises in the wood shed at the back of the house. I soon extended the hundred yards to half a mile and began to feel very much fitter, but unfortunately the more exercise I took the more hungry I became.

My hair had grown very long by now, so Pierrot brought home a close friend of his who could use a pair of shears. He was a woodcutter (perhaps the most appropriate tradesman for the job!) and told me how he had found in a large forest a crashed aircraft, for which the Germans had been searching for weeks. They had seen it come down and wished to remove all ammunition and machine guns, lest they should fall into the hands of the partisans. He produced one or two odds and ends which he had found on the bodies of the airmen, by which I knew that they were British. He said the areas of flesh not covered by clothing had been eaten away by the animals and insects of the forest. This was not a very pleasant topic for a barber's chair, and I was not sorry when the job was finished. Shaking hands, the woodcutter reaffirmed his promise of secrecy as he departed. During my stay in France, I shook hands more times than throughout the rest of my life in England. It is the custom in France to shake hands on meeting and again on departure, even if this comes only half an hour later – and no matter how many people there are to go round.

There was news in the village of two more airmen who had been taken prisoners a few miles away. They had both been wounded; one poor fellow had a head wound and one eye missing, and the other had burns and a broken arm. They staggered along with one idea only in their semi-conscious minds – to keep going and evade capture. The pitiful pair made their way through the forest to a lumber camp, but the man in charge (an ex-army officer) saw they were too badly hurt to be hidden and told the Germans, who took them to hospital. One died within a few hours but the other, with the broken arm, was said to have been spirited away by members of the Resistance Movement after he had received treatment.

The letter from the curate was now overdue, and I began to lose confidence, but fresh hope came from Henri. He believed he could put me in contact with yet another organisation which had already smuggled airmen to the coast and taken them across the Channel in fishing smacks.

Instead of running round the field to keep fit, I now began to accompany Pierrot for the milk each evening. This meant passing through the village, but there were never many people about on dark nights. At the dairy I would stay out of sight leaning against a wall farther up the street while Pierrot went inside and got his can filled. I soon got to know my way round the village quite well. The days passed slowly by till 22 December, my birthday. I shall always remember that morning. After pinning all my hopes on the curate's assurance that I would be in England by now, I felt almost heartbroken. From my little bedroom I heard Mme Barbierri cursing foully and kicking the two cats round the kitchen; she was in a terrible temper. Slipping on my clothes, I opened the door, and bade her good morning. She replied bluntly and thrust a piece of paper in my hand.

I could read very little French, but managed to get a rough idea of its contents. It was from the curate. Handing it back to the old lady, I listened as she read it aloud in English:

"Twelve of the very best executed in Paris. All

communications cut, movement disorganised".

"PATIENCE — SILENCE — PRUDENCE".

"Burn this".

We faced each other in silence, but my thoughts were hundreds of miles away. I was imagining another kitchen, this one on the outskirts of Liverpool. My father, mother, and young brother would be thinking of me. Today was my 22nd birthday and it was three and a half months since I had been posted 'missing'. I wondered if any of the boys I had flown with were prisoners of war, and if the Red Cross had notified their next-of-kin. If this were the case, my family would at least know that I stood a chance of still being alive.

I was abruptly brought back to reality. The old lady was wagging her finger at me and carrying on in a wicked rage. She was telling me to get out of the house. There would not be enough potatoes to feed three mouths during the winter. "Get out! Get out!" she screamed furiously. I went back to the bedroom and gathered together my few treasured belongings; my trusty sheath knife, a little celluloid black cat which I had carried for many years, a Women's Land Army badge I had received from my fiancée on my last leave, a tiny purse which contained a lock of my mother's hair, and my maps and compasses. During my stay in the cottage I had dyed my white aircrew sweater to a dark brown so that it would be less conspicuous. Pulling this on, and Pierrot's jacket over it, I bade farewell to Mme Barbierri, thanking her for all her kindness and expressing my deep sorrow that we should be parting on such unpleasant terms. She was worked up into too great a frenzy to give a civil answer, and I was glad to shut the door and stop the sound of curses coming through it.

Taking deep breaths of the cold fresh air, I strode across the thin carpet of snow which had fallen during the night. My first intention was to visit the other family, thank them for all they had done and say goodbye. I went briskly along with a feeling of freedom, like a rabbit out of a hutch who is yet aware that in the open field a farmer might shoot it at any moment. Coming towards me I saw the huddled figure of M.Barbierri outlined against the white background; he was returning from Mass. His eyes widened in amazement at seeing me out of the house in daylight, and when I said I was going away he earnestly implored me to come back. Since the beginning of the week he had been kneeling in church four times a day making special prayers for my return home. He was confident that once he had finished that seven days' praying session, something unforeseen would happen. So great was his belief in prayer that the idea of this not coming true was absolutely not to be thought of.

With tears rolling down his cheeks, he stood there in the snow appealing to me to come back with him, for he knew help was close at hand. Although his wife made him so unhappy, he told me that she had a heart of gold. He felt sure that if we both returned to the cottage together we would find that her temper had subsided and she would be pleased to see me back. I was not sufficiently hard-hearted to withstand the old man's pleading, so I turned and retraced my footsteps through the snow, walking slowly beside him. Re-entering the house I found that the old lady's rage had died away. She was very sorry that hard words had been spoken and quickly made a special pan of black coffee, and even produced some of her whisky. Although we were back on friendly terms again, I decided I would definitely leave the cottage within the next few days.

CHAPTER FIVE

𝒟𝒾-𝒟𝒾

When dusk fell I made my way as usual to visit Pierrot and his family. I told them what had taken place during the morning and said it was impossible to wait any longer for Henri to make further contacts. I told them how grateful I was for everything they had done for me, and how I realised the risk they had taken in helping me, but I thought it better for all concerned if I set forth on foot until I found someone who could put me in contact with the Maquis.

We had the usual meal of potatoes and I could not help feeling hurt that even Jeanette had not wished me a happy birthday, for I felt that they all knew the significance of the date. As we ate our food in silence, my mind kept wandering to my home in England and picturing what lay ahead of me when I left my French friends in a few days.

A knock came on the door and I grabbed my plate and dived into the bedroom, where I had already spent many hours awaiting the departure of visitors. But this time Pierrot caught my arm and led me to the other bedroom where he and his parents slept. Alone in the darkness I silently finished my soup, sitting on the floor with one eye at the keyhole to see who the visitor was. Often I had spent as long as two-and-a-half hours in this position. Tonight, however, I was fortunate. Within a few minutes handshakes were being exchanged, the door was reopened and the guest departed. Pierrot opened the bedroom door and I entered the living room. By the glances between them and the whispered conversations, I realised that something unusual was in the air, and I heard the mother saying she hoped they would have no more visitors that night.

Jeanette disappeared into her own bedroom on the other side of the room and returned a few minutes later wearing her Sunday clothes. Her eyes were sparkling with excitement. Putting down one of her walking sticks, she took my hand and led me through the doorway. There on the dressing table stood a cake, and on it twenty-two candles were burning. So this was why I had been obliged to hide in the other room! All round the walls were paper decorations, and behind the cake stood a bottle of wine. Each of the family came to me in turn, shook hands, kissed me on both cheeks and wished me a happy birthday.

I was speechless with emotion and surprise. I wanted so much to thank them, but my heart was too full. Never in all my life had there been a moment like this. Nobody in the world but myself knew how much they had sacrificed for me. My eyes smarted; I felt the hot tears roll down my cheeks and could not check them.

The homely celebrations lasted throughout the evening until it was once more time to creep back along the canal and to bed at Mme Barbierri's. Tip-toeing through the garden, I silently let myself into the little homestead. The old couple slept separately, and each night I would stand in the darkness by Madame's bed and tell her all the latest news I had heard from the BBC broadcast. This evening, as I stood there in the darkness, I told her what a wonderful time I had had and of the cake specially made for my birthday. I could see the dark outline of her head on the pillow and could tell by her voice that she was extremely annoyed and jealous. Peevishly, she suggested that perhaps I had forgotten my desire to return to England. I replied with a laugh and struggled to conceal my anger at the remark. Whereupon her voice changed to a triumphant sneer as she told me she had some information which I would appreciate even more than Jeannette's delicious birthday cake. I hated this insinuation and did not commit myself, but I was exceedingly anxious to learn what it was the old lady had to tell me. Slowly she unfolded her secret sentence by sentence, deriving pleasure from the hungry way in which I listened to every word and asked for more.

Whilst I was away, my aged helper had actually spoken to a member of the Resistance Army who had assisted several airmen towards repatriation. Declining to reveal all her knowledge, she told me to go to bed and I would learn more on the morrow. Whispering my thanks, I wished her a peaceful night and withdrew to my own tiny bedroom.

The following morning seemed unbearably long until at last Madame broke her stubborn silence and told me a friend would definitely come to see me at two o'clock.

Early in the afternoon he came. He was a small, round-faced fellow who spoke only in a whisper, as if someone in the kitchen might overhear the conversation. He was introduced to me as M.Colin, a cheese merchant, who lived on the other side of the village. After the usual handshakes he leaned forward and told me that a fortnight previously he had spoken to two American airmen and helped them on their way to England. Looking through the window, he pointed to the stationmaster's house a hundred yards away. "While you have been here, the Americans have been hidden for one month in that attic". It seemed almost unbelievable that all the hours I had spent peeping through the curtains of the cottage had been shared by two men in similar circumstances, peering through the shutters at the same scene. I wondered if they had seen the two German soldiers who had passed in front of the station and entered the cottage, little knowing there was an Englishman behind the door.

M.Colin said that a false identity card would be made for me and in a few days he would take me in his van to a place where I would be introduced to an English-speaking lady. From then onwards, we would travel as man and wife by train all the way to the Spanish frontier, where I would be passed over to guides who would lead me over the Pyrenees into Spain.

When I thanked him for the part he was playing in this wonderful plan to help me, he smiled and shrugged his shoulders and said nothing was too much risk for him if it was for France and her Allies. He was a widower and said he had very little to lose. He carried a revolver and assured me coldly and calmly that the Germans would never capture him alive. Little did he know that a few weeks later his bold statement would come to nothing. The Gestapo caught him unawares in his own courtyard with an empty pocket. Found guilty of assisting young Frenchmen to evade their conscription for forced labour, he was sentenced to life imprisonment. Transported to Germany, he suffered the horrors of existence between life and death in various concentration camps including Buchenwald. His merciful release by Allied troops almost at the end of the war came just in time to save his life. Had the Gestapo known he was also involved in helping the other airmen and myself, he would have been executed.

Mme Barbierri made me promise not to breathe a word to Pierrot and his family about M.Colin's visit. She began to gloat over the prospect of getting me away without the assistance of Henri, whom she now disliked as much as anyone in the family. When I visited my other friends that evening I felt very guilty keeping the great news from them, but could not break my word.

The evening following M.Colin's visit, I found Jeanette very excited. She said I would be introduced that night to an old friend of hers named 'Di-Di' Valiant. "He has just escaped from Germany" she whispered. Pierrot hurriedly finished his evening meal and left the house to tell the expected friend the coast was clear. The door reopened a couple of minutes later and Di-Di hobbled into the room, leaning heavily on two walking sticks. He collapsed into a chair, his chest heaving up and down as he struggled to regain his breath. His cheek bones stood out, the skin was tight over them, and his eyes were sunken deep in their sockets. He grinned at everyone in the room, running his hands nervously up and down his thighs and pushing back his long blond hair.

Twelve months before, he had been a healthy nineteen-year-old boy whose ambition in life was to become a professional footballer. He was the outstanding player in the local club and there were excellent prospects of his entry into the game as a professional, had he not been conscripted for forced labour by the Nazis. At Saarbrücken he was put to work in a railway engineering factory under abominable conditions. Food was insufficient, the living quarters overcrowded and rat-infested and he was obliged to work day in and day out standing in his wooden clogs in water. He fell ill, but received no medical attention, only jabs in the ribs from a rifle butt to keep him working. One morning, as he left his bunk, he collapsed in a heap on the floor. As he tried to crawl towards the door, he was kicked unmercifully. He realised that if he did not escape soon he would die in the labour camp.

The first week in December, he and three other young French boys managed to hide on board a goods train bound for France. They entered a van loaded with rubber tyres and concealed themselves in the stacks, building up the tyres again round them and over their heads. Each man took with him a bottle of water, some pieces of black bread and a bottle which contained a mixture of vinegar and paraffin.

All trains were thoroughly searched as they crossed the Franco-German frontier. Bloodhounds and Alsatian dogs were used to track down possible stowaways. When the four escapees were sure they were reaching the frontier, they sprinkled vinegar and paraffin all over their heads, clothes and the floor near them. The train rumbled to a standstill and they trembled breathlessly as they heard the guards going from wagon to wagon. The dogs must have found the smell of the mixture distasteful and they turned away without making a close investigation.

The train restarted, and a few minutes later the four Frenchmen were in their home country. But their troubles were not yet over. Guards were posted at each end of the goods train armed with machine guns, primarily for use in air attack, but also to shoot at any refugees. The fugitives had by this time spent three days and nights in the tyres, and the temperature had been below zero throughout the journey. Since the first day Di-Di had been numb from the waist downwards. On the fourth day his friends ventured to leave their hiding place and peep outside. They told him that the train had come to rest a few miles outside Leroville, and he realised that he was quite near home. When darkness fell they helped him out on to the track. His legs were useless, but he managed to drag himself into a field. The thought of being so near home kept him going, and foot by foot he made his way across country. In the early hours of the following morning his parents heard a knock on the door, and on opening it they found their son lying unconscious on the step.

Taking the local doctor into their confidence, they summoned him immediately. A bed was made up in a neighbour's attic and the poor boy wrapped in blankets with hot-water bottles. The doctor fought against bronchitis and frostbite, and the patient who had so strong a desire to live responded to his treatment. Tonight was Christmas Eve, and the first time he had left his bed since reaching home. As I watched him, sitting on the chair wrapped in blankets, I could see in his eyes the wonderful happiness and relief he felt at being among his friends.

During the evening I talked a good deal with my new acquaintance, asking him many questions about life in Germany and particularly of the effect of Allied bombing attacks. He spoke of the colossal devastation, the thousands of deaths and of how some of the towns were obliged to spray the streets with disinfectant to keep down the smell of rotting flesh buried beneath the rubble. Before returning to his hideout nearby, Di-Di arranged that his father, who was an engine driver visiting Bar-le-Duc daily, would make enquiries on my behalf of the organisation who were supplying the necessary forged documents to safeguard his own existence.

Lying in bed that evening before dropping off to sleep, I carefully thought over my position. Although I found the time in hiding long and tedious, I realised how lucky I was. Although I had travelled no nearer home for several weeks, I felt that my chances were now better than ever. From three different sources, patriotic people were endeavouring to help me – Henri in Paris, M.Colin in the village, and now the engine driver at Bar-le-Duc. When I awoke, it was Christmas morning. I dressed with the determination to make the day as cheerful as possible, and to get on friendlier terms with Mme Barbierri before the end of my stay as her guest.

When I went into the kitchen, we exchanged the compliments of the season, and then I dashed round making myself useful, dusting the furniture, peeling the potatoes and chopping the firewood. By dinner time, I had got Madame into an excellent humour. One of the precious chickens had been sacrificed for the occasion, and when the old man returned from Mass it was served on the table with potatoes, cabbage, turnips and a delicious gravy which I found French housewives could prepare exquisitely. This was followed by a fruit tart made with home-ground flour, after which we sat back talking contentedly of other Christmases we had known. I poured out a glass of black coffee each, and at Madame's request brought forth her precious home-made whisky. We drank toasts to France, to England, and my safe return home.

In the evening, I made my usual journey through the darkness to my second home. Sitting by the radio, I tuned in to London, and with the volume almost at a whisper I heard the BBC announcer open the programme by saying "A happy Christmas and good luck to all members of the Forces wherever they may be."

On Boxing Day, a young boy came round to the 'Home sweet Home' with a package containing cigarettes, biscuits and a camera. He was the village grocer's son, and said his father was a close friend of M.Colin. The camera was brought for M.Barbierri to take a photograph for use on my false identity card; by now I had no RAF ones left.

The next time I saw Pierrot he had good news from Bar-le-Duc. Some members of the Resistance would definitely call in a car after dark to take me away, either the second or third day of January. The following six days, I waited as patiently as I could. Mme Barbierri believed that her own connection through M.Colin was due to materialise any day, but insisted that this be kept a secret from the other family. Pierrot's family also believed that their scheme was about to materialise, and they too requested that I 'keep it dark' from Mme Barbierri!

On New Year's Day we sat in silence round the table and there was a melancholy atmosphere over the household. This would probably be their last meal with the *aviateur anglais* as their guest. Jeanette remarked how long the winter evenings would seem without my company, and tears came to her eyes. Pierrot said hopefully that

Winter 1943/44, the aircrew sweater now dyed
a less conspicuous brown. This was the photo
taken to enable M. Colin to make false papers

after I got home perhaps I would get shot down in France again, and live with them a second time! Unable to frame an appropriate reply without hurting his feelings, I remained silent. The mother spoke of how happy my own parents would be to see me safe and well again, and the father remarked that I would be glad of a few pints of English beer when I got back, with which I heartily agreed.

I stayed later than usual this night, and when I left, the usual handshakes and wishes of *"Bonsoir"* were supplemented with kisses on both cheeks and expressions of *"Bonne chance, Denys"* which I knew came from the very depths of their hearts.

Walking cautiously back to Mme Barbierri's, I cast repeated glances back towards the moonlit silhouette of the little wooden house where I had been so welcome and spent so many happy evenings.

Quietly opening the garden gate, I lowered my head in the porch and gingerly entered the door of the 'Home sweet Home' for what I thought would probably be the last time. Turning the key in the lock behind me, I tip-toed to Madame's bedside. She was lying awake as usual, waiting to ask what I had heard on the news from England and what I had eaten during the evening. I felt sorry for her and wished she could get over the jealousy towards her neighbours, for I knew that both families had hearts of gold. I am sure the prospect of reward from the Air Ministry had no influence upon them whatsoever.

CHAPTER SIX

Leaving Sampigny

The second day of January arrived at last. I borrowed M.Barbierri's razor and underwent the slow and painful process of shaving without soap. Stuffing my various sentimental little belongings into my pockets, I paced around the house, watching the clock as it ticked nearer and nearer six o'clock. Several times before I had been worked up into a similar state of eager anticipation but, although previous plans had failed and led to bitter disappointment, I felt fully confident that this time I was moving into the hands of the Resistance Movement.

A few minutes before the vital hour, Mme Barbierri, who was still unaware of the anticipated events of the evening, had occasion to leave the house. Heading towards the village, she was met in the path by a gentleman wearing a navy blue overcoat and black beret. He quietly asked if she was Mme Barbierri, then moved closer and told her he had come to take away the Englishman. At first the old lady was suspicious of him, but after a while she believed he had come from M.Colin. During the conversation, however, he mentioned he had received information about me from Pierrot's family. This annoyed the old lady so much that she unleashed her temper and stamped away to tell M.Colin what was happening. Then Jeanette came stumbling into the kitchen crying "*Vite! vite!* they are here to talk to you."

At that moment, Mme Barbierri burst through the doorway, her eyes blazing, and ordered Jeanette out of the house. She created a terrible scene and used all the swear words she could think of. However, the stranger came into the house and with a few quietly spoken words soothed her down. He had two colleagues waiting in a car which stood under the trees a short distance away. After speaking to them, he had realised that M.Colin was actually a member of their own organisation. But they had both heard of me from different sources, each intending to pass me into the hands of an English-speaking lady.

Once aware of the misunderstanding that had arisen, Mme Barbierri endeavoured to make amends for her behaviour by producing the whisky, and the stranger lifted his glass and toasted *"Général de Gaulle et la Victoire."* Thanking the old couple for their kindness during my long stay, and assuring them that some day when the war was over I would return, I shook hands with them and departed.

Reaching a group of trees, I saw the car, and standing in the shadows were the two Resistance men with Pierrot and M.Colin. Exchanging a few words of farewell and handshakes, I stepped into the back of the saloon and was driven away.

M.Althuser, the stranger, had told Mme Barbierri that I would be in Paris the following day. His last words to Pierrot and M.Colin were that I would be in Nancy before dawn. But when I questioned him in the car, he said the less people knew of a plan, the better and safer it was. The driver had not yet spoken, but he now turned round and said he knew his instructions and we were going neither to Paris nor to Nancy. If anyone were arrested in the village we had just left, no one could possibly divulge to the Gestapo where I had gone to or what route I had taken.

Seated beside the driver was a short broad-shouldered man wearing a leather overcoat and beret. He was M.Clément, another engine driver, through whom the original contact had been made. Leaning over the back of the seat, he told me they were taking a chance and hoping I was not a Gestapo agent in disguise, but I would be under suspicion until I had proved otherwise. If I were an agent, M.Clément assured me, I would soon be *kaput*. As I did not understand, they explained that it was German, and meant I would be finished. To illustrate this, they poked an automatic into my ribs. Quickly I replied with a laugh that if I were a member of the Gestapo the three of them would soon be *kaput* long before I would, and I dug a finger into M.Althuser 's ribs. This amused them immensely and they laughed heartily. The atmosphere had previously been grim and tense; Resistance work is a ruthless game of life and death but now my little joke had cleared the air, so I felt more at ease. M.Clément pushed an identity card into my hand, saying the photo bore a slight resemblance to me. If we were stopped by a patrol, I was to stick the card out of the window and leave the talking to the others. M.Althuser had lived his early life in Alsace; as he spoke fluent German, he would take charge of any situation that might arise.

The driver had a pocket-full of licences and permits with which, he assured me, he could get almost anywhere and travel at any time of the night, irrespective of the curfew. Laughingly, he told me that he and the car were both on hire to the German Army for the convenience of officers and important officials; in this manner he acquired considerable information and was a very valuable member of the underground movement. Speeding through the country roads for about an hour, slowing down occasionally as we passed through the villages, then accelerating again with moonlit fields slipping by on either side, I felt at last that I was really getting nearer home.

The scenery changed as we entered a built-up area. Zig-zagging through narrow streets, the driver crossed the town in a way which would confuse anyone who might be interested in our destination. Stopping on a deserted corner for a few seconds, he allowed time for me and the other two passengers to jump out. Then, with a wave of his hand, he drove away.

Clément and Althuser took hold of an arm on either side and quickly hustled me round more corners and through back streets until finally we entered a narrow road which ran steeply uphill. Clément advanced alone while I remained concealed in the shadows with his companion. A low whistle from a doorway told us the coast was clear, and walking farther up the hill we entered the narrow hall of a house. The door was closed and locked behind us, and an electric light switched on. I was now in the home of M.Clément, where I was introduced to his wife and Jacques, their schoolboy son.

M.Clément explained that I was in Bar-le-Duc, and that I would stay in his house three days before continuing my journey. During this time, M.Althuser would take my photo and carry out the forgery of a complete set of identification papers.

The house consisted of two rooms upstairs and two down. The one at the front downstairs facing the street was a kitchen and living-room combined, while the smaller one was a bed-sitting room and looked out on to the garden at the rear. Taking me outside the house at the back, my host showed me the garden which I could see rose steeply up the side of the hill to a dark patch on the sky-line made by a small wood. He explained that I was to sleep downstairs in the back room; if anything should happen, I was to jump out of the window and scramble up the slope to the trees as fast as I could.

The front door would always be kept locked and whenever he or his son wished to enter they would give five short rings on the bell. If anyone came to the door and did not give this signal, I must immediately pick up all my possessions and stand by my bedroom window ready to jump out, leaving no evidence of my presence behind. Mme Clément was told that on no occasion must she unlock the front door without peeping through the kitchen window or the letter box to see who was there. I was now living in a town with enemy troops wandering up and down the streets all day long, and I would have to take far greater precautions than I had done living in a country village. The Gestapo usually carried out their searches and interrogated citizens between midnight and 5am. So if any suspicious sound were heard outside the house after curfew time, I was to get out as fast as I could – taking the chance that I should not find myself confronted by sub-machine-gunners surrounding the garden.

The German Army parading along the Boulevard de la Rochelle in the centre of Bar-le-Duc
(photo. Harbulot)

CHAPTER SEVEN

Denis Lebenec

The night passed uneventfully and at eight o'clock in the morning M.Clément went to work, followed soon afterwards by Jacques on his way to school. Left alone with Mme Clément, I helped her to prepare dinner and she told me something of the family history. When the introductions had been made the previous evening, I had noticed that Jacques was described as Mme Cléments' son in a way which implied that her present husband was not the boy's father. As we peeled the potatoes, I learnt that this was indeed her second marriage. I could tell by her accent that she was not a native of this part of France. She told me she was a Parisian and had married at the age of seventeen in Paris, where Jacques was born a year later. After four years her husband left her. Obtaining a divorce, she was given the custody of the little boy, and leaving him to the care of his grandparents, took up employment as a shorthand typist. This went on until 1940, when she happened to make up a foursome with a girl friend and two sergeants of the French Tank Corps. Her partner for the evening was M.Clément, who was spending a few hours' leave in Paris at the time. He, too, had been married but his wife had died in 1937, leaving him with a young son who was then nine years old and living with relatives in his home town of Bar-le-Duc.

When the Germans broke through the defences and overran France, he saw a lot of combat. His division fought a rearguard action right down to the South of France, in the course of which he won the *Croix de Guerre* for gallantry. When the Armistice was signed he was released from a prison camp with other railway workers and allowed to return home and recommence his job as an engine driver. Reaching his home town after weeks of being without news, he found that his young son had been killed by a German hand-grenade in the course of the fighting.

M.Clément had lost both his wife and son, but in Paris there lived an attractive young woman with a son almost the same age as his own. After the marriage they came to live in Bar-le-Duc, Mme Clément bringing most of her modern furniture, and it was upon her ultra-modern bed-settee that I had slept the previous night.

Sgt Clément, 47th BCC 4th division, 1939

In the bed-sitting room stood a modern chromium-plated slow-combustion stove, into which a shovelful of coal was put each morning. This was the first coal I had seen in France and was really a very dusty slack which the husband brought home from the railway. It was sufficient to keep the room warm for twenty-four hours. Each morning I would go down into the cellar and sieve the coal from the dust; the dust was then made into briquettes with plaster of Paris to make them firm, and these were used for cooking.

Jacques only attended school for a few hours each day because the air raid shelters could only accommodate half the children at once. He showed me his exercise books and said the work was very easy, for although he was fourteen years old and attended a secondary school, he was only doing work of pre-war twelve-year-olds. The Nazis did not wish the youth of occupied countries to receive an education comparable with their German standard.

The days seemed to pass more slowly than in Mme Barbierri's cottage. I could not move about the house and missed the walk in the darkness on my own to visit Pierrot. There were no cats in the kitchen to tease, and I could not feed the rabbits at the rear of the house in case I should be seen by the neighbours on either side. However, there were three bicycles belonging to the household. I cleaned these each in turn. There had been a good harvest of haricot beans from the allotment that summer and they hung in dozens of bundles from the rafters in the attic, waiting to be shelled. Also in the attic, hanging to dry, were large tobacco leaves, which had been cultivated by M.Clément. He often offered me his tobacco pouch and a cigarette paper, watching with amusement my ungainly attempts to roll a cigarette between my fingers. Sometimes it was packed too tightly and went out after a couple of puffs: at other times it was too loose and burnt away like a bonfire.

When the third evening arrived, my friend returned from work and told me I was to be his guest for a little longer. Before I could be issued with identification papers it would have to be ascertained that I was a genuine British airman and not a member of the Gestapo masquerading with evil intentions. Someone would come to the house the following evening and ask me various questions, my replies to which would be radioed to England. He would probably want to know where I was born, my home address, names of members of my crew and so on. Within a few days a reply would be received confirming whether these details were correct. The visitor would be the head of the Resistance Movement in the town, whose identity was known to very few. Even M.Clément only knew him as 'The Chief' or 'Monsieur X'.

Next evening, the supper things had been cleared away and young Jacques sent to bed early when the five short rings sounded on the front doorbell. It was our friend M. Althuser. Glancing quickly round the room, he inquired if it was safe to bring in 'The

Chief' and his interpreter, then stepped out into the darkness again. A minute later a dark-haired young woman entered. She was Micheline, the interpreter, and behind her came the man with whom I was to become more and more closely associated in the months to come, the mysterious M.X.

Micheline was dressed simply in dark clothes and wore horn-rimmed glasses. At first I imagined her to be a school teacher, possibly a language mistress in the local secondary school, but I was mistaken; the only teaching she had done was during a few months' stay in England. My initial impression of the nameless gentleman was by no means favourable. He had a sinister manner and never seemed to look me in the eye, usually speaking with his face half turned away from me as he exhaled cigarette smoke. We both regarded one another with suspicion. However, a few weeks later, when I knew more about his character and activities, I felt a great admiration for him and the dangerous undertakings in which he was engaged.

Taking pencil and paper, M.X proceeded to take notes of the colour of my hair and eyes. Then with the aid of his interpreter he asked my full name, RAF number, rank, date I was shot down, and a complete list of my crew. The questioning could quite well have been carried on in French, for by now I had very little difficulty in understanding the everyday conversation of my hosts. The complete list was then carefully folded and M.X slipped it down the inside of his sock, as an extra precaution in case he were stopped and searched after leaving the house.

Now that the interrogation was over, the tension in the room relaxed. Mme Clément handed round glasses of wine and we quietly toasted *"La Victoire"*. The pretty little interpreter told me the names of three American airmen she had helped during recent months, thinking perhaps I might know them. This was, of course, a thousand-to-one chance, for, although I had carried out my flying training in Canada and America, I knew very few members of the US Air Force and had to disappoint her.

I was told that my stay in this house would last a further seven days. At the end of this week, confirmation of my identity would have been received, identification papers forged and I would depart for another district, where I would be picked up by aircraft. At first this sounded fantastic to me, but I learnt later that dozens of saboteurs, secret agents and Resistance organisers were actually put down and picked up again months later by aircraft in the heart of the occupied countries. Lysanders were generally used for this purpose and sometimes a lucky airman was flown back as an additional passenger.

There was much more activity for me to watch through the lace curtains into the street than there had been at Mme Barbierri's. The local prison was a few hundred yards higher up the hill and on two or three occasions I saw the French *gendarmes* marching some unfortunate individual up the road to spend a few months behind iron bars – perhaps for stealing his neighbour's chickens or some similar offence. There was linoleum on the kitchen floor, its patterns formed by bunches of flowers. I spent hours pacing round the table stepping from flower to flower until I felt dizzy, then I would turn in the opposite direction, stepping round and round on all the spaces and missing the flowers.

One evening, the secret signal was sounded on the door. It was the interpreter again, bringing with her a shirt, tie, jacket and a pair of trousers. I changed into them and Mme Clément noted how much needed taking off the bottom of the trousers. Micheline promised that if my identity card were completed within the next couple of days she would take me round the town for a walk before I departed for England.

Five days passed and still M. Althuser had not come round to take my photo, so M.Clément called at the studio on his way home from work and it was decided that I should accompany him to M.Althuser's house the same evening. Putting on my new clothes and the traditional black beret on the side of my head, I stepped out into the street beside the leather-coated engine driver. Walking through the town my eyes soon became accustomed to the darkness, and as people passed us on the footpath I could see the outlines of uniforms and hear the guttural mutterings of the soldiers. Side by side, we made our way across the town in silence. Near the approach to the railway station, my escort whispered to me to stand in the shadows while he knocked on the door. All was well inside, so I was beckoned to enter.

When my eyes had adjusted themselves to the bright electric light, I was introduced to Mme Althuser, her nineteen-year-old daughter Janine, and her schoolboy son. The black-out in the studio was imperfect; we could not risk intrusion by the police, so a pair of floodlights and a camera were carried into the dining-room. While the mother and daughter held a sheet behind my head, M.Althuser took the portrait. Someone suggested that while I was there I had better have my thumb marks put on the identity card, whereupon the photographer got down on his hands and knees and began to grope about in the ashes at the back of the kitchen grate. He found a piece of wire, and pulling steadily on it drew forth a metal box which had been concealed half-way through the wall of the house. Brushing away the ashes, he brought the box into the living-room. It was divided into two sections, one containing a variety of rubber stamps and the other with two or three dozen printed cards of various colours and sizes. Picking out a black and white card, he revealed a blank identity card. Fitting it into his typewriter, he asked me under what name I would like to be known. I asked if my Christian names could remain almost the same, so that they would always come readily to me in any circumstances. This was agreed upon, and M.Clément suggested that I should bear a surname which was common in Brittany, and that my birthplace should be there to account for the flaws in my accent.

The typewriter clicked, and a new Frenchman came into existence. He was:

DENIS THOMAS LEBENEC,
Born at the little coastal town of Carnac, in the
département of Morbihan, Brittany.
Height: 1·65 metres.
Eyes: Blue.
Hair: Fair.
Occupation: Labourer.
Date of birth: 22 December 1918.

This was my own birthday moved back three years, making me twenty-five – an age group which had not yet been completely conscripted for work in Germany. I moistened my thumbs on an inked pad and then made the required impression in the two squares on the card marked *droit* and *gauche*. M.Althuser licked some form of taxation stamp and stuck it in position, then sorted out his set of rubber stamps which represented 'Départment Council of the Meuse,' and others bearing the German eagle and the swastika. On the back of the card he added further stamps, which indicated the dates on which it was supposed to have been recalled, inspected, and reissued.

While I was practising my new signature on a spare piece of paper, my friend the forgery expert created a *Certificat de Travail*

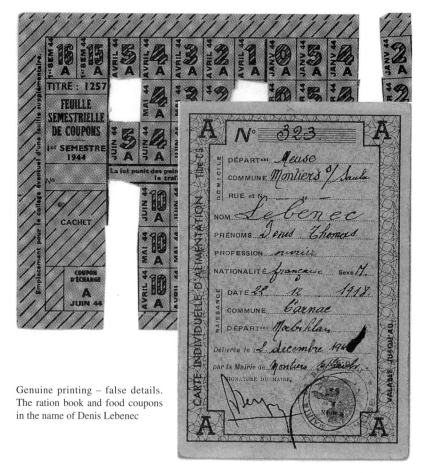

Genuine printing – false details.
The ration book and food coupons
in the name of Denis Lebenec

with the use of more rubber stamps on a buff-coloured printed card.
This certified that I was engaged in essential work at a certain
cheese factory in a town about ten miles away. The employer's
signature across the factory stamp looked very effective, but of
course the person was non-existent. The address looked plausible
enough – Nos. 80-82 of a certain street, although in actual fact the
last building in the row was 78.

Another assortment of papers was unearthed, from which I was
equipped with a ration book and all the necessary coupons. The
following day, my portrait would be developed, stuck into position
on the identity card and embossed with a final stamp. I would then
be able to move about the country more freely.

My hosts told me of the recent escape of a British Secret Service agent who had been living as a Frenchman not very far away. When the Gestapo came to arrest him, he shot his way out, killing two Nazis, and made a successful getaway through the window clad only in his pyjamas. The story sounded very romantic to me and too much like a 'twopenny thriller', but I had not yet been acquainted long enough with the Resistance Movement to realise that incidents like this were taking place almost daily in different parts of France. In most instances the Gestapo came off best, and successful escapes were few and far between.

The blank cards and forgery equipment were all carefully replaced in the metal box and pushed back into position under the fireplace. It was agreed that M.Clément should call again on his way home from work the following evening, by which time the identity cards would be complete. This he did, and we spent the evening carefully folding and dirtying the precious documents to make them look as though they had been used for months. Every so often my hosts would turn suddenly to me and demand to know my name. "Lebenec, Denis Thomas," I would reply. They would continue to ask my age, where I was born, whom I worked for, and where I lived (this was, of course, another fictitious address). The process was repeated time and again until at last I could snap back the answers without hesitation or mistake, as though I had been giving them all my life.

CHAPTER EIGHT

Moved on

The following evening Micheline called to take me for a walk. Before we left the house, M.Clément flashed an electric torch in my face, demanded to see my identity card and barked out in the abrupt German manner:

"Where are you going at this time of night?"

"I'm going to visit my cousin who lives on the other side of the town," I replied. He laughed and said my French was better than that of most of the *Boches* who had been occupying France for three years. The night air seemed cool and refreshing after being shut up in the house all day. The young interpreter and I went through the streets arm in arm like a courting couple, with only an occasional whispered word passing between us. We walked boldly together into the main thoroughfare, passing the darkened doors of various cafés from which flowed the almost continual sounds of accordion music. In the darkness we rubbed shoulders with the German troops as they stumbled along from café to café in the black-out. At one street corner, as we groped in the inky blackness for the footpath, a German shone his flashlight at our feet to illuminate the way. *"Merci, Monsieur"* said my escort, giving my arm a squeeze.

Leaving the activity of the main street behind, we made our way into the quieter part of the town. Pausing in front of a church, Micheline asked in a whisper if I wished to go inside. Knowing that she herself was a regular churchgoer, and having noticed that most of the French population with whom I had already come in contact were far more devoted to their religion than the average Englishman, I nodded lest I should hurt the little interpreter's feelings. Pushing open the big wooden doors, I could see the candles flickering at the altar. This was the first time I had been inside a Roman Catholic church, so I carefully followed behind my guide and repeated her actions. Dipping our fingers into the holy water, we made the sign of the Cross. Micheline uttered a prayer as she did so, and I murmured some incomprehensible imitation behind her. There were rows of chairs, and in the candlelight I could see two or three figures kneeling and praying.

Tip-toeing silently to a dark, deserted corner of the church, we knelt down side by side in silence. Meditating in the silence, I thought how unjust life seemed to be. I myself had never said a prayer since I had been able to form my own opinions, yet here I was, alive, in good health and somehow confident that come what might I would eventually reach England again. Then I thought of the really decent fellows I had flown with and remembered how many of them had become a mass of splintered bones and torn flesh, or been burnt to a cinder in a blazing inferno of exploding petrol tanks.

Glancing at the bowed head of the plucky little Frenchwoman at my side, I thought of all the misfortune she had had to contend with during her thirty years on earth. Her father was killed in the 1914-18 war and her widowed mother had struggled for years to support herself and her daughter. When the Germans swept through France in 1940, the whole town was evacuated. Mother and daughter pushed a handcart containing all their precious belongings along the road, in an endless procession of homeless people fleeing to the south, in many cases for the second time in their lives.

As the pitiful, defenceless civilians struggled along the road, the Italian Air Force – which seemed to do so poorly against RAF opposition – took an opportunity to display their murderous abilities. With machine-guns blazing they dived towards the roadway. Micheline's mother was hit in the leg and lay for hours in agony by the roadside with dozens of others before medical assistance arrived. A bullet was extracted from her calf; she still bears an ugly blue scar and will never forget those terrible days of evacuation.

Tip-toeing out of the church, we continued our cautious meander through the streets, returning to M.Clément's a different way. We passed in front of a large sinister-looking building outside which stood an armed sentry. A few yards past it, my escort squeezed my arm and whispered one single word: *"Prison"*.

We had been away for nearly two hours, and found M.Clément waiting anxiously. *"Comment ça va, Lebenec?"* he asked. *"Ça va bien, merci,"* I replied, and told him how we had spent the evening.

Before leaving the house, Micheline arranged to call for me again the following evening to visit her home. Wearing my new suit, and knowing that in my pocket I carried a perfectly forged identity card, I felt full of assurance and began to believe myself fully capable of bluffing my way out of any emergency which might arise.

My confidence was shattered the following evening. The signal sounded on the doorbell and Micheline was admitted into the house. I saw immediately that her dark eyes no longer bore the calm, self-possessed expression I had come to know. She brought bad news. The man who operated the secret radio transmitting set, and had the various particulars of myself, had been arrested at five o'clock that morning. She did not know whether the information concerning my identity had already been destroyed or not, and wondered whether the slip of paper had fallen into enemy hands. M.and Mme Clément stood in silence; it was a foregone conclusion that the poor man would be executed. Yet it was not his death that we were all secretly thinking about, but the murderous flogging and torture to which he would be subjected before he died. Micheline knew him; he was a local man and would leave behind a wife and five young children.

We decided that it would be best for me to stop going out in the evenings, and in the following days I concentrated more and more on getting word-perfect in my false identity. Each day we listened carefully to the broadcasts from London. The war was going well for the Allies. The Russians were forcing their way forward day by day, Bomber Command was pounding Germany in increasing numbers almost every night, the USAF was continually obliterating objectives with their daylight bombing, and the second front was expected to open up in the near future.

I was busy helping Madame to prepare her husband's meal on the seventeenth evening when the doorbell sounded five times. Glancing at the clock she remarked, "He's home early tonight," and went to open the door. She was surprised to find an unexpected visitor standing outside; it was Micheline.

"Put your coat on, Denis, and come quickly," she said, and told me a gentleman was waiting at a certain rendezvous in the town to take me to England. This was the glad news I had been waiting for; needless to say, I slipped on my coat, jammed the beret on my head, and was ready, with my face wreathed in smiles, within two minutes. Micheline said we would not be able to wait until M.Clément came home as time was too short, so Jacques dashed off on his bicycle to see if perhaps he could meet his stepfather on the way home from work and tell him to hurry.

"*Au revoir*, Madame Clément; thank you with all my heart for all your kindness," I said.

"Goodbye," she whispered, with tears in her eyes, and told me I would have to return after the war to give her a few more lessons in English.

Outside, my escort led me to a quiet alleyway and stopped. Looking up into my face in the moonlight she offered me an apology.

"They were all lies I told you about going back to England, Denis. I am so, so sorry for you," she said softly. She said trouble had broken out in the first village I had stayed at. Arrests had been made, and lest my trail should be picked up and followed to M.Clément's, it was best that I should move on. It was essential that no member of the Clément family should know where I was moving to. Micheline had been ordered by M.X to call for me and get me away from the house under a false pretext; I felt very much as though I were deserting a sinking ship, but, as Micheline pointed out, if there were trouble in the district, it was better that I should keep moving. If arrests were made and I was actually found in hiding under the same roof, the entire family would be executed. She had no idea where my new home was going to be, but said that shortly we would meet M.X and he had made all arrangements in advance.

Walking through the town arm-in-arm with her, I suddenly became aware that a dark figure had fallen in step at my side. It was our mysterious unknown friend. On a secluded corner, I shook hands with Micheline and we continued alone. Walking through deserted back streets, M.X told me that at the moment there was great danger and that I had already stayed in the one house longer than was prudent. When I met my new friends, I was told not to say where I had previously stayed, or who had helped me, but that from time to time I would meet the interpreter again.

Coming to a halt in a deserted road, I found we were standing in front of a pair of ornamental gates. Putting his hand through the bars, M.X slid back a bolt and I followed him into what appeared to be an extensive garden surrounding a large house. The gate swung shut with a clang, the bolt was pushed into position and the key turned in the lock. I felt as though I were inside a prison and wondered anxiously what my new benefactors would be like.

Walking side-by-side up the gravel path we reached the front door, where my new friend gave three short rings and then stood back in the shadows, waiting. The door swung open, and silhouetted against the shaded light in the hallway I saw the slim figure of a young girl. She beckoned us in, re-locked the door and bolted it. We were standing in the hallway of a large old-fashioned house.

Most of the building had been requisitioned by the Germans and used as offices in connection with food distribution. The owners had been obliged to withdraw from their spacious, luxuriously furnished rooms and inhabit the servants' quarters at the rear of the building. This was where M.X and I were now being guided. Mounting a short staircase at the end of the passage, we entered a living-room. A quick glance round showed me the vast difference in the standard of living of my new helpers compared with the homely, working-class people with whom I had spent my time in France so far. The furniture was all heavily carved dark oak, looking very solid and impressive. A large radio set stood in one corner and a telephone in another.

I was introduced to the family. First, M.Hesling, a small, nervous, middle-aged businessman in horn-rimmed glasses and going bald on top. Then I shook hands with his wife, a small, dark-haired, bright-eyed lady who walked with a slight limp. I soon found she had a keen sense of humour. The girl who had opened the door was Colette, their nineteen-year-old daughter. As they employed no servants now, she stayed at home and helped her mother with the housekeeping.

M.X explained that he was expecting to get some more news in the near future which would help my position considerably. In the meantime, I could hide there with a reasonable amount of safety. Wishing me good night and assuring me of some word within a few days, he departed. M.Hesling escorted him off the premises and then returned to the room.

Once more I was a curiosity in a strange household. The family bade me sit down and then stood round smiling and staring. They began to discuss me amongst themselves, and were surprised when they realised how well I understood and spoke their language. Taking me to a map that was pinned on the wall, the bespectacled gentleman asked me to indicate my home. I did so, much to the surprise of Colette who had imagined I came from the United States. I answered dozens of questions about my experiences of bombing Germany and my impressions as I baled out by parachute, but they knew it was indiscreet to ask any details about the length of time I had been hidden in France and my whereabouts during that period.

We gathered round the radio, listened to the drum beating the sound of 'V for Victory' and heard the familiar *"Ici Londres"*, then carefully moved the pins on the map indicating the day's advance by the Russian Army. Immediately the news was finished and the customary fanfare of trumpets and patriotic anthems began, M.Hesling grabbed the volume control and cut down the sound until it was almost inaudible; he thought it most imprudent that the BBC should broadcast these tunes so loudly. Although an eavesdropper would be unable to distinguish the words of an announcer, the sound of a popular tune (particularly the *Marseillaise)* could not be mistaken no matter how faintly it was played.

Showing me to my bedroom, my host produced a form of miniature sledge, and, noticing my curiosity, explained it was used to warm the bed. Taking a small tin tray to the fireplace, he shovelled on to it a few pieces of red-hot charcoal This was hung from the sledge in such a manner that as it slid under the bedclothes, it warmed a large area without scorching the sheets. Our discussion of flying and the war in general was continued late into the night. When I finally retired, I found that the sledge-like contraption had warmed the bed comfortably from top to bottom. Before going to sleep, I inspected the shutters over the window to make sure that they could be opened with speed and in silence and estimated the drop to the ground. A peculiarity I had noticed in French houses was that all the windows opened inwards, and I now realised the advantage, for although the shutters were securely locked into position, I could still open the windows and admit a certain amount of fresh air.

I slept well in M.Hesling's pyjamas, the first I had seen since leaving England, and awoke the next morning to hear the radio already switched on. My host was carrying out his early-morning routine quest for news. He always listened to three different versions of the war situation: that of London, Switzerland, and the German-controlled French radio. In this way he formed his own opinions of losses and gains by both sides. The Swiss radio maintained a strictly neutral atmosphere, and M.Hesling had a high respect for the authenticity of their news bulletins.

Colette was already busy polishing the floor. She had dusters tied to her feet which she rubbed vigorously up and down the oak parquet. Mme Hesling brought me my *petit déjeuner*, which consisted of a bowl of coffee made with milk and sugar and a piece of toast spread with real butter. My hosts were in a far happier financial position than my previous helpers, and able to augment their meagre rations from unofficial sources. When I had finished eating, I wished to make myself useful and offered my services in the kitchen, but Colette and her mother would not accept my assistance and bade me join M.Hesling in his office in another part of the building.

I was given an abundance of geography and history books with which to amuse myself while the little businessman carried on with his work. He was a wholesale dealer in wines and spirits, but, due to restrictions, his business was almost at a standstill. His day was spent making occasional phone calls and dictating one or two letters to his daughter, who played the role of shorthand typist.

The time I looked forward to each day was eleven o'clock, when we would adjourn to the dining-room to sip an *apéritif*. This was a small glass of the most delicious wine I had ever tasted. When I expressed my appreciation of it, M.Hesling winked and said, "The Germans think they have taken all the best wines from France, but they are wrong. The very best still gets put on one side, and the labels stuck on the bottles for transportation to Germany are often misleading."

Very often, as I sat in silence with a book in my hands, my thoughts would wander many miles away. Almost four months had passed since my descent into France, and still I was very little nearer home. All this time had been spent waiting and waiting for the Resistance Movement to arrange for my return, and I often wondered where I would have been had I taken the law entirely into my own hands and kept on running across the country towards Spain. Remembering lectures given by Intelligence officers to all aircrews before flying on operations, I recalled how it had been impressed upon us that once an airman was in the hands of the Resistance Movement he must realise that these people had a far better knowledge of actual conditions than he could possibly attain. If an evader were expected to hide in a tiny attic or a dark cellar for even a couple of months, he was to remember that his helpers advised him to do so for his own good.

One particular instance was quoted of an airman who was hidden in one room for fourteen days, but grew impatient, and, ignoring advice, put on his coat and left the house. Fifty yards along the road he was challenged by a German patrol who had seen him leave. He was taken back, and before the whole of the village he saw the entire family lined up with their backs to the wall of their home and machine-gunned. Such stories as this seemed incredible, and I had thought the airmen who had returned safely to England through occupied countries were 'shooting a line', but I appreciated now the truth of their experiences. I had been extremely lucky so far; I was getting well fed and even had my bed warmed at night. My mysterious M.X was taking a keen personal interest in my welfare.

He told me to be patient, and surely he knew better than anyone else the safest procedure for me to adopt.

Considering how conversant I was now with the French language, and that I possessed a fairly good knowledge of local customs, M.Hesling suggested that we should take a walk together one afternoon. I washed, shaved, and cleaned my shoes in preparation for my first venture outside the house in daylight. Leaving by the front door, we walked together up the gravel path towards the ornamental iron gates. Stepping into the street, we headed for the outskirts of the town. My little benefactor was apparently highly respected in the neighbourhood. From time to time he would raise his hat, politely returning the greetings of passers-by.

Working our way through narrow back streets, with the drainage from the sinks of the houses running down the centre, we began to climb out of the valley. Soon we had left the buildings behind and were walking among the well cared-for allotments on both sides of the hill. Pausing for breath, we looked back across the rooftops, and my guide pointed out the railway station, prison, post-office, and various other places of interest. Recalling the walks I had taken in the dark with Micheline, I was able to judge in what part of the town my previous residence had been. I knew M.Althuser 's studio was almost opposite the railway station; in an emergency I could probably find my way there and recognise the house again. Most of the allotments possessed a tiny summer house, where the owners could come out of town and spend the weekend. Some were little more than a couple of sheets of tin, but others were well built and brightly painted, with roses growing round the door and a few yards of lawn in front. We meandered amongst the rows of vegetables past the reservoir and then reached the open fields. Standing behind a hedge, M.Hesling pointed out a German flak tower in the centre of the field. It consisted of a sand-bagged platform mounted about fifteen feet off the ground on wooden beams and I imagined it could accommodate several machine guns for use against low-flying aircraft, but nothing of a heavier calibre.

Retracing our steps down into the town, my companion resumed his graceful smile and salutations to his numerous acquaintances. We rounded off a very pleasant day playing draughts and backgammon, a new game which I soon learned.

CHAPTER NINE

Preparations for a Journey

The following morning, M.X visited the house and the wine merchant told him of the pleasant stroll we had taken together the previous afternoon. The hue and cry of recent arrests had died down and no members of M.X's organisation had been seized except the radio operator, whose execution had already been carried out. My visitor considered that an occasional cautious venture in the outside world would be beneficial and give me confidence for my journey home, which would probably involve travelling by train and crossing Paris.

My hair had grown very long and looked out of place when I wore a collar and tie with my suit. With a twinkle in his eye, M.X suggested that I should visit a hairdresser. It was then I noticed his sense of humour and daring character. Casting behind him a witty remark to Mme Hesling as she warned him to take great care, he led the way out.

We walked together down the street towards the centre of the town. Before reaching the main shopping centre we turned off into a deserted little alleyway at the rear of some houses. Here my companion took out of his pocket a piece of lint and a small roll of sticking plaster and said "Members of the hairdressing profession are usually very talkative." He told me that from then on I was to imagine I had a boil on my upper lip and proceeded to stick the plaster and lint into place, explaining that he would do all the necessary talking in case my accent aroused suspicion.

Round the corner we found a vacant chair in the hairdresser's. M.X said his little piece about my supposed boil and informed the barber that I wanted my hair short back and sides. I grunted my appreciation of the lengthy expression of sympathy offered by the gentleman with the scissors, then settled down in the chair listening to an exchange of views between my friend and the barber on the various boils they had been afflicted with from time to time.

"Is this the first one you have had?" I was asked, in between the snipping sounds of scissors. I nodded my head, whereupon the barber assured me I would most probably have two or three more elsewhere before I got rid of them. In the mirror I could see a smile flickering across the face of my fellow conspirator. When the job was finished, I fumbled in my wallet while my companion had time to step forward and pay, saying that it so happened he had the exact number of francs in his pocket.

Leaving the shop, we returned to the alleyway and he removed the plaster. "You might as well take a little fresh air before you go back," said my companion, and we set off towards the outskirts of the town.

I was curious to know more about this mysterious man who was doing so much to help me and yet guarded his identity with such care. Judging by his appearance, his clothes, the cleanliness of his hands, cultured speech and intelligent conversation, I imagined him to be a doctor. The production of the sticking plaster and lint strengthened my suspicions, but it would have been very indiscreet to ask questions.

Each day since my arrival in France had improved my vocabulary and I could now understand almost everything that was said to me. Apart from some grammatical mistakes I could carry on a conversation reasonably well.

The more I spoke with my unknown companion the better I liked him, and the mystery of his identity was an additional fascination. Strolling along together through the countryside he asked me if I were happy in my new home and if there was anything I needed. I told him that M.Hesling and his family were extremely kind to me, but needless to say the uppermost thought in my head was the desire to see England.

Now that I had received a smart haircut there was only one thing which marred my appearance – my boots. Apparently, M.X had noticed that they were falling to pieces and had already made arrangements for their replacement. The following evening Micheline would call and take me to a house at the back of a shoe shop where I would be fitted with a brand-new pair.

Walking and talking together, we made our way back towards the town and I was soon once more in the shelter of M.Hesling's home. Here we discussed the possibility of a slightly more adventurous outing. There was no bath in the portion of the house which had not been requisitioned, so M.Hesling regularly visited a public wash-house in the town. I had not even seen a bath since leaving England, and after careful discussion it was ultimately agreed that I should accompany M.Hesling when he paid his weekly visit the following morning.

Having listened to the news report and finished our coffee and toast, M.Hesling and I set off down the main street in the direction of the public baths. We went by the post office in the main boulevard to post some letters. Looking at the large shops, cafés, and the lines of trees on either footpath, I tried to visualise exactly where I had passed in the dark with Micheline. There were plenty of Germans about, and we passed in front of the building in which they had established their

Monsieur'X'

headquarters. Several military vehicles were parked outside and a steel-helmeted sentry stood on guard at the entrance.

Arriving at the baths, we found a small queue waiting at the pay-box. When our turn came, my friend bought two tickets, hired two towels, and then we both stood on one side waiting for a shower to be vacated. One portion of the building was devoted to ladies and the other to gentlemen, and while we stood by the wall waiting, a familiar young lady stepped out of the curtained partition. It was Janine, the photographer's daughter. She looked directly into my face, but, although she realised who I was, she did not pause or betray the slightest outward sign of recognition. She knew only too well the risk her father was taking in his Resistance activities, and together with her young brother she had been schooled in the art of controlling her emotions and concealing her surprise.

While we patiently awaited our turn, two German soldiers walked into the building. They had come for a shower and had priority, so took the next two which became vacant. By now

M.Hesling and I had advanced to the head of the queue, and when my turn came I found my shower in between those occupied by the Nazis. Frequently they called to one another over the partition, and eventually both burst into song. The feel of hot water spraying down on my body, washing out my pores after such a long time, was extremely invigorating. This, together with the singularity of the whole situation, made me feel very cock-sure and I had to suppress a desire to join in the singing. Looking at my civilian clothes hanging on the hook and knowing that a short distance on either side hung two green German uniforms made me chuckle to myself as the water streamed over my face. The voices on either side began to render the popular German Army song *'Lili Marlene',* and I couldn't help whistling a meek little accompaniment to the catchy tune.

That evening, Colette returned to her father after answering the front doorbell to tell him a young lady had called to see him on private business and was waiting in the office below. The visitor was Micheline, whom I was to accompany in quest of a pair of new boots or shoes.

Making our way through the pitch-dark streets, we reached the side door of a little cobbler's shop. The young French woman gave the prearranged signal of four light taps and the door was opened. When we stepped inside, the door was re-locked and I was introduced to the cobbler and his wife. Three or four pairs of brand-new shoes were brought into the room. The uppers were of leather but the soles were made of a thick piece of plywood which had saw cuts from alternate sides every half-inch, making them reasonably pliant. When a pair had been selected which gave as much comfort as one could expect from a semi-wooden article, glasses of wine were produced and quiet but sincere toasts were drunk to the victory of the Allies. The cobbler told me with a proud smile on his face that I was not the first Allied airman he had helped; a few months earlier an American flyer had been sitting in that very same chair.

Leaving my old boots behind to be repaired, I shook hands with my two new acquaintances and walked away uncertainly on my wooden soles. Gradually the stiffness wore off and the wood became more flexible, and by the time we had wandered round the town and returned once more to the big iron gates of my sanctuary, they bent quite freely with each step I took.

The following day M.Hesling was too busy to go out for a walk and asked me if I would care to leave the house alone. I agreed very enthusiastically and spent an hour wandering in and out of the narrowest streets I could find, avoiding the busy shopping centre. I had a wonderful feeling of confidence, knowing I was dressed as well as, if not better than, the average young man-about-town.

From time to time I touched my identity card as it lay in my pocket, together with some money. I had almost forgotten that I was associated in any way with the RAF, so often had I repeated to myself that I was none other than Denis Lebenec, born in Carnac and working at a cheese factory. The thought that pleased me most was that M.Hesling actually regarded me as being able to speak his language sufficiently well to wander round the town and to be capable of looking after myself if anything unforeseen should arise. Repeatedly glancing sideways at my reflection in the various windows, I could not help thinking to myself, "Yes, you certainly look as much like a Frenchman as anyone else in the town."

A German guard outside the Préfecture, Bar-le-Duc
(photo M. Althuser)

Returning exactly on time, I found M.Hesling looking eagerly out of the office window for me. A big step forward had been made, and from that day on I used to take short walks morning and afternoon.

The time passed quickly, and at the end of a fortnight I ventured into the centre of the town. I had conquered the feeling that every German in uniform was looking for me, and if I was looking in a shop window and suddenly found a Nazi soldier standing beside me with a rifle in his hand, my hair no longer stood on end. I would just continue my examination of the window and then casually turn and walk away.

I had been living in the Hesling home for three weeks and knew my way in and out of every back street in the little town. Although I appeared to walk about casually enough, I never took a step forward without having in the back of my mind a fixed route by which I could extricate myself if any dangerous situation arose. I kept a sharp look-out ahead, and casual glances behind me as I looked into shop windows or stooped to tie my shoe-lace, gave me a fairly good idea who was following me.

On the first morning of the fourth week I was busy helping M.Hesling with some odd jobs round the house. Mme Hesling had asked us to move a stove for her, and in dragging it along the passage I got my thumb wedged against a sheet of tin underneath. As soon as the stove was in position, Colette and her mother insisted that I should bathe my hand in hot water and disinfectant. Sitting there with my thumb in hot water, I heard the front doorbell and Colette went to see who it was. She returned with my very welcome friend, M.X, who told me that a man was waiting downstairs in the office who would take me a step nearer England. I jumped for joy and dashed round the house collecting my coat and beret. When M.X looked at my thumb, my suspicions that he was a doctor were again aroused by the prompt and efficient way in which he bandaged it.

Down in the office I shook hands with a dark, serious-faced young man about twenty-five years old. He was the agent whom M.X had been expecting for the past three weeks. Briefly, it was explained to me that when this gentleman left the house I was to follow him at a distance of about fifty yards or so. He would lead the way into the railway station, and while he bought a ticket I was to stand at a newspaper kiosk looking at the postcards until a ticket was slipped into my hand. I was to follow wherever he went, and get into the same carriage as he did, but on no account was I to reveal that I was associated with him. When we reached our destination the procedure was to be the same. I must hand in my ticket at the barrier and then continue to trail the young man at a safe distance.

Looking at his watch, M.X said that we had very little time to spare, so M Hesling quickly poured out four glasses of whisky and we drank to each other's health, safety, and to the victory. As I shook hands with Colette, she gave me a little bracelet with tiny figures attached and told me to keep it as a lucky charm. I shook hands with M.and Mme Hesling and thanked them sincerely for their kindness towards me, asked M.X to give my kindest regards to the little interpreter and my other friends in Bar-le-Duc, and said that I looked forward to seeing them all again someday. M.X gripped my hand tightly and I noticed for the first time that his face looked rather pale. Quietly and calmly he told me that M.Colin, the rosy-cheeked little cheese merchant of Sampigny, had been arrested the previous evening, and M.Althuser, the photographer, had been dragged from his home by the Gestapo only a few hours ago. No one knew where the next Gestapo raid would be made, and once I was on the train I could consider myself extremely fortunate to be getting away from the town alive.

There was no time to say anything in reply, for he wished me luck and turned to follow the younger man, who was already walking up the gravel path. Giving them fifty yards' start, I began to follow them. Half-way through the town they separated; M.X crossed the road and stood on a corner until I came level with him. With his hands in his pockets and a cigarette drooping from his mouth, he gave a slight wink and half-smile which no one else in the street could possibly have noticed. But I knew it meant: 'Cheerio. Think of me, still in France, when you are safely back in England!'

CHAPTER TEN

The Chenu Brothers

The young man in front was so typically French that it would have been very easy to lose him, so I determined to keep my eyes glued to his distant figure. Each time he turned a corner I lost sight of him, but he must have appreciated my difficulty for he walked slowly for a short distance after each turning before hurrying on at his normal speed. Entering the station a few seconds behind him, I spotted the newspaper kiosk and was standing beside it casually surveying the items for sale when I suddenly became aware of someone close beside me. My arm was hanging loosely by my side and I felt a ticket pressed into the palm of my hand. The moment my fingers closed, my guide moved quickly away and passed through the barrier on to the platform. A train was standing farther up the platform with all the doors closed and the guard signalling it away. Casting a quick glance behind him to make sure I had come through the barrier, my friend broke into a run, grabbed a door handle and swung himself into the carriage. The train had started to move away before I had reached the open door, and as I sprinted alongside and got aboard, I heard a porter shout his disapproval. But it was so very, very important for me to catch the train that I think I would have tried to jump on an express if it had been necessary.

There was one seat vacant in the compartment, so I took it, directly opposite a fair-haired youth who was all smiles and seemed dying to start a conversation by remarking how nearly I had missed the train. Next to him sat my new friend, whom I had decided to think of as Monsieur 'Y'. I wanted to look at him carefully and try to assess his character, occupation, and so on, but each time I turned my head towards him I seemed to meet the eyes of the smiling youth. I began to think perhaps he, too, was in the conspiracy and looked at M.Y questioningly. He must have read my thoughts, for bringing his handkerchief to his nose he pressed his forefinger to his pursed lips, indicating that I should not speak to the youth. Finding I was more interested in watching the countryside than in talking, he turned towards my colleague and two or three times tried to get into conversation with him.

As the train rumbled through the countryside, I began to wonder where it was taking me. After sitting there for a few minutes I realised that there was one obvious way in which I could find out. I took the ticket out of my pocket and read on it the name Revigny. This told me my destination, but I had not the slightest idea whereabouts in France it was or whether it was a village or town. At first, I hoped it would be somewhere on the outskirts of Paris, but remembering the size of the train and the non-corridor coaches, I came to the conclusion that it must be a local which would only be travelling a short distance.

Twice the train came to rest at country stations, and peasant folk bundled in and out of the compartment with their baskets. When it slowed down for the third time, I read the name on the platform — Revigny. M.Y stood up and opened the door, but unfortunately the youth also got out and obviously intended they should walk off the platform together. But my guide had other intentions, and I saw him deliberately push his way into the crowd as they walked towards the exit. Reaching the barrier, the elder man handed in his ticket and passed on, but the young fellow started rummaging in his pockets and could not find his, so I pushed my way through with the rest of the passengers. Just as I drew level, he waved his ticket, and, turning to me with his face covered with smiles, said triumphantly, "Hurray, I've found the darn thing." I grinned in reply and tried to shake him off as quickly as possible.

Outside the station, I caught sight of the man whom I knew was leading me nearer to England. Assuring himself that I was following, he set off down the street and led the way through what I found to be a much smaller place than Bar-le-Duc. But the two towns had one thing in common: they were both divided by a river. The roadway took us over a newly constructed bridge and I saw on either side a mass of twisted girders half out of the water, evidence of the effort made by the French Army to stop the Panzer Divisions as they rushed through the country earlier in the war. In the centre of the town, I saw further indications of street fighting having taken place, bullet marks and shrapnel scars spattered at the street corners.

M.Y was joined by a younger but bigger and more heavily built man, whom I learned later was his brother. Still keeping the fifty yards distance between us, I followed the pair until we reached a deserted stretch of the road. There the brothers stopped and beckoned me to join them. When I drew level they shook hands warmly and walked on, one on either side of me.

Reaching the edge of the town, we stopped in front of a gate made of sheet iron half an inch thick, built in a high stone wall. The elder brother produced a key and led the way through the opening, shutting the door with a clang and re-locking it. We were standing in a courtyard about twenty yards by forty yards. The two longer sides were formed by a large old-fashioned house and a long wooden workshop which faced each other at right angles to the roadway. The far end was closed by a lower stone wall surmounted with spiked iron rails, through which I could see a garden and orchard beyond.

Entering the house, we mounted the staircase in single file. At the top, the landing led off in two directions; turning to the right we entered a kitchen. There was the usual wood-burning stove with which I had now become familiar in every French house, and a stone sink with the largest water-pump I had yet seen. The handle was at least five feet long; when it was used it was raised above the head and brought down to the knees. The furniture consisted of a fairly modern kitchen cabinet, a table covered with oilcloth, and a few chairs. A quick glance round told me that the presence of a woman in the house was missing. The top of the stove was dirty and the table top covered with cigarette burns; although the floor had been swept, it had obviously not been washed for a long time.

My two new friends introduced themselves. The elder one, whom I had called M.Y, was Louis Chenu, twenty-five years old, and the other was his eighteen-year-old brother Jean. They apologised for the state of the kitchen, saying they did all the housework themselves as they had no mother to look after them. They began to unfold the sad story of their family.

Pre-war, there had been the father, mother, and three sons, Henri, Louis and Jean, and with them lived an elderly uncle. The father was a proprietor of the joiner's shop on the other side of the courtyard, and the two elder sons worked with him, together with ten other carpenters. Jean was still at school, and the uncle spent all his time pottering about the garden and orchard, which he kept in immaculate condition. The business flourished; the family owned their own car and employed servants. Fate turned against them in 1937, the first blow being the death of their mother. Shortly afterwards came the war. Louis entered the Army and was away from home when the Germans overran France in 1940. The father, uncle and two sons piled on to their car as many treasured belongings as possible and joined the pitiful trek of refugees fleeing southwards. Returning after the Armistice, they found their home and workshop still standing, but they had been ransacked. Louis showed me some of the furniture which he had repaired – a door, the panels of which had been kicked in, and several pictures which had been deliberately smashed. The evacuation had told badly on the elderly uncle and he passed away not long after the return home. M.Chenu, who had been badly wounded in the 1914-18 war, died a few months later. Louis was at this time a prisoner-of-war but obtained his release to carry on the business. The three brothers then lived alone, but Henri, the eldest, had never been strong, and less than a year later was buried beside his parents. Louis and Jean were now the only survivors of what had been a happy family. Realising how great a part the war had played in their misfortunes, they had developed a hatred of the Nazis even greater than that of their fellow-countrymen, and from then onwards put their heart and soul into the Resistance Movement. They had already done a great deal of excellent work, regardless of the risk to which they exposed themselves.

'Denis Lebenec' flanked by the fearless Chenu brothers, Louis and Jean

Louis pointed to a calendar. It was 10 February 1944, and, indicating a day five days ahead, said that on that date I would be home. Immediately I bombarded him with questions, for the news seemed too good to be true. I knew very well that one was not supposed to ask questions regarding Resistance activities, but I had been disappointed on so many occasions that I longed to know more solid facts about my repatriation.

Louis told me that the actual place where the aircraft would come down was several miles away from Revigny. This would necessitate another train journey and an overnight stay in a house in Nancy. A few weeks previously, three American airmen had stayed a few days with the brothers and then returned through this particular organisation. This sounded very convincing, but I still pressed for more details. Louis had not accompanied the men to Nancy, so how could he know they got away successfully? He assured me that a radio message had been received from the London BBC. Still inquisitive, I asked him if he or his brother had ever seen an aircraft come down and take-off again in Occupied France. On one occasion, they said, Louis had formed part of a guard of patriots round a field where one of these secret landings had taken place.

At last I was on the trail I wanted and eagerly asked him what sort of aircraft it was, but beyond recalling that it had two engines he could tell me very little. He could give a better description of the pilot, who had stood at the side of the machine for a few seconds. He was exceptionally tall, wore a moustache and a flying kit with many zip fasteners. Louis said that he saw four men get out and four others take their place before the aircraft took off again, but he was not one of the privileged few who knew who these eight men were. He thought they were all Frenchmen, but he had had no opportunity to speak with these mysterious passengers who passed to and fro into enemy territory at the break of dawn.

Jean produced some photographs showing how beautiful their home had been in earlier years, and, looking through the shutters into the courtyard, he pointed out the goldfish pond, rose bed, and various garden ornaments which were now partially covered with piles of timber and weeds.

Louis left the house and returned a short time later with a lady who was introduced to me as Madame Marie Stef. This thirty-year-old brunette with dark, flashing eyes lived nearby and helped the boys in many ways, cooking most of their meals and doing all she could to help them with their Resistance activities. When she saw how appropriately dressed I was and found I could understand and speak French reasonably well, it was decided that I could go along to her house with the brothers for my meals without the suspicion of the other neighbours being aroused.

Jean was very keen on flying and soon began showing me his piles of magazines on model aircraft building. His ambition was to be a pilot in the Free French Air Force, and he asked me what exams had to be passed before being considered for training, and if I thought he would be eligible. The afternoon passed quickly and at five o'clock Louis suggested that we should go along to Mme Marie's. Slipping on berets and coats, we descended the stairs. Louis walked ahead up the road while Jean and I trooped behind with hands in pockets. After a hundred yards, Louis turned off, and, passing through a gateway, entered a small bungalow. Sauntering along, we saw him reappear and signal that all was well for us to follow. Entering the bungalow we found Mme Marie pumping water at the side of the sink. Standing beside her were her two children, Claude, aged seven, and his four-year-old sister, Annie. Each came forward in turn and shook hands with me, whispering a quiet *"Bonjour, Monsieur"*.

Here was yet another French family with a sad background. Before the war, Mme Marie and her husband had operated a little market garden which made enough profit to support themselves and their baby son in comfort. The husband, Robert Stef, was called up for the Army, and while he was away little Annie was born. He was given a few days' compassionate leave to see his wife and baby daughter and that was the last time he had been home, for shortly after his visit he had been taken prisoner and had been in Germany ever since. The German Army began to surge through the North of France and Mme Marie had evacuated with the rest of the town, pushing a handcart with her most precious possessions, three-year-old Claude and her very young baby. The pitiful little party did not get very far south and was soon overtaken by the onrushing German divisions. There was no point in running any farther, so she turned her handcart round and trudged wearily back to Revigny. At this time she did not know whether her husband was alive or dead, and as she plodded into the town the poor young mother received a further shock. Smoke was rising from various parts of the town and as she got nearer she found her own home was ablaze. It had been deliberately set alight by the German troops for their own amusement and they were standing round enjoying the scene of destruction. With her children in her arms she stood crying and screaming at them until she dropped to the ground exhausted, but they only turned away and laughed.

The Chenu family were still in the South of France, and as their big house was empty and her own in ruins, she went to live in one of the rooms there. A few weeks later, when the rightful owners returned, M.Chenu told her she was welcome to stay with them until she could find somewhere else to live. Eventually, the Government erected a home for her on a plot of land belonging to her husband. This was the bungalow in which I was now standing. It was a very roughly built affair, in no way comparable to the prefabricated houses constructed in England. It was a square building divided into five sections. The doors and windows were poorly made and fitted badly, and the entire floor was bare concrete. The largest section of the home served as kitchen and living-room, containing the sink and water-pump, the usual wood-burning stove with the flat top and tin pipe passing through the ceiling, a sideboard, kitchen table, six chairs and a small radio. I learnt later that nearly all the furniture had been made by Louis. Our hostess said something to Louis about some haricot beans which needed shelling, and as he left the room I offered to go with him and help. Walking round the back of the bungalow past the chicken run, we came to a barn. Inside were lots of rabbit hutches, a goat in a pen, a disused pigsty, a handcart, and a lot of gardening tools. Hanging from the rafters were dozens of bunches of haricot beans which had been there since the summer and were now quite dry. I had spent hours and hours in my various hiding places shelling similar bunches and imagined there was enough work here to last many days. Louis had a quick way of shelling them. He put a couple of bunches in a sack, laid it on the ground, and started beating it heavily with a garden fork. Taking another sack and fork, I did likewise, and after a few dozen blows we pulled the bunches out of the sacks and found the dry pods had all split open. The beans lay at the bottom of the sacks ready for tipping out into a large dish we had ready for them. The light was failing, but we continued this rapid method of shelling until it was impossible to see. Re-entering the bungalow, we found the evening meal waiting on the table. I certainly lost no time in disposing of my plateful of deliciously cooked rabbit and mixed vegetables. The two children were put to bed while the rest of us crouched round the radio and listened to the impressive beat of the drums and the announcer's voice calling *"Ici Londres"*. The news from the Russian front was excellent and our troops were still advancing slowly but surely in Italy. When the announcements were over, my three friends turned and asked the inevitable question: "How long will it be before an invasion is made across the Channel?"

The evening amongst new company had passed quickly, and we suddenly realised that it was almost curfew time. Donning our berets, we wished Mme Marie *"Bonsoir"* and departed. Louis walked ahead and opened the door into the courtyard while his brother and I concealed ourselves in the shadows until we heard his low whistle indicating that all was well. Inside the house, the brothers showed me a room on the ground floor where I was to sleep. Before retiring for the night, I was given an old rifle and twenty rounds of ammunition for use in emergency. The brothers were sleeping in a room directly overhead and it was agreed that if three taps were given on the floor I was to grab my weapon and join them upstairs. From there we could make our way along through the bedrooms to the extreme end of the building and descend a small disused staircase leading to a door in the corner of the courtyard. Louis also had a rifle and his brother carried a heavy American automatic pistol. If the house became surrounded we would do our best to shoot our way out into the open country. Wishing me a good night's sleep they promised to give two trial taps above so that I could identify the signal. I listened to their footsteps mounting the staircase and then came two sharp, unmistakable knocks from above. Picking up the rifle, I used it to sound a similar reply on the ceiling and then sat down on the edge of the bed to examine the weapon thoroughly.

It was an old French cavalry-style rifle with a short barrel, and had probably not been fired since the last World War. Opening the breech, I found a further five rounds. The mechanism was oily but badly needed cleaning. The barrel was filthy but I could at least see light through the end. The firing pin was in the bolt and there seemed no reason why the gun should not operate. The ammunition was approximately the same size as the standard ·303 with which I was familiar, but a closer examination of the cartridge cases revealed various years of manufacture between 1918 and 1939. Selecting the five bearing the most recent dates, I reloaded the rifle, hoping the ammunition would fire if the necessity arose, and leaned it against the wall beside the bedpost.

The brothers had told me that men of all nationalities had slept in that particular bed during the previous two years, and when I pulled back the clothes I certainly believed them! Partially undressing, I laid my trousers where I could grab them at a second's notice. In spite of the electric fire, I found the bedclothes rather damp because they had not been slept in for several weeks.

Unable to sleep, I lay thinking of M.Althuser and M.Colin, each locked in a cell somewhere, and of their families who would be waiting for the dreaded news of their execution. I thought of

M.Clément, M.Hesling, Micheline and the cobbler and his wife, hoping that they had taken sufficient precautions for their own safety. I knew M.X would now be lying in hiding miles away from Bar-le-Duc; he had told me so.

Four more nights in France and then I would fly back to England! What a glorious thought! I began to imagine opening the garden gate at home, running down the path and bursting through the front door to tell my family that I was alive and well. I dropped off to sleep with these thoughts. The next thing I remember was imagining I heard my mother's footsteps approaching the bedroom. The door opened, the light was switched on and I sat up in bed expecting to see her standing there with my breakfast on a tray, as she did when I was on leave. Instead, there was a dark-complexioned fellow with untidy hair and badly needing a shave, holding out a bowl towards me. I blinked my eyes and brought my senses to reality; I was still in France and Louis stood at my bedside with a bowl of black coffee. Slowly sipping the dark liquid consisting mainly of chicory and scorched oats, I said how lucky I was to be so well looked after by a couple of splendid patriots. Jean came through the door and said that they were very proud to have the opportunity of helping an Englishman. They had rendered assistance to Frenchmen, escaping from Germany, American airmen, and escaped Russian prisoners of war, but never before had an Englishman slept in the house.

CHAPTER ELEVEN

The Underground

For several days Louis had been awaiting a message regarding my departure, but when at last he did get news it gave me yet another disappointment. The people through whose hands I was to pass in Nancy had been arrested, the rest of the organisation were all lying low and my departure would be delayed for at least another fortnight. I had now become accustomed to the disasters which always seemed to foil attempts at my repatriation, and I realised how lucky I was that I had not actually been in the houses when the Gestapo raids had been carried out. I had been told of other airmen who had passed through the hands of the underground movement and returned to England within a few weeks of being shot down, but somehow Fate seemed against me.

The brothers had a precious hoard of old-fashioned guns hidden in a cellar, but it would require several days of hard cleaning to bring them into a reasonably reliable condition, so I set to work with renewed vigour. By now, I was rapidly becoming as enthusiastic as my two companions and hoped an occasion would arise before my return home when I could take part in a small ambush or any offensive action which would give me my revenge on the Nazis for the sufferings they were inflicting on some of my French friends. I paid particular attention to a German Mauser automatic pistol, for which I found several rounds of ammunition. The moving parts were soon put into working order, but the clip in which the rounds were secured and then pushed into position up the handle was missing. I considered the possibility of making one with the aid of pieces of metal lying around the workshop, but without the original object to copy from I found the task beyond my ability. This meant that each individual round would have to be loaded separately. Placing one cartridge in position, I moved over the safety catch and slid it into the inside pocket of my jacket, feeling that now as I walked along the road to Mme Marie's for my meals I would not be entirely helpless if an emergency arose.

I knew that by wearing civilian clothes and carrying a gun I was violating my rights in international law as a military person who was evading capture. I had already decided, however, that if trouble arose, I was certainly not going to raise my hands above my head, shout "*Kamerad*", plead to being a defenceless airman and end up behind barbed wire as a prisoner of war, while my friends Louis and Jean would be executed for helping me. They were risking their lives daily in the attempt to get me back home and I was prepared to take the same risk to shoot our way out of trouble, side by side.

The following Sunday morning, the three of us set about our weekly toilet, sharing the razor blade and tiny piece of soap, wetting our hair, then combing it into position. Brushing the dust off our best clothes, we prepared to go round to Mme Marie's little home for our Sunday dinner. At the bungalow, little Annie opened the door for us, and stepping inside I found a stranger sitting there. He was elderly and quietly spoken, and his bent back, weather-beaten complexion and rough hands showed that he had spent the majority of his seventy-odd years working on the land. Mme Marie introduced him as her father-in-law, who lived on the other side of the town in a little cottage and visited her once a week to have a Sunday dinner. Today's menu included a rabbit, vegetables, and some of the most delicious gravy I had yet tasted in France. The steaming platefuls were put on the table and quickly devoured by hungry mouths, and within a few minutes each plate was being carefully wiped clean with pieces of black bread. Fruit tart and custard followed; then we sat back, contentedly smoking cigarettes and sipping black ersatz coffee. All the meals I ate at Mme Marie's were plain and wholesome, but I usually left the table feeling that I could easily eat the same amount again. I never had anything to eat in the morning except perhaps a piece of toast and coffee, and the next meal, after dinner, would not be served until seven or eight in the evening.

The winter afternoon was crisp and fresh and it seemed a shame to stay indoors, so Louis suggested we should all venture out to take a walk through the town together. An overcoat hung in Mme Marie's wardrobe, unused since the day her husband had joined the Army. It fitted me perfectly and there was even a pair of gloves in the pocket. We set off down the road with Claude and Annie, each holding one of my hands. If anyone should happen to ask who I was, Louis would say I was his cousin. There were several other families taking advantage of the pleasant afternoon. Occasionally greetings would be exchanged across the road, but no one looked at me with suspicion. The old gentleman was rather nervous of walking beside me and seemed only too pleased when we reached a point where he turned off towards his home. As I shook his hand, I felt it trembling. There were not many people who could take risks so coolly and with such outward unconcern as the two brothers and their generous little neighbour.

The following week I saw further evidence of Louis' Resistance activities. He had a collection of printed cards and rubber stamps similar to those which had been used to make my own set of false documents. I helped him to make them out and stick into position the photos of several young men who were evading conscription. Already, several dozen had passed through the house and were now living on out-of-the-way farms up and down the countryside.

The brothers were in daily danger of being arrested, and Louis sometimes said that he himself doubted whether he would still be alive to join in the celebrations when France was finally liberated. Their plans for escape in the event of a Gestapo raid on the house were very vague and I told them that a few additional precautions could increase their chances considerably. The three exits from the house all led into the courtyard, so that the moment the Germans entered it we would be like rats in a trap. There were no windows whatsoever along the rear wall of the building, which looked on to the outhouses of the large mansion next door, but the loft over the woodshed had wooden walls. So I suggested that an emergency hatchway be cut by which we could drop to the ground on the neighbour's territory at a point that was only a few feet away from the shrubbery. We could then make our way through the bushes to the small wood at the bottom of the garden and ultimately into open country.

Louis went round to the neighbour's, and under the pretence that he wished to carry out some repairs to the gutters on his own property, obtained permission to carry round a ladder and his bag of tools. While Louis worked on the outside, Jean and I worked in the loft. At the end of a couple of hours, hinges had been fixed to three of the boards in the wall so that they would open outwards like a trap door but would fall back into their original position again as soon as released. The ground below was so hard and uneven that it would be very easy to sprain an ankle jumping down in the darkness, so we constructed a special ladder. To one end we attached metal bars, bent in such a fashion that they could be hooked over a thick wooden beam forming the ledge from which we had previously intended jumping. The ladder was short enough to be fitted across the limited space in the loft, but by climbing down as it hung in, we could drop off the end on to the ground quite comfortably. In the event of an emergency, the last man to descend would reach up from the foot of the wall and unhook the ladder, use it to knock away the stick propping open the secret door and finally hide it in the bushes nearby. The side of the loft would then look quite normal and only the most thorough examination would reveal the carefully concealed hinges.

This was a definite improvement, but the next thing was to plan our manoeuvres once we were clear of the house. We spent a couple of days reconnoitring the fields behind, and I learnt that the river ran a short distance away. This was about 25ft wide at its narrowest point. Jean and I would have no difficulty in swimming across the current, but Louis would have to be towed. The prospect of having to do this was not very inviting, for I knew how easy it would be for a non-swimmer to panic in midstream – especially if the Nazis were following along in hot pursuit. Moreover, there was very little in the way of cover for a quarter of a mile on either bank. A more practical idea would be to follow the hedge from the foot of the garden until it reached a ditch. Dropping into this, we would be completely out of sight and could move along, following its wide curve to where it passed below the roadway via a tunnel just big enough for us to squeeze through. Once we were safely under the road, a further hundred yards could be travelled along the bottom of the ditch until we finally emerged in the open fields, heading in the direction least expected by any pursuers who might by this time have realised that we had vacated the house from the rear.

The furniture production was now almost at a standstill. Louis was too much occupied with his Resistance activities, Jean had never been trained as a joiner and had very little interest in woodwork. The young Spaniard they employed was not turning out enough work to merit his wage, so Louis regretfully informed him that he would have to look for a job elsewhere. His departure increased my freedom considerably, for I could now go to and from the workshop as I pleased. Every day I spent hours enjoying the privilege of working with an array of tools and machines extensive enough to make any amateur green with envy.

Each day brought springtime nearer and there was a great deal of work to be done in Mme Marie's garden, making preparation for the vegetables to be planted which would feed her own little household, the two brothers, and whatever 'guests' they might have throughout the coming year. This was an excellent opportunity for me to use some of my stored-up energy. It was arranged that I should spend the mornings in the workshop helping Louis to cut logs on the circular saw, or whatever jobs needed doing, and then after dinner work in Mme Marie's garden.

A high hedge separated the plot of land from the roadway, behind which I could spend my time digging without much danger of interruption. My first job was to go carefully between the rows of tiny plants which had been in the ground throughout the winter, forming ridges with a spade just high enough to cover the plants completely with soil. Each day afterwards I was to look out for any leaves pushing through the surface and cover them. When I told Mme Marie we did not eat any vegetables like these in England she looked at me in surprise and said that surely the *"pissenlit"* grew in England, pointing to the dandelions in the hedge bottom. I soon learnt that the seeds which I had often blown off dandelion clocks when I was younger were a potential winter salad in France. The seeds were planted at the end of the summer, and because the leaves were not allowed to see the sunlight, they remained crisp and white, resembling miniature celery. There was quite a demand for them in the neighbourhood, and every day I dug a fresh basketful for Mme Marie to sell.

There was a lot of work to do; the ducks, hens, rabbits, and goats had to be fed and cleaned out, so my time passed less monotonously than before. The two goats – Marie's, which was called Ninette, and Louis' fiery little creature which guarded the entrance to the secret cellar – were both in kid, so I endeavoured to give them the best attention possible.

I was introduced to another young man from the town known as 'Petit Lefumer'; he was an undersized little fellow who visited the house each week to see his old school pal Jean. An old pipe was always clenched between his teeth, even when he was amusing us with his acrobatic antics such as walking round the kitchen table standing on his hands. He was the local cinema operator and told me of all the precautions the Nazis took before a film show for the German troops. Two soldiers walked up and down each row of seats looking for bombs before the rest were allowed to enter. While the film was in progress, one man mounted guard outside the entrance, while another stood in the projection room keeping a watchful eye on little Lefumer. Another week slipped by without any message being received, and once more it was Sunday, the day of rest. A rabbit was reduced to a small pile of cleanly picked bones and each dinner plate carefully polished clean with a piece of bread lest any of the precious gravy be wasted. Mme Marie served hot coffee, Louis handed round the cigarettes and then we set out for an afternoon stroll in the sunshine. Back once more in the homely warmth of the bungalow, we played a few card games and the evening soon slipped by. It was almost curfew hour when we made our way cautiously down the road to the bleak-looking house where we slept. Another week in France had passed without mishap, but I was determined that further precautions would have to be taken in the very near future before the luck which the brothers had enjoyed for so long gave way with fatal results.

It had been the custom, whenever the doorbell rang, for Louis to go out into the courtyard and shout "Who's there?" before unlocking the iron gate. This seemed a very inefficient arrangement so, on my suggestion, Louis would slip off his clogs, silently approach the door, and peep through a little hole that we had made to see who was there. If he saw a German uniform he could tip-toe quietly away and warn us and we could carry out our evacuation as pre-arranged. The hole was bored about three feet six inches from the ground in order to be below the eye level of the person outside, and when it was first done it was quite a novelty for Louis to peep at each visitor before allowing admission. But even so, Jean and I stood behind the shuttered windows with rifles in our hands.

During the week I met a new friend, Raymond Picot. He was one of the many who were going around the countryside with the aid of forged identity cards. He had deserted from *Les Sapeurs-Pompiers de Paris* because his particular section had been destined for transfer to Germany. The *Sapeurs-Pompiers* were the Parisian Fire Brigade, noted for their high standard of physical fitness and discipline. I had already seen photos in various magazines showing them giving gymnastic displays and holding parades in Paris. As the bombing of the Reich increased, the Germans requisitioned a large percentage of the force to operate in Germany and it was to avoid this that Raymond was 'on the run'. He was a powerfully built, happy-go-lucky young fellow in his early twenties. He had had several narrow escapes and swore that he would not remain alive long enough after capture to be interrogated by the Gestapo. He always carried a razor blade sewn in the turn-up of his trousers with which to sever his wrists and bleed to death if captured. There are not many men who would have the will-power to do this but as I came to know Raymond better, I believed that he would have carried it out if the necessity arose. He brought news from the outlying villages of how many men could be called upon to fight, once they had the arms.

Arms! That was the problem. There were plenty of men longing for the opportunity to strike at the enemy, but all over the country the plight was the same – only old-fashioned, obsolete weapons were available. The RAF were dropping supplies, but this was a tremendous job. The Gestapo knew well enough how dangerous partisans could be if armed and organised. All the time, secret radio transmitters were being found, arms depots discovered, Maquis groups located, hostages taken for sabotage, and each day patriots were being tortured and executed. Raymond spoke of fresh arrests having been made in a district he knew well and of new and more terrible methods of torture being used to extract information.

We had a long discussion of the situation and decided that the invasion was bound to come soon. Almost every night the German industrial areas were getting hammered by heavy RAF bombing forces, and in the daytime the Americans were blasting the railways and other targets in occupied countries. A suitable place for the dropping of arms had already been selected and messages exchanged with England. Eventually we would be supplied with the hand-grenades, machine guns and explosives which we were longing to use. Until then we decided to start laying in a stock of food for ourselves and all the other patriots whom we could count on once we had the arms, but who, until that moment arrived, were remaining in hiding or continuing their everyday occupations.

The three main things to get hold of were flour, meat and potatoes. Once a good stock of these was laid in and we received arms, we would be prepared to carry out guerrilla warfare – operating either from a hideout in the woods or some derelict farmhouse in the country. Spring was approaching, and we felt sure that open fighting would break out in all the occupied countries. Each night the broadcasts from London were telling people to prepare to strike at the enemy when the signal was given, and they emphasised that one of the best things to do until that moment arrived was to lay aside in some secret place as much as they could possibly spare from their meagre rations. Groups of Maquis were urged to steal or destroy as much foodstuff as possible which was destined for Germany, so we discussed the various farmers in the district who were known to be profiting by selling their stocks to the Nazis and started to make our plans. Raymond knew a building a few miles away in which the Germans had stored several tons of grain commandeered in the region, prior to shipment to Germany by rail. This grain was unguarded. He planned to carry out a careful reconnaissance, and Louis said he would borrow a horse and cart. At one time Raymond had spent a couple of years as a butcher. He said that if we could rustle a cow he would kill it and we could cut it up and preserve it. We all went round to Mme Marie's for dinner but told her nothing of our plans, so that when we went out on our food raids she would not need to worry about our safety. No arms or the slightest scrap of evidence was ever left in her house, and if Jean and Louis were arrested it was agreed that they should swear that Mme Marie was absolutely ignorant of their activities, and with a bit of good luck she would be released. Of course, if my identity were discovered and Marie accused of feeding an English parachutist, there would be only one sentence – death.

For this reason I had decided that I must never be taken prisoner: I knew too much. I would already be posted as 'missing' in casualty lists, and no doubt would have been mentioned in the local newspapers with my age, name, home address and so on, and I was confident that the enemy had full access to all information published in the British press. If they had noted my name, they might easily have connected it with my flying kit left in the wood. Then there was the wireless operator who had been executed in Bar-le-Duc. The slip of paper with all my particulars on it might well have been discovered at the same time as his hidden radio. If I were captured and gave my number, rank and name, in accordance with international law, they would know I had been shot down the previous summer and had been with the underground movement ever since.

Previously I had looked upon reports of torture and atrocities as mainly propaganda, but I knew now that if the Nazis wished to extract information from anyone, they would show no mercy. Stories I had read where the hero had died rather than betray his friends always appeared too romantic to me. I do not think many men would be able to stand all the agonies inflicted by the Gestapo without at least giving away something – least of all myself. I am no hero and I felt afraid that if I were captured and subjected to torture I would weaken and talk. In my heart I knew that I would rather die than betray the friends who had been so good to me, but to be kept alive in agony would be more than I could bear.

I had acquired a considerable amount of information about the Resistance Movement in the district – far more than the majority of members themselves, who usually knew only the person who formed the next link in the patriotic chain. Even then, they probably knew only a number, whereas I knew several separate links and had a strong clue as to the identity of the chief resister in the region, M.X. During one of my afternoon strolls I had caught a glimpse of a figure in a white smock as I passed the door of a chemist's shop. As I walked on, I began to realise that there was something familiar about the figure. The next time I saw M.X my suspicions were aroused again by a remark he made revealing a knowledge of medicines, and I felt sure that the white-smocked figure in the shop was none other than M.X. If this information were forced from my lips in a Gestapo cell I would not wish to live any longer. I thought the matter over very carefully for several days and decided coolly and deliberately that, like Raymond, I would never allow myself to remain alive for interrogation. I would move heaven and earth to escape, and would either get away or die a quick death from a machine gun in the attempt.

GERRARD 9234

TELEPHONE :

Extn...............

Any communications on the
subject of this letter should
be addressed to :—

THE
UNDER SECRETARY
OF STATE,

and the following number
quoted :—

Your Ref. .... P.408419/3/P.4.(B.6.)

AIR MINISTRY

(Casualty Branch),

73, OXFORD STREET,

W.1.

4th March 1944

Sir,

      With reference to the letter from
this department dated the 24th January 1944,
I am directed to inform you, with great regret,
that in view of the lapse of time and the
absence of any news concerning your son,
1438430 Sergeant T. D. G. Teare, since he
was reported missing, it is now proposed to
take action to presume his death for official
purposes.

      I am accordingly to ask that you
will be good enough formally to confirm that
you have received no further evidence or news
regarding him.

                  I am,
                   Sir,
                    Your obedient Servant,

              for Director of Personal Services.

J. G. Teare Esq.,
    268 Higher Road,
      Halewood,
        LIVERPOOL.

Missing, presumed dead...

CHAPTER TWELVE

Laying in Stores

The days passed much more quickly in the company of the two brothers than during all my previous months of hiding. Each day something new happened; we were constantly making plans for acts of sabotage and discussing means of stealing arms from the Gestapo and Gendarmes.

Quite frequently the troops from the Caserne would pass the house in a route march. Often wearing full kit on their backs, they would go through the streets of Revigny out into the country, singing their rousing marching songs. A few hours later we would hear them approaching once more and they would go stamping through the streets back to the Caserne again. I always ran to the window to watch them through the shutters, and I was very impressed indeed. Their singing was not like that of the British soldiers on the march, where the order 'march at ease' is given, and then any Tom, Dick or Harry would pipe up with "It's a long way to Tipperary" or "Pack up your troubles". Instead, the NCO in charge became a choir leader, giving the note and the order, and then every man would burst into song at the same moment, all in perfect harmony – the bass being taken by the deep-throated men, whilst the younger men (perhaps sixteen or seventeen years old) took the high-pitched descant. The tramp of feet kept time, and in some of the songs the voices would cut off in sudden silence while the boots stamped out perhaps two or three beats, and then the voices would continue. This sounded very smart indeed, and when between 100 and 200 troops gave this pause in the music and emphasised the stamps whilst passing through the town, it echoed up the alleyways and certainly created an impression of strength and military efficiency. I soon came to know their tunes quite well and knew when the pauses for stamps came in, but I never knew what the actual words meant. I often heard the strains of 'Lili Marlene' coming from stationary troop trains, since Revigny was an important railway junction. Here again the singing seemed to be disciplined with the entire train-load singing the tune, usually to the accompaniment of many mouth-organs.

I continued to work each afternoon at Mme Marie's until the

weather made it possible to go ahead with preparations for the next year's crop in the market garden, and I decided that I might as well work full days. The living of Mme Marie and the children depended upon the sale of vegetables; since there was very little work in the business, Jean and Louis were more or less dependent upon the garden also. Where the farmer had gone round with the plough I had to get the soil ready for sowing the seed. This was quite a big job, for Mme Marie wished to keep the garden up to the standard which her husband had maintained. I spent hours breaking up the large lumps of soil left by the plough, dragging a small harrow over the ground several times. It was hard work, and although it was only spring I often worked stripped to the waist. When the earth was finally broken up small enough, Mme Marie gave me a pair of short boards which were attached to the soles of my shoes. With these, the soil was trodden down flat until it looked as if it had been lightly rolled. For the first few mornings Louis accompanied me along the road to Mme Marie's, but after I had been working full days for about a week I started to go alone between eight-thirty and nine each morning. I worked hard all day long, taking a break for dinner from 12 o'clock to 1 o'clock and a glass of wine and a piece of black bread and cheese at 4 o'clock, and then working again until dark before coming in for my supper.

The people I met became familiar. Sometimes I would meet a gendarme cycling towards the police station, and after a few meetings we used to give each other a nod and say *"Bonjour"* as we passed. I wondered what he would do if he discovered who I was. Some of the force of gendarmes were very patriotic Resistance workers, but they never knew whether to trust each other because there was a definite percentage of the members who were pro-German. Patrols were carried out along the country roads in pairs on bicycles. One day, two of them were cycling along a few miles from Revigny when they came across a party of five dirty, unshaven, frightened-looking men dressed in rags. When the gendarmes asked for their identity cards, one of them spoke in broken French and pleaded to be allowed to go free, saying that he and his comrades were Russian prisoners of war who had escaped from a camp. They said they would be punished severely if they were taken back. One of the gendarmes was a keen patriot and would have liked to let the men go free, but he had not known his colleague long and could not trust him. So the only thing to do was to march the men along at the point of a revolver to the police headquarters. Inside, the leader did not plead for mercy. Instead, he produced papers to prove he was a Gestapo officer, and demanded in perfect French to use the phone. He contacted the German headquarters and in a short time a car came along containing an officer who certified that the five men were Germans, and then drove away with them in his car. The patriotic gendarme thanked his lucky stars that he had not let the 'Russian prisoners' go, otherwise he would certainly have been executed. News of this and similar incidents spread like wildfire through the force, and all the men were kept on tenterhooks, hardly daring to help in any Resistance work whatsoever.

Mme Marie herself worked like a little slave. She had the children to look after and meals to prepare for us all, and also put in several hours on the land. I think the strain was too much for her; although she was tired she would not stop but became quite short-tempered. Most of the time I got on pretty well with her, but poor Louis repeatedly felt the rough side of her tongue. Some days everything he did seemed to be wrong.

I was becoming much fitter with the work and the fresh air, and some nights Jean, Louis and I would have a strenuous half-hour of unarmed combat before going to bed as part of our preparations for an emergency. I still had my RAF stop-watch, so I suggested we should have periodical practice-evacuations from the house, timing ourselves and reducing the number of seconds required to an absolute minimum.

We would undress and get into bed in the usual way, switch out the light, and then, giving the word 'go', I would start my stop-watch. The most important things to grab in the dark were our rifles and ammunition, then our boots; it is a great handicap to run across country barefoot. Next came trousers, but these were not really essential and if the emergency had arisen I think I could have made much greater speed without them. However, for practices we always took them with us and endeavoured to put them on *en route*. We dashed through the bedrooms, Jean and I going ahead to the loft over the woodshed, opening the trap-door, hooking the ladder down the side of the wall and climbing down, while Louis came last, locking the doors behind him. Once down the ladder, he unhooked it and used it to knock away the stick holding the trap-door open, and it swung shut with a bang. In the meantime, Jean and I scouted ahead for opposition. Once I heard the door shut I stopped my watch and we saw how many seconds it had taken.

The first attempt was pretty hopeless. We stumbled against the furniture, knocking over chairs and making a terrible amount of noise in our attempts to get away as quickly as possible. We had put our boots on in the bedroom, so there had been a terrific clatter of hobnails through the house. Then the trap-door had shut with a bang that would be heard a hundred yards away.

The next morning we arranged the furniture so that we could run straight through the rooms from one end of the house to the other without colliding with anything. We also decided that it was best to go barefoot as far as the trap-door, and deaden the sound of the door shutting with rags. After two or three practices we were able to slip silently out of bed, withdraw down the ladder, and be in the wood with our rifles at the 'ready' within two minutes.

We were gradually acquiring our food supplies – potatoes, corn and two live calves. Louis and I rigged up a block and tackle in the woodshed, and with the aid of my sheath knife the poor young beasts were slaughtered. Raymond's previous experience helped greatly. He knew just where to plunge the knife down on top of the head while the three of us held it still. When the animal dropped to the ground unconscious, Raymond quickly cut its throat. The blood rushed out and we did our best to catch it in a bucket. Then the carcass was hoisted up to the roof by its hind legs for Raymond to start skinning and cleaning it. The procedure was repeated with the second calf, but, having seen the operation performed once, I was able to play a more active part and helped Raymond.

The carcasses were cut up and each of us set to work in the kitchen removing the meat from the bones. Raymond worked quickly, while I hacked away as best I could, gradually improving. As we removed the meat we passed it to Jean and Louis, who cut it up in smaller pieces and put them in glass jars. They sprinkled each jar with salt and inserted a small onion for flavouring, poured on a spoonful of water and secured the lid. I had not seen meat preserved in this way before, but the boys seemed to know what they were doing so I said nothing. The following day Louis produced a dustbin and put in it the jars of meat, packing them round with rags to prevent the glass from cracking. Water was then poured over the lot and the lid put on.

We all went round to Mme Marie's for dinner, then Raymond left on his bicycle, promising to be back again within a few days.

Louis hinted to Marie that something was going on at the house that would prevent us from working in the garden that day. He handed her a sack containing the livers, hearts, kidneys and tongues of the calves, and she knew better than to ask any questions.

In the afternoon we stood the bin on bricks in the courtyard and lit a fire underneath. Once the water was brought to the boil it was easy to keep it going. While the meat was cooking we folded up the skins and took them down to our hideout under the goat-pen, then buried the bones at the bottom of the garden. After the jars of meat had been boiling for three hours or so, we opened one of them and found the result delicious. So now we had a fairly good supply of potatoes, flour and meat, and impatiently awaited the day when the second front would be opened and the whole of the French underground movement came out to fight the Germans in the open. If we received our quota of arms parachuted down, so much the better; if not, we would fight with what ancient weapons we already possessed, and gradually equip ourselves with the arms we took off the Germans we ambushed.

In the town was a wine and champagne factory which was maintaining its normal pre-war output, although almost every bottle was transported to Germany. We decided that a stock of wine would be very welcome, and every bottle we took would be one less for the Germans. We made a daylight reconnaissance one afternoon. Strolling past the main gates, we saw the lodge of the watchman, and a dog chained up outside. In the courtyard were several carts, and dozens of barrels were lying around outside the doors of the factory. The rear of the building faced open fields and we saw that by climbing over a wall we could drop into an orchard, go through into the watchman's garden, and from there probably gain access to the courtyard. A farmer had several head of cattle in the field behind the factory, and although the hedge and the ditch would prove no difficulty, there was an electrified wire running round the four sides of the field. It was the first I had seen in France and I could only remember seeing an electric fence in operation a couple of times in England. The shock such a fence gives is not dangerous, but it would certainly be an unpleasant surprise if we touched it in the dark. We knew that the farmer brought his cattle in each night, but did not know if he switched off the current.

We decided to make an expedition the same night. We fitted a cover over an electric torch so that only a pin-point of light shone through. Louis wore a pair of sandals, I found a much-worn pair of galoshes, and Jean managed to get his feet into a pair of PT shoes that fitted him when he was fifteen. I also wore my dark brown sweater, pulled my black beret down over my head, and concealed my face as much as possible with a scarf. The brothers did likewise, and then we darkened our hands and foreheads with charcoal. We emptied our pockets lest anything should rattle or fall out, leaving behind incriminating evidence.

Louis had already proved himself a fairly good lock-picker and had a pretty good assortment of keys, so he was to be No.1 of the party and lead the way, carrying the keys and the flashlight. Silence was essential, and so I carried a cosh strapped to my right wrist and a knuckle-duster in my left hand pocket. The rubber truncheon was actually a German weapon which had been found in the house by Jean when he returned from the 1940 evacuation.

If opposition were encountered, Louis would whip off the cover of the flashlight and shine the full force of the beam in the person's eyes. At this moment I would move forward and administer the necessary blow. Jean was to bring up the rear with his ·45 automatic, which he could use as a club or, in case of absolute emergency, could fire. If there were one or two persons we would endeavour to dispose of them, but if there were three or more no doubt a rapid withdrawal would be the most judicious course to pursue. That was the theory of the operation, but in reality we were a most unlikely trio of burglars: two law-abiding French brothers and an English bank clerk. Young men who had been brought together, under quite remarkable circumstances while fighting for their respective countries, but who still had so much to learn.

Taking advantage of the fact that people sleep most heavily during the first couple of hours they are in bed, we slipped silently from the house shortly before midnight. We passed under the electric wires, through the hedge, across the ditch and through the nettles to the wall. It was not very high and we soon found footholds and climbed over. Slowly and silently we passed through the orchard. Our eyes were well accustomed to the dark and we did not need the lamp. We reached the garden, Louis opened the gate into the courtyard without difficulty, and we entered the yard and moved slowly foot by foot towards the factory doors. The dog was only twenty-five yards away but made no sound. Jean stayed at the gate while Louis tried various keys, and I stood by with my truncheon ready. After trying for about quarter of an hour, we moved on to the next entrance. This was a large double door with a small wicket gate. Louis found a key which fitted perfectly and the door was opened slowly. I tip-toed stealthily back to where Jean was standing in the shadows. He had not heard a sound while we'd been away, so the three of us entered the building and silently shut the door.

In the light of the torch we explored the building. There were dozens and dozens of barrels, but as we tapped them lightly with our finger nails we found they were empty. We went up and down the rows, but every single one was empty. We came to some huge wooden vats about ten feet high with pipelines leading from the bottom, but the stop-cocks needed a spanner to turn them. We looked around but there was none near by and it was impossible to get at the wine without one.

We moved about this department and then on to the others, right through the factory, until we came to another locked door. It was a very solid-looking obstacle, but we could see through the space between the wall and the door that it was only secured by a large iron bolt. Working with a penknife we moved the bolt back a fraction of an inch at a time until finally the door was opened.

Inside we found more rows of barrels, but this time a tap on the sides made a different sound and revealed that at last we had found some full ones. Padding silently along in our rubber footgear, we found steps leading down to the cellar. Cautiously we descended and Louis opened the aperture of the flashlight to let out a little more light. It was cool in the cellar and the floor was dry earth, and there we found our objective. There were dozens of wooden boxes each containing twenty-five bottles of champagne; they were labelled ready to go to Germany. The cellar was divided off by a barred partition, the door of which bore a heavy padlock. Shining the torch through the bars we could see shelves lined with bottles of various shapes and sizes. Louis tried to open the padlock and failed. The whole lock could have been removed with a screwdriver but unfortunately, not being experts at the game, we had forgotten to bring one.

We had already been in the building over an hour, and decided the best thing to do was to retrace our steps silently, leaving everything as we had found it, and come back another time. We went up the steps again, past the full barrels, then shut the door, put the bolt back in place with a penknife and left by the door we had entered, out once more into the fresh air. Louis quietly locked up again and we started to move back across the courtyard. A few feet from the garden gate we heard a slight sound in the direction of the dog kennel. We each froze stiff and remained still as statues in the shadows for several minutes before continuing, suppressing an urge to run away in a panic. Probably the dog had just turned round and gone to sleep again. We passed on through the garden and orchard, over the wall, and reached home again without incident – but we had safely gained some interesting information.

CHAPTER THIRTEEN

Bar-le-Duc

There was only one thing that we really needed now, and that was money – the international passport. With sufficient money such things as boots could be obtained, and although I had repeatedly offered the remainder of my 'escape' money issued by the RAF, Louis would never accept it, telling me to hang on to it as it might help me in an emergency some time.

Raymond Picot knew where he could easily dispose of meat at 200F per kilo (at that time equivalent to 10 shillings, now about 50p) in Paris. Nearly all restaurant proprietors were prepared to buy in the black market at that price, so we disposed of another pair of calves and Jean and Raymond left by train for Paris early the following morning, each carrying two heavy suitcases. They returned the following day with the suitcases empty, having sold a hundredweight of calf meat and received assurance that cash was waiting for them and the more meat they could bring, the better.

Later the same week, while I was working at Mme Marie's, Jean came running round, calling to me to come and see what they had brought home. I went with him and there, in the courtyard, was a bull sticking its head over the high sides of a cart. Louis and Raymond beamed all over their faces when they saw my surprise; they had bought the bull from some not-too-scrupulous farmer at a price well above the controlled rate with the profit from the calves. We got the bull out of the cart and into the woodshed – not without a lot of chasing around and difficulty – then we gave it some hay.

It was essential that the meat should be sold absolutely fresh, for it was now spring; the weather was quite warm, and we had no place to keep it cool, so Ferdinand was sentenced to die at five o'clock in the morning and part of his form would travel to Paris in suitcases by the 9am train.

Raymond had acquired the head of a poleaxe, Louis had fitted it with a long shaft, and we had a good supply of ropes. The following morning our victim looked at us with curiosity but was too sleepy at that early hour to protest. We gave him hay to keep his mind occupied while we slipped the rope round his ankles and horns. Then came the deathly hush while Raymond took his aim. If he did not hit the exact spot in a few seconds, Jean, Louis and I would be hanging on to the ropes trying to stop a mad bull chasing round the woodshed.

He adjusted his grip on the axe and shuffled his feet on the floor until he was in the right position, like a golfer taking the most important stroke of his life, then raised the poleaxe in the air. Just as he was about to make the downward swing, the bull moved and looked round at us. Louis and I exchanged a look. The atmosphere was very tense; there was only one small point which Raymond had to hit in order to penetrate the brain.

Once again Raymond adjusted his stance and grip. Again he raised the axe in the air, then down it came with a sickening whack as the circular metal point sank two inches into the top of the bull's head. It jerked forward, throwing all its weight against the brick wall in a final charge. The building shook with the impact and then the bull dropped to the ground – dead. Raymond quickly cut its throat open with my sheath knife and the blood gushed out by the bucketful.

There was little time to spare, so the carcass was hauled up on the pulley system straight away and we set to work immediately, skinning it completely before the blood had all drained away and the legs were still kicking feebly. Having gained experience with the calves, I was by now quite a help to Raymond and could work almost as fast as he once he showed me how to tackle the job.

This time Louis was accompanying Raymond to Paris, and before 8.30am the pair of them were walking towards the railway station, each carrying two suitcases containing several thousand francs worth of Ferdinand.

The rest of the day I carried on removing the flesh from the carcass, so that when Louis and Raymond returned from Paris the following day the meat was ready to load up the empty suitcases once more. After only a couple of hours in which to wash and have a meal, Raymond set forth once more, this time accompanied by Jean.

We decided that after this bull had been disposed of we would discontinue the black-market practice; if the boys were searched on the train, the consequences would be serious. Raymond would be charged with black marketing, using a false identity card and desertion from the *Sapeurs-Pompiers*, and he would almost certainly end his days in a German concentration camp. If Jean or Louis were arrested and their home searched and I was discovered, they would both be executed for harbouring me. In other words, each trip to Paris meant extra risk to our lives for the sake of few thousand francs.

Louis and I stayed up all that night helping to bring a kid goat into the world. I was surprised to see that the little animal tried to stand up and bleat like a lamb when it was just a few minutes old. It was covered with fur and had tiny little hoofs. I dried it with a sack and put it in a straw-filled orange box lest it should catch cold. The little creature struggled out and, walking with very shaky steps, went to its mother, and knew by instinct where it could drink. When it had finished I replaced it in the box and left it. Next morning it was perfectly dry and walking round the pen. It was difficult to realise that the little creature was only a few hours old.

Later that day the others returned from Paris. Jean had brought back a cigarette case which he gave me as a souvenir – I still have it.

Our position was now much better than it had been a month previously. We had a good stock of flour, potatoes, meat, wine, and money although we were still awaiting our consignment of arms by courtesy of the RAF. An invasion on the western front was expected any day, for hardly a day passed when we did not see American bomber formations flying overhead. Occasionally we would see combats taking place as the Luftwaffe tried to stem the armada, but there was always a heavy fighter protection consisting of Lightnings and Thunderbolts and most of the time the bomber force went along unmolested. At night we would hear the heavy drone of RAF four-engined bombers, flying much lower, with a heavier bomb load than the Americans and without any fighter protection. The German night fighters were always active, and many nights we would hear the exchange of fire and see the tracer patterns in the sky.

One particular night the sirens had gone as usual but we heard no aircraft. Instead, there were terrific detonations miles away, and we knew that a heavy raid was in progress. The windows and doors shook, but every time the explosions ceased the silence was broken by the sweetest bird-song I have ever heard. It was a nightingale in the wood at the bottom of the garden; it was marvellous to listen to it. I have never heard anything so clear and sweet. Then more bombs would fall, the windows and doors would rattle, then, in the following silence, the bird would sing once more.

The next day we learnt of great devastation that had been caused at 'Mailly-le-Camp'. The BBC said the raid had been an enormous success; one of the largest military depots and ammunition dumps in the world had been completely gutted by thousands of tons of bombs, all showered down on it within a couple of hours.

For days afterwards rumours kept coming in from various sources of the devastation caused. People told of how the bodies were being picked up by lorries and carts and loaded into goods wagons and taken away. There were even rumours of bodies being loaded into the carts before they were completely dead, and of seeing slight movement of limbs amongst the corpses. A very pleasing and important point about this raid was that, as far as was known, there were no French victims amongst the casualties. This was quite a change, for all over France civilians were being killed every day in air raids.

Along the Atlantic coast all railway communications were being cut time and time again. The time for us to strike could not be far off, and each week Louis contacted M.X in Bar-le-Duc to receive fresh orders and news of Resistance activities. All the time M.X was making plans and endeavouring to contact organisations to get me back to England. One day Louis returned from Bar-le-Duc with the news that all arrangements had been made for my repatriation via Paris. I was to meet a certain gentleman at 2pm the following day. The rendezvous would be the Church of Notre Dame in Bar-le-Duc. We received the news with mixed feelings. Jean and Louis did not want me to leave, but realised that this was a great opportunity for me. Mme Marie did not want me to go but she well knew how worried my family and friends would be back in England waiting for me. I myself knew that I would miss the pals I had made in Revigny, but all the time I was their guest I was more dangerous than a charge of dynamite. Just giving a parachutist a piece of bread and a drink of water was sufficient qualification for the death sentence.

That evening we celebrated my departure with a couple of bottles of champagne which we took around to Mme Marie's. We laughed and joked about the happy times we had had together, and then finally we played the old card game which involved the blacking of the loser's face with the frying pan. The time soon slipped by; it was nearly midnight when we crept back to Louis' house via the garden and through the wood.

The next morning I fed Louis' goat, then went round to Mme Marie's and fed her rabbits, poultry and goat, and played with the little kid for the last time. We had an early dinner, then Louis and I set forth on bicycles for Bar-le-Duc, leaving Mme Marie behind with tears rolling down her face, trying to assure young Annie and Claude

Annie with 'Uncle Denis'

that I would come back and see them again. She had made some special little buns out of white flour for me to take on the journey. As I rounded the corner and entered the town I turned and gave a farewell wave to Jean as he stood in the road.

We could have travelled by railway, as we did when I arrived in Revigny several weeks previously, but the trains were not reliable. Even on short routes they were often several hours late, and we could not afford to be late at the rendezvous. It was a glorious day as we pedalled along. We had left Revigny at noon, so we had plenty of time to ride along at a comfortable speed.

The fruit trees which lined the route all the way were shedding their blossom; the apples, pears and cherries were in tiny fruit. Halfway to Bar-le-Duc we came to a spot which Louis had before described to me as an ideal place for an ambush. It was indeed. The road dipped down into a valley and on either side was a soil embankment and woods. With a few machine guns carefully concealed it would be possible to trap a convoy of vehicles, wipe out all the personnel, remove the arms, ammunition, food, etc., and then set fire to the vehicles. The idea certainly had grand possibilities, and I tried to picture the ambush taking place, with Jean, Louis and Raymond in the thick of it, almost regretting the thought of myself back safely in England.

As we cycled on I tried to thank Louis for all he had done for me, and told him that he must come to visit my home as soon as possible after the war had ended. When we entered Bar-le-Duc I knew my way along the side streets to Notre Dame just as well as Louis did, if not better. We entered the church, shook hands, kissed one another on both cheeks, and wished each other good luck; then Louis withdrew.

It was only eighteen minutes to two, so I had a look round at the inscriptions on the walls and the various statues on either side. There was a woman kneeling in prayer, but she went out after a few minutes and I was left in the church alone.

When the church clock sounded two, I took up my position, kneeling, apparently deep in prayer. I was waiting for someone to come and kneel beside me, whisper a few words, then get up and leave the building and I would follow behind him. I knelt there for five, ten, fifteen minutes. It seemed a very long time and my knees were aching, so I got up and walked round the church once and then knelt down again – this time choosing a more comfortable bench.

Another fifteen minutes passed, and I stretched my legs once more. I wondered what could have happened to the person, whoever he or she was, who was due to meet me. The minutes dragged slowly on and on. One or two people came in, crossed themselves, prayed for a few minutes, then went out again. Eventually, the clock struck three. Good heavens! I'd been on and off my knees for an hour; no wonder they were feeling a bit sore.

A door opened and a couple of dozen children trooped out of their classroom, crossed the church and went out by the main door. A young woman, apparently their teacher, followed behind, and as she approached I saw it was none other than Colette, M.Hesling's daughter. Our eyes met and she recognised me, but despite her surprise she betrayed not the slightest hint that she knew me, turning her head away as if I were a complete stranger to her. She thought I had been back in England a couple of months, and must have suspected some sort of trap laid by the Gestapo when she saw me.

I waited a further half-hour, then the door opened and in walked M.X. He crossed himself, then knelt down while he had a careful look round the church. Seeing that we were alone, he beckoned me over to a corner and explained that something had gone wrong and the agent had not reached town. The best thing to do was to return to Revigny with Louis. He said I would find Jean's bicycle outside the church and that if I rode out of town the way I had entered I would come across Louis along the road. The only thing to do was to wait as patiently as possible, and he assured me that a message regarding my whereabouts had been received in England and acknowledged, so my parents' minds would be at rest.

I waited for ten minutes after he had gone before leaving so that we would not be associated with one another, found the

The church of Notre Dame, Bar-le-Duc

bicycle outside, and set off in the direction of Revigny. Glancing up at the clock as I left, I saw it was almost four o'clock – I had been in the church two hours.

On the outskirts of the town I caught up with Louis at the side of the road. He did not say much; he knew that all my dreams of reaching home had once more been dashed to the ground. On the way back, we called at a roadside café and had a drink. We took a table in the corner and Louis ordered a couple of glasses of wine. We were the only customers, and the waitress seemed glad of someone to talk to. She discussed the weather, the news and the air raids, and Louis carried on the conversation, except for an occasional "yes" or "no" from me.

When we reached Revigny, Jean, Mme Marie and the children were very surprised to see me again. Jean was sympathetic over my bad luck, and we decided that, if some arms were not received shortly, the pair of us would set forth in the direction of the Pyrenees.

CHAPTER FOURTEEN

Second Assignation

During the next week, many troops and armoured columns drove through the town and it became common knowledge that the Germans were making preparations for a defensive line along the Meuse if the Allies succeeded in landing on the Normandy coast. There seemed every indication that Revigny would become a battlefield, and lots of rumours ran around about the compulsory evacuation of the entire region. I found Mme Marie sobbing in the kitchen; she visualised her home being burnt down again for the second time within five years. We talked the whole thing over. It was no use being optimistic and hoping it would not happen; there was every possibility that fighting would take place, and the people of the north of France knew only too well what that had meant to the countryside in 1914-18.

The possibility of moving the furniture elsewhere was out of the question, for until the actual battles were taking place one could not tell if the Germans would make a stand or not. So we decided to dig a large hole in the garden into which, at a few hours' notice, we could put all Marie's bedding, curtains, clothes and linen in boxes. We would surround these with imperishable objects such as pots, pans, cutlery, crockery and garden tools, pack the lot with hay and straw, put boards over the top and then cover the whole cache with about a foot of soil. Marie could then evacuate, leaving the house and what remained of the furniture to the tender mercies of the gods. Louis, Jean and I would take as much poultry and as many goats and rabbits as possible to the woods from which we would be operating, and turn the rest of the livestock loose to fend for themselves.

The three of us worked for many hours until we had a hole six feet deep and about eight feet square. We boarded the sides and floor and placed some fairly stout timber on one side to be used as the roof. If the order came for the evacuation of the town, or common sense suggested the time had come, in a couple of hours we could have the majority of the household valuables buried in comparative safety below the surface. Everything would remain in reasonably good condition throughout the summer, but if the district were not liberated or the fighting had not ceased by then, all the bedding and linen would be ruined in the winter.

On several Sundays we had walked along the river banks, and I had often wondered if I would still be at Revigny when the weather would be suitable for swimming. Jean had a canoe, which we carried down to the river bank on our shoulders. We found several people down there and two other canoes already in the water. We quickly changed in the nearby bushes, Jean into a pair of trunks, while Louis and I each sported a pair of football shorts. Though the water was rather chilly and the wet shorts clung uncomfortably to our legs, we enjoyed ourselves. Louis could not swim, but he was a game trier, and repeatedly came up smiling after launching himself forward and apparently going straight to the bed of the river like a stone! I held his head above water and he struck out in the frantic breast stroke so typical of the average learner. In spite of swallowing many mouthfuls, he was still keen to learn. I finally slowed down his movements and got his arms and legs and breathing synchronised, but even so he sank as soon as I took my hand away from under his chin.

While he rested on the bank to get his breath back, I tried to teach young Claude, but he had soon had enough; in any case the conditions were not very good for a beginner. The bed was uneven and very stony, a current ran down the centre of the river, and in the still water near the sides one's feet kept catching on tree-roots and reeds.

While we splashed around, a party of German soldiers came along, changed in the same bushes and then, while one member guarded the clothes and the rifles, the rest swam. Jean and I boarded the canoe and moved downstream away from them. It could comfortably accommodate the pair of us as long as we kept still; it was lovely gliding along with the current, with just an occasional movement with the paddle to steer round the bends.

We went about half a mile downstream in a very few minutes, then turned round, but it took us half an hour to paddle back against the current. We returned to our starting place and found Louis and the kiddies had got dressed and were waiting on the bank for us. We dragged the canoe out and then quickly dried in the bushes. The German troops were still playing around in the water, quite unaware of the fact that the canoeist with the white shorts was none other than an enemy parachutist. We carried the canoe up on our shoulders back once more to Louis', fed the goat and rabbits, then settled down to our evening meal, for which we were very ready.

I was just settling down to work in Mme Marie's garden after the midday meal on Monday when Louis came running round to tell me we must go to Bar-le-Duc again to meet an agent and catch the Paris train which left at ten minutes past two. It was already almost one o'clock, so we had not a minute to spare. I changed into my best clothes, bade a hurried farewell to everyone, and then Louis and I jumped on the bicycles and started pedalling hard for Bar-le-Duc.

We said very little as we rode, for we needed all our breath. I eagerly looked at each signpost we passed; gradually the distance to go decreased. At each village I glanced up at the church clock and realised we would have to keep up a good speed to get there before two o'clock.

The rendezvous was in Notre Dame Church, as before. At last we could see the town ahead and put on a final spurt. We were in such a hurry that we failed to notice that since we passed through the last village we had met no oncoming traffic whatsoever. When we entered the streets of the town there was not a soul in sight, but still we pedalled on until suddenly two *agents de police* (special constables) ran out into the street and grabbed hold of our handlebars. "Where do you think you are going – don't you know the air raid warning has sounded?" I left all the talking to Louis, who explained that we had just ridden into the town and had not heard the sirens, probably due to the wind.

The chain had come off my bicycle when I was stopped so abruptly, and I remained bent down busily replacing it while Louis replied to questions from both *agents*; he even produced his identity card before they asked for it, and made such ready answers and apologies for not having heard the sirens that they did not ask anything about my identity whatsoever. They just bustled us into the nearest air raid shelter and said we would have to keep off the roads until the all clear had sounded.

It so happened that we were just outside the gasworks, and the nearest shelter was actually inside the yard; a small sand-bagged affair amongst the heaps of coke. We were only a short distance from Notre Dame and heard the clock strike two. We were so near and yet so far; in ten minutes' time another chance to get back to England would be lost.

We heard aircraft approaching and hoped to goodness that the gasworks was not one of their objectives today. The noise increased until they were directly overhead. We listened tensely for the whistle of bombs; the seconds passed by slowly, and nothing happened. The noise gradually diminished until the aircraft had passed overhead, and then they were completely out of earshot.

Ten minutes later the all-clear sounded, and Louis and I jumped on our cycles and dashed along to Notre Dame. We hastily looked round the inside, hoping against hope that we would find the agent still waiting, although it was now half past two. Alas! the building was empty; the agent had either been and gone or had never been there at all. Louis went off to contact M.X, while I repeated my performance of the previous week, kneeling as if in prayer, then stretching my legs and looking at the paintings and statues.

A quarter of an hour later the church door creaked slowly open and I saw the familiar face of M.X. He looked cautiously round, then came across and knelt beside me. With head bowed, he started murmuring his prayers, or at least so it would have seemed to anyone else in the church. He was actually muttering just loud enough for me to hear and understand what he was saying.

He told me that the agent had definitely come to the town to collect me and take me to Paris with him. He had actually been in the church at two o'clock during the air raid, but had dashed off to catch the train as soon as the all-clear had sounded because it was essential that he should be back in Paris that evening. However, M.X was able to assure me that he had definitely contacted a very well-organised movement which received its orders direct from London, and that once I was in their hands I would be returned to England by the same channels as the many spies and experts who repeatedly arrived in France (often by parachute) and returned to England once their particular mission was completed. I know now that some of these agents made as many as two or three entries into France and returned again to England each time. M. X told me that an agent was visiting the town again the following week – either the man who had come that day or perhaps a woman, possibly English. The only thing to do now was to return once again to Revigny and be prepared to leave at a minute's notice some time the following week. He said my bicycle was still outside and I would find Louis waiting for me on the outskirts of the town as before. Then he got up and left the church.

A few minutes later I, too, rose to my feet and tip-toed across the stone-flagged floor to the door. As I opened it, the sound of heavy feet tramping up the street came to my ears. My heart beat a little faster as I stayed with my hand holding the door a couple of inches ajar while a column of German soldiers marched past a few feet away. When they had gone, I stepped out once more into the sunshine and closed the church door behind me.

As I cycled through the town, I saw many more troops than usual, but I knew all the streets like the palm of my hand and rode through them and in and out amongst the troops as if I had lived there all my life.

Once again on the road to Revigny I found Louis waiting for me. We said nothing, but rode in silence as on my previous return from Bar-le-Duc. We called at the same little wayside cafe and had a refreshing drink, served by the same girl whose conversation was practically the same as the week before – just the weather and the war. Then we pedalled along the dusty road, with its line of fruit trees on either side, back to the familiar village of Revigny which by now I had cause to look upon as my second home.

When we reached the place of the proposed ambush, Louis turned to me and said perhaps we would be fighting side by side after all. I found some consolation in that. After all, I thought, this idea of getting back to England as soon as possible is all right for me, but I will be leaving all my friends just before the fighting starts. I would be safely at home when they were fighting desperately, with inadequate arms and hopelessly outnumbered. I was even beginning to feel a little guilty at leaving, because, after all, I had helped to prepare all their plans – in fact, half the sabotage schemes had been of my devising. And now, when Louis looked at me and said that I might be fighting with them, I felt quite proud and forgot my dreams of England.

CHAPTER FIFTEEN

A Change of Plan

During the previous week someone in the village had contacted Louis and told him there were rumours that he was occupied in Resistance activities. Of course, he promptly denied the suggestion in case this should be a trap, but he had known the person all his life and eventually decided to listen to what he had to say. He spoke of two members of the *Garde Mobile de Réserve* – 'GMRs' – who wished to desert and go to England. Louis was cautious at first, but finally agreed to meet them at a certain café. He was very suspicious because the GMRs could not be trusted. They were a corps of Frenchmen who had volunteered to do guard duty at strategic points in France against saboteurs, paratroops, etc. They wore a uniform and were fully armed. Many of its members had joined to avoid being conscripted for work in Germany, and as regards saboteurs coming to wreck the particular object they were guarding, they might be only too pleased to assist them! However, one could not pick the sheep from the wolves and there were definitely some true Nazi sympathisers amongst them.

Louis disguised himself to meet them and had an automatic in his pocket to be on the safe side, but in the course of the conversation he gained confidence and took them to be genuine. As they could not talk freely in the café, a second meeting was arranged. Louis disclosed his address and told them how to reach it via the garden at the rear.

It was agreed that it would be unwise and unnecessary for them to know my identity, so I was to remain in the background during this meeting. At the appointed time, I went and hid in the bushes at the bottom of the garden, waiting to watch them as they walked up the garden path. After hiding a few minutes I suddenly wondered if Louis had removed the lock and chain which fastened the gate at the bottom of the garden. I stepped out of the bushes and bent to examine the gate, and as I did so I came face to face with a uniformed fellow who had just struggled through the hedge. While we both looked at each other with mutual surprise, a second man stepped cut of the hedge.

These were the GMRs; I hardly expected them to come in uniform and it was quite a shock. However, they smiled and said "*Bonjour*", to which I replied, then I showed them the way up to the house. In the courtyard we were met by Louis, who concealed his surprise at seeing me with them and asked them to step into the house. While he talked with them in the sitting-room, Jean and I listened to the conversation through the keyhole.

They both said they wanted to get to England as soon as possible to join the Free French Air Force. The eldest, Charlie, aged twenty-five, had been a pilot at the outbreak of war, but France had been overrun before he had had an opportunity to make any operational flights against the enemy, and now he wished to offer his services again to his country. The younger one, Bob, aged twenty, had no flying experience but wanted to train as a pilot once he reached England.

Louis told them that everything was very, very difficult at the moment, and as the second front was expected to open up any day the Germans had doubled their precautions. Many underground organisations had already been found out, and hundreds of Resistance workers arrested and tortured to death. No one knew when the next Gestapo raid would take place; people who were doing Resistance work hardly dared breathe.

The boys insisted that they wanted to try to get to England as soon as possible in spite of the risk. Louis promised to do what he could to help them and said he would get a message to them as soon as he knew something definite.

When we heard the chairs scrape on the floor as they rose to their feet to leave, Jean and I tip-toed from the door and went upstairs to get a further view of these newcomers through the shutters as they walked through the courtyard below and down the garden path.

During the next week we were all on tenterhooks waiting for a message from M.X. Each time anyone came to the door I immediately jumped up and wondered if my moment to depart had come. Finally, the doorbell rang, and somebody from the village came and said that Louis was wanted on the phone at the post office. When Louis returned he said he had spoken to M.X and that a rendezvous had been arranged again at Notre Dame for that afternoon at the same time as before.

The usual preparations were made and then I bade farewell to Marie, Jean and the children for the third time and cycled along in the direction of Bar-le-Duc with Louis. I knew the route quite well by now, and as I cycled along I could not help imagining that I might be pedalling back again in the opposite direction in a few hours' time. On the two previous occasions I had ridden full of thoughts of England, where, if all had gone well, I would have been a couple of days later. On this third occasion I could not muster up the same enthusiasm; ever since the Resistance Movement had started to help me I had been receiving continual disappointments. Something had always happened to upset the plans for my repatriation.

We reached Bar-le-Duc without incident, and at a certain point I said goodbye to Louis and carried on to the church alone. Once inside, I bowed my head and crossed myself, then knelt in a praying position without any feeling of self-consciousness or embarrassment, as if I had been accustomed to doing it all my life.

I looked around at the now familiar statues, the altar, and various paintings on the walls, then settled down to wait until the clock struck two. Two or three people came through the door and departed again after a short prayer. Finally the church clock struck and I waited tensely; in a few minutes from now I might be on the train bound for Paris. I felt in my pocket to ensure that my identity card was there – yes, it was. I repeated to myself over and over again my fictitious name, age and birthplace to make sure I would not slip up in the event of a check being made on the train, which was most probable.

The minutes passed and no one came near me. I walked round to stretch my legs and then returned to the usual position. After about twenty minutes the large door creaked open and out of the corner of my eye I saw Louis enter. He saw there was no one else in church, and then tip-toed across to me and whispered that once again things had gone wrong and the agent had not arrived at Bar-le-Duc that morning.

He had seen M.X, who had suggested that, instead of returning to Revigny, I should stay in Bar-le-Duc until the meeting was finally successful, and that the best place to stay would be with M.Hesling, the wine merchant who had sheltered me in his house about three months previously.

We crossed the town together, opened the large iron gates and walked down the drive to the large house. Colette answered the doorbell and ushered us to her father's study, where we found M.X already talking with M.Hesling. The room was the same as on the day when I first met Louis and followed him to the station. I remembered the sad news M.X gave me on that memorable morning and asked if he knew anything more about M.Colin and M. Althuser. He told me that M.Colin had been found guilty of helping French *réfractaires* and had been sentenced to life imprisonment in a concentration camp. Fortunately the Gestapo knew nothing of his

A German feldgendarme...

activities in assisting American airmen or he would have been executed. His sentence was bad enough, because very few people survived more than a year in a concentration camp, and the longer the war lasted the less was the poor fellow's chance of seeing again the France he loved so well.

... and a prison guard, both photographed in the studio of Jean Althuser

M.Althuser was luckier. His house had been thoroughly searched from top to bottom by a Gestapo officer who had boasted, when he was a friend of M.Althuser, that if he and his men searched the house of a suspect they would miss nothing – not even a button. However, they had not found the little metal box at the back of the grate which contained sufficient evidence of M.Althuser 's Resistance activities to bring about his execution. So he was just sentenced as a common criminal for being in possession of a large number of forged bread coupons.

He was sentenced to eighteen months' imprisonment in the local jail, the one which I had walked past on several occasions with Micheline the previous winter. M.X told me that M.Althuser was not too uncomfortable there, and a little extra food had been successfully smuggled to him. His cell was almost dark and very small, but on two or three occasions he had been seen walking across the town under armed guard to the prison governor's house where he did a couple of hours' gardening occasionally.

M.Hesling served us each with a glass of whisky and we made the usual toasts: to the Victory, to France, to England, and to my return. Then, with a shake of the hand, a kiss on either cheek and a wish for good luck, Louis left me.

There was now such a large number of Germans in the town and there had been so many arrests made lately, that it was decided that I had better not leave the house unescorted. This was unfortunate; the days would seem very long in the house after a reasonably active life at Revigny, but I realised how dangerous everything was at the present moment. At the rear of the house in a small courtyard were vines growing up the wall together with several apple and pear trees. All badly needed pruning, so, with a pair of clippers and a ladder, I spent a few days trimming them into shape. I had plenty of time, so I deliberately adopted a go-slow policy. I had looked through all the books in the study on my previous visit but I spent hours turning over the pages again. The days dragged slowly by until they totalled one week, and then it was announced that I had a visitor in the office to see me.

It was M.X, and he brought very bad news. He told me that the British Secret Service agent who was to have met me at Notre Dame had been arrested by the Gestapo the very morning he was supposed to have come to Bar-le-Duc. The interrogation had started straight away, to gain information about others acting in the area.

He was stripped, flogged to unconsciousness, then thrown into a cell. The very brave man had revealed nothing, but when the guards opened the cell door the next morning, they found that he had bitten through his wrists.

M.X and I looked at each other in horrified silence. I ran my fingers over my own wrists, and had a wretched feeling in my stomach as I wondered if I would have the guts to die rather than betray those who had helped me and the knowledge I had acquired of the Resistance movement.

When the intricacies and tragedies of activities carried out by the Special Operations Executive, MI5, MI6, MI9, the Jedburghs and the Special Air Service were gradually revealed after the war, I learnt much more about the courageous people I had been privileged to know.

Monsieur X had initially made contact with these cloak-and-dagger people when he kept a rendezvous in a bar at Place d'Erlon in Rheims. There, he was introduced to a certain Capitaine Nicholas, who was said to be a Canadian, and who arranged proof of his direct connection with London by agreeing that certain meaningless phrase be broadcast by the BBC at a particular time two days later. The words, 'Le goujon peut avoir confiance' (The gudgeon can have confidence) were duly transmitted.

In the spring of 1944, the region around Rheims suffered a major Gestapo raid, in which thirty people were arrested, but the 'Capitaine' was not caught. The man who died in the cell was said to be his colleague, an Englishman only recently arrived in France.

I have also read that the 'Capitaine' was elsewhere known as Lieutenant Lafleur, such was the grimly secretive life in Nazi-occupied Europe.

CHAPTER SIXTEEN

Robert Lhuerre

Another week dragged wearily on. Each night M.Hesling and I listened to the radio, turned down very softly, and heard the news in French from London. The air raids were becoming heavier and heavier; the French coast was being hammered almost unceasingly now. The second front seemed imminent – but was this bluff? Would the Allies make a landing in Yugoslavia where the partisans had already got a foothold in the country, or would they just keep pressing on steadily up Italy and then come into France that way? We could only guess, and hope that the day of liberation would come some day – the sooner the better.

After hearing the radio, we would adjust the pins and cotton on the maps of the Russian and Italian fronts, discuss what the next move would be, and then settle down to playing draughts for the rest of the evening, just as we did earlier in the year.

I felt very depressed. All chance of reaching England seemed at the moment completely lost. It was too dangerous now to try setting off on my own by cycle or on foot down to the Spanish frontier. France was full of troops and Gestapo agents, and I used to shudder when I thought of what would happen if I were caught.

One afternoon at the beginning of my third week with M.Hesling, I was sitting in the cellar on a wooden box. A sack of potatoes had started sprouting and M.Hesling had asked me if I would pick off all the sprouts so that the potatoes would not be wasted. In my black mood, as I pulled each sprout off, I was saying to myself, "I will get home – I won't get home. I will get home – I won't get home." For nine months I had been hiding in this foreign country eagerly looking forward to the day when I would speak my own language and meet my parents and fiancée again, but I had gradually lost hope. The last failure had been a heavy blow to my morale.

Most of the potatoes seemed to have an even number of sprouts, so that I had to cheat myself and count the same one twice so that it would come out "I will get home". Then I heard someone coming. It was Colette, who said, "M.X is here with good news".

My mysterious friend said that he had come into contact with an organisation which was still able to repatriate airmen, and that someone would call at the house at 10am the next day. Before taking this for granted, I asked M.X to tell me outright if this was going to be a genuine move to go home, or if I was just going with the stranger who would come the next day to hide out somewhere else until the liberation. If this was the case, I said, I would rather go back to Revigny again, and fight when the time came side by side with the two brothers and the local partisans. He assured me that this was definitely a move to go home and that he hoped I would have better luck this time.

I lay in bed that night thinking of all the different people who had helped me since I arrived in France, wondering what the man would be like with whom I would leave tomorrow, and where I would be in twenty-four hours' time. I got up earlier than usual the following morning, was dressed, washed, shaved, and had had my customary drink of *ersatz* coffee, ready to leave long before ten o'clock. Sitting quietly in the study, I listened to M.Hesling dictate letters to Colette and watched tensely out of the window.

At exactly ten o'clock a man came down the drive and M.Hesling answered the doorbell. During a few seconds' whispered conversation at the door the stranger proved that he was the person we were waiting for and was duly ushered into the study.

I was introduced as 'Denys from England', and we shook hands. The newcomer was about forty years old, medium built, with dark hair and a sun-tanned complexion. He wore ordinary, well-worn clothes and the typical black beret. As I walked up the drive with my escort, I turned and waved a farewell hand to the Hesling family at the window and then looked ahead and wondered where I was being taken. My guide did not speak a word as we went through the town. We walked along side by side in silence, but each of us was very much on the alert for anything that might happen.

At a certain point a second man stepped out of an alleyway and walked on the other side of me. He told my first friend (whom he called Jules) that everything was in order. The three of us continued in the same direction. After various turnings left and right, we halted in a narrow side street, Jules opened a door and I followed him down a passage between two houses to a smaller building at the rear. He opened another door and the three of us entered a kitchen. Here he spoke to me for the first time since we left M.Hesling's. He just said, "So far, so good", and then put three glasses on the table. While we

drank some red wine, he told me that my next acquaintance would
be an American-speaking young man who would help me on my
way to reach a point where an aircraft would pick up myself and one
or two others and return to England. He said he knew I had been in
France many months, although he did not know where I had been
living and did not wish me to reveal it to him, but he insisted that
from now onwards I should deny having been in France more than a
month. He made me promise to say that I had been living in the
woods during that time. Finally, he said that on no condition
whatsoever must I tell this American-speaking fellow that I had
passed through the particular house I was in at the present moment.
After I had promised faithfully to abide by these three promises,
Jules looked at his watch and said that it was time to move on.

   This time I left with the second man and Jules stayed behind. We
walked along in silence through the streets towards the railway.
Shortly before the road crossed the railway line, my friend nudged
me and said that on the other side of the bridge there would be two
men with whom he would leave me.

   Just as he had said, there were two men standing near the walls.
With a casually muttered greeting, my friend walked on along the
footpath, the two new men fell in on either side of me and we
ambled easily along in line together. As we continued our walk we
looked at one another, weighing each other up. My friend was a
dark-complexioned, good-looking young fellow about my own age,
with jet-black wavy hair and dark brown eyes. When we reached a
point where there was no one near enough to hear us he said with an
American accent, "How are you feeling, pal?"

   It was wonderful to hear my own language again after such a
long time, and several seconds passed before I could think what to
say in English in reply. Eventually, I managed to grin and say
quietly, "Fine, thanks, chum".

   "Do you speak French?" he asked. Remembering what I had
promised a short time before, I replied, "Yes, but only a little",
although at the time I could speak the language with the local
accent so that people would hardly suspect me to be anything other
than French.

   We were now walking back towards the centre of the town and
in one of the main streets I followed my friend into a building, up
the staircase, up one flight, two flights, three flights, until we were
finally on the top floor. Passing along a corridor, we entered a room

on the left at the end. My friend locked the door behind us and then introduced himself. He said his name was Robert and that he was really an American, although hardly anyone knew it. His father had been American, but was dead; his mother was French and at the moment living in South America. He was a student in France when war was declared, and had joined the French Air Force, in which he became an air gunner. He showed me photos of himself dressed in flying kit standing by various aircraft. When France was overrun by the Germans he had simply taken off his uniform and put on civvy clothes as thousands of others had done, thus avoiding becoming a prisoner of war. He had been living like that ever since.

Robert Lhuerre (furthest from camera) whilst he was serving in the French Air Force

He looked at his watch and said he would have to leave me for a quarter of an hour, and asked me to remain quietly in the room during his absence. He locked the door behind him as he went and I was alone in the room. From the only window I could see the traffic going up and down the street. At the far side of the room was a door which was ajar, so I tip-toed and peeped through. It led into a dingy little store room full of dusty bundles of papers and books. Both tables were covered with papers, and from them I gathered that this was an office which was in some way connected with the distribution of flour.

Eventually, I heard footsteps outside; they stopped opposite the door and a key was turned in the lock. I waited tensely behind the door as it slowly opened, and was relieved to see it was my new friend, Robert.

We descended the three flights of stairs and emerged into the sunshine at street level once more. Little did I guess then that the most dangerous and exciting moment of my life was to take place in that very building within a few days.

German soldiers marching along Boulevard de la Rochelle, directly outside Robert Lhuerre's office

We crossed the town and headed towards the country, passing quite near M.Clément's where I had hidden several months previously. Those good people would think I had been in England a long time by now and would certainly have had a shock to see me walking through the streets. As we walked past the prison, Robert whispered to me what it was and I pretended that this was news to me, although I actually remembered the road quite well. Just past the prison we went up a steep, stony cart track towards a farm. On the way, Robert told me that I would be picked up by an aircraft in two days' time and until then I would be able to stay at this farm. He knew the son was a keen patriot and he did not think the family would mind sheltering me.

We entered a courtyard, where a sheepdog barked noisily at the end of a chain. Through the open door of the farm house we could see the family having dinner. A tall, fair-haired young lad left the table and came towards us. Robert explained who I was and the son asked his father if I could stay there for two days. His father looked me up and down, glanced towards his wife, and finally consented. Robert said he would return that evening to see me, bade everyone goodbye and retraced his steps towards the town.

Another chair was placed at the table and another plate of thick soup put out. I sat down, and as I ate everyone watched me. At the head of the table sat the father, a tall, lean, bony fellow with a farmer's typical sun-tanned face. Near the stove sat his wife, also a rather lean-looking woman. Next to her sat a thin, pale-faced daughter about thirteen years of age, who helped her mother to serve the foodstuffs from the stove to the table. The tall lad who had spoken to Robert sat next to his sister, and then on my side of the table sat two younger brothers aged twelve and fifteen.

Each time I looked up from my meal they seemed to be watching me. Finally, the youngest boy spoke. He asked the others if they thought I could speak any French, to which the eldest brother replied that I probably knew a few words as I had been living in France for a month already.

Deliberately speaking slowly, I told them that I knew a few words of their language, and could understand a small part of their conversation. It was amusing to listen to them discussing me amongst themselves, thinking I could not understand them when they spoke at a normal speed.

After the meal, I went out with the farmer, and while he cut the grass with a scythe I loaded it into a cart. When we had a good load we climbed on top and the horse trudged slowly back to the farm. There the grass was distributed among half a dozen cattle and a mare which M.Lefeure told me was due to foal in a fortnight's time. I worked with the farmer until the evening meal was ready at seven o'clock. Shortly after we had finished, Robert returned and we walked round the garden and orchard together talking quietly in English about the present situation, about air raids, and about conditions in England. I asked him why he was not going to England in the same way as I was, and he told me that he would have flown over several months before but that he was in love with a girl in Bar-le-Duc and as soon as hostilities ceased they were going to be married. In the meantime, he preferred to stay beside her and at the same time help Allied airmen as much as he could. He had already conducted four American airmen to a certain point not very far from Rheims where an aircraft had picked them up. When he mentioned their names they seemed vaguely familiar, and then I realised that some of them were men who had stayed with Louis at Revigny. So Robert and Louis were links in the same organisation, although they had no idea of each other's identity and had actually never met.

I became fond of Robert and felt an absolute worm to have to abide by my promise and keep deceiving him time and time again when he asked me what England was like when I had left a month ago. He even spoke of Christmas and the New Year that had passed and asked me what sort of celebrations went on in my squadron. I detested having to keep lying to him, especially as he trusted me so implicitly when I told him I had only come down a month ago, and never asked me where I had been during that time. However, I still kept faithfully to my promise.

He told me that the following night would probably be my last in France, and he would bring his fiancée up to the farm and introduce her to me. The following day we would set off for the place where the aircraft would touch down for a few seconds and I would be back in England a couple of hours after that.

The message would come over the BBC confirming the date and time of the landing the following evening. I had heard lots of these 'personal messages' to France coming from London after the news bulletin. The announcer would read short sentences, such as "The black cat has had five kittens", or "The goldfish swims round and round", or "The frying pan is black, Mother". Each seemed meaningless – but all over France there were groups of saboteurs, Maquis, underground workers and agents who waited anxiously for some pre-arranged sentence which might mean that the time had come to blow up a certain bridge or a long-awaited arms container would be dropped at a certain point that night. In our particular case, the message would confirm that a plane would be landing at a pre-arranged point at dusk the next day or the following dawn.

During the next day I helped with the normal farm routine as much as possible and got to know the family better. The middle brother was very pleasant, hard-working and easy to get along with, but there seemed something sinister about the eldest. He did not always seem to be on good terms with his father and did not work on the farm.

He told me about patriotic exploits that had been carried out by himself and three pals. I listened politely to the stories coming from this seventeen-year-old lad, but wondered if he was letting his imagination run away with him.

After supper, Robert arrived with the fair-haired young lady who was his fiancée. Apart from when we were introduced, she hardly said a word. Robert spoke quietly to me in English as before, and told me that the BBC had made an announcement cancelling all 'personal messages' for that day and that it would be no use going to Rheims until further arrangements had been made. We walked round the farm talking together for about half an hour and then Robert and his fiancée left me in order to get back into town before the curfew.

I slept with the eldest son in a bedroom on the ground floor. That night, instead of getting undressed, the lad produced some old army equipment from behind the wardrobe. Sitting on the bed in the candle light, he showed me a belt, haversack, and some ammunition in a couple of pouches. After blowing out the candle, he quietly opened the window and looked out. He said that at midnight his three pals were coming to collect the ammunition to take it to hide in a better place and asked me not to mention a word about it to his father.

We lay there quietly listening to the kitchen clock ticking until midnight, and then we heard a slight movement outside the open window. The lad tip-toed across the room, and as I lay there hardly breathing, I watched the three figures outlined against the sky and listened to the whispered conversation of the boys' voices. The articles were handed over and then the three visitors tip-toed away.

I lay awake for some time after they had gone thinking how foolish and inexperienced they were. If any patrolling Germans spotted them at that time of night they would be arrested immediately and shot for carrying ammunition. There were only a couple of dozen rounds and it would have been far safer to walk along in broad daylight with them in their pockets. By more experienced resisters, revolvers, ammunition and even hand-grenades had been carried across towns successfully in ladies' shopping bags covered only with a few potatoes. Yet I had a real admiration for these three boys, for they had the same courage and desire to fight for their country as had their fathers and elder brothers.

CHAPTER SEVENTEEN

D-Day

The following morning was 6 June and all Europe was buzzing with the news that the Allies were attempting a landing on the Normandy coast. I could imagine people like Louis, Jean and Raymond jumping with joy, but at the farm where I was nobody seemed particularly excited except myself and the eldest son. The BBC announced that hundreds of ships had crossed the Channel that morning and had made a foothold, supported by unceasing waves of bombers. I thought of all the thousands of men who would be fighting bitterly at this very minute. There would be paratroops, glider-borne troops, landing craft, tanks, artillery. This was the time for all saboteurs to strike, the moment the Maquis had been waiting for, and yet here I was, waiting helpless on a farm doing nothing.

That day I listened to every bulletin that came over the radio, hardly daring to think what would happen if the invasion were beaten back. Perhaps the Allies would not be able to make another attack for two or three years; that would be terrible for me and for all the millions of people in Europe who were waiting to be freed.

In the evening I was very pleased to see Robert enter the farmyard. He was as excited as I was at the news, and hoping against hope that the Allies would be successful. He said his own position was becoming rather precarious and the possibility of flying to England seemed to be out of the question. I myself had been more than the agreed two days at the farm, and I think my hosts were beginning to get a bit nervous. In the town a rumour was becoming strong that the Germans were erecting barbed-wire enclosures at various places and intended rounding up all Frenchmen in the country and putting them inside – in this way stopping Resistance activities.

Robert suggested that the pair of us should take food and set off together to live in the woods, and that he should say he was a machine-gunner shot down in the same aircraft as myself. He was very worried and wanted to get away from the town. I knew it was far easier said than done; we would only be able to take a week's supply of bread with us, and once this was gone it would be difficult for us to come out of the wood and get some more unless we had an arrangement with someone who lived fairly close and was willing to help us. Robert did not even know what direction to take in order to come across an organised group of Maquis in the woods. I thought of my old friend M.X. He was the one person who could help us both now. I did not know where to find him, but I knew M.Hesling knew his identity if only I could contact him. I told Robert that I had a friend in Bar-le-Duc who could help us as he was the chief of Resistance activities in this district, and that I knew a way of contacting him once I was in Bar-le-Duc. Robert and young Lefeure looked at one another doubtfully. I had been speaking in French, and Robert asked how was it that I was speaking fluently now but only a few days ago knew only a couple of words. I managed to pass it off with a laugh by saying that I was rather shy when I first arrived. but Robert was still uncertain.

"Are you quite certain your friend is not a member of the Gestapo?" he asked.

"Probably my friend would think the same thing about you," I replied.

Finally, we agreed that as neither could have confidence in the other, the three of us should go into the town and at a certain point I should leave them. I would contact my friend alone and then return with news in half an hour. They need not wait for me at any appointed spot, but could watch me approach the agreed place from an alleyway or café, and convince themselves that I was not being followed before making themselves known. The only alternative was for me to go down into the town alone and come back later with news. They did not approve of either idea, but eventually I persuaded them to come with me.

I put on my coat and beret and the three of us set off down the rough cart track to the main road. We headed straight into the centre of the town. Everything was more or less as it had been before. People were still walking up and down the streets and the cafés were full of German soldiers, just as they had been before the invasion. We all knew what was happening at the coast, although the Germans denied it. Every vehicle travelling on the main road was stopped and searched, and the atmosphere was tense throughout the country.

Near the Town Hall I left my friends and promised to be back, alone, in half an hour. I was only about three hundred yards from M.Hesling's house, but I dodged about the back streets, making certain I was not being following, before approaching the house.

The large iron gates were not locked, so I went through and down the drive. I rang the doorbell and M.Hesling himself answered. He got a shock when he saw me, but quickly opened the door to his office for me to enter. I told him I simply *must* see M.X and that I could only stay for twenty minutes. Poor M.Hesling could not understand what had happened and I felt I had not time to spare to tell him, so he hurried off to bring M.X.

Mme Hesling came and spoke to me while I waited and I told her the purpose of my visit; unfortunately, this surprise call had given her a nasty shock also. As long as I was walking about the streets I spelt a potential death sentence to all the people who had helped me. I kept glancing at my RAF stop-watch and when fifteen minutes of my half-hour had ticked past I saw two figures hurrying down the drive. M.Hesling was quite out of breath with hurrying both ways.

I explained everything to M.X. He was worried lest anyone had followed me to this house, but I quickly set his mind at rest. I told him of the promise I had made to Jules, as apparently he did not trust my Franco-American friend and said that, so far as he and the people at the farm knew, I had only been in France for one month. M.X asked me again if I were sure I had not been followed, but I assured him I was absolutely certain on that point. He then suggested that I should stay there instead of meeting the other two as arranged. I was a little annoyed at this and told him that I believed Robert to be genuine and that, had the invasion not started, he would have helped me to return to England. Now the tables had turned, I could perhaps help him instead.

The minutes were ticking by; if I were not at the meeting place in a few minutes, the other two would think I had been arrested and would not know which way to turn lest the Gestapo forced me to betray them and the family at the farm. It was common knowledge throughout France that the Gestapo now had an injection to give their victims, after which they would go into a coma and in that state would answer any questions that were put to them.

M.X tried again to persuade me to stay but I told him that I certainly was not going to leave my friends in the lurch. We had no time to argue. In three minutes the half-hour would be up. I suggested returning to Revigny and taking Robert with me. M.X was still doubtful but eventually agreed this was the best thing to do, as long as I was absolutely certain that Robert was not in the pay of the Gestapo. After telling me to be very, very careful, and not to get caught after being so lucky for nine months, he shook hands with me and I left the house. There was only one minute left as I passed through the iron gates. I hurried through the side streets and got to the agreed point about one minute late.

There was no sign of Robert and young Lefeure, but after I had stood alone on the corner for a couple of minutes they revealed themselves up a side street. I walked up to them and we started our journey back to the farm. It was not safe to talk until we had left the town behind and were walking once more up the rough track to the farm. I told Robert that I knew where we could go, only twenty kilometres from here, and hide out with reasonable safety. Unfortunately, Robert had become doubtful and suspicious and, rather than agree definitely to the pair of us setting out then and there, he said he would see what he could find out during tomorrow and then we would make our decision. He was probably wondering how it was that an Englishman who was only supposed to have been in France a month knew his way round Bar-le-Duc so well and seemed to have such a knowledge of other places round about.

During the next day I hung around the farm, hoping that Robert would come along and that we would set off by foot to Revigny straight away. I waited until bedtime, but, alas, he never came. It was a decision that was to cost him his life.

Young Lefeure and I lay in bed that night talking quietly. I told him that I was not going to wait here any longer; each day that passed made it more dangerous to travel, and as Robert had not come up to see me that evening I meant to see him first thing in the morning and tell him that if he could not make up his mind to leave Bar-le-Duc with me, I would go off by myself.

Earlier that month Monsieur 'X' had offered me the chance to be smuggled over the Swiss frontier, about sixty miles away, where I would be interned until the end of hostilities. I declined; to me the word internment just meant being locked up in another foreign country; whereas I still cherished the thought of being whisked away by some secret organisation, all the way home. London had acknowledged radio messages that I was alive and active, so I presumed that my parents would have been notified accordingly. Sadly, however, this information had been retained for my own safety. My distressed parents actually received a letter from Buckingham Palace in May 1944 expressing deepest sympathy for the loss of my life.

BUCKINGHAM PALACE

May 3rd 1944.

The Queen and I offer you our
heartfelt sympathy in your great
sorrow.

We pray that your country's
gratitude for a life so nobly given
in its service may bring you some
measure of consolation.

George R.I.

J. G. Teare, Esq.

The Buckingham Palace letter, and the end of hope for my parents

By now a very strong bond of friendship and respect had developed between myself and the people of the Resistance. The landing in Normandy meant the time had come to fight in the open, and all the ambushes and acts of sabotage, that we had planned for so long, were about to become reality. Arms and explosives were being parachuted down for enthusiastic amateurs to hurl themselves against the occupying enemy. So, the place for myself – a trained machine-gunner, who even had instruction in throwing hand grenades – must surely be alongside the people who had already risked so much to give me food and shelter.

CHAPTER EIGHTEEN

Arrival of the Gestapo

Next morning, after the usual bowl of coffee and piece of bread, I thanked the farmer and his wife for their hospitality and told them I was leaving. They wished me luck, and I think it was a great relief to them to see me go off the premises.

The eldest boy came with me to the town and headed for the office where we expected to find our mutual friend. We entered the building, but instead of going up the three flights of stairs to the top floor where Robert had taken me a few days previously, we stopped at the top of the first flight and young Lefeure asked a typist if we could speak to M.Lhuerre. She said he was not in at the moment but would be back at 11am. This meant that we had an hour to wait, so we descended the stairs and started to saunter round the town.

We wandered slowly along the road under the trees at the side of the river; the sun was warm, the birds were singing and everything seemed peaceful. We crossed over the quaint old bridge which had a small shrine in the middle where passers-by would pause and pray before the tiny altar. It was one of the most historic and beautiful sights of the district.

Entering a café on the other side, we sat quietly in the corner drinking a glass of beer. At 10.45 we rose and began to retrace our steps towards the office. Along the side of the river we saw three figures approaching. As they drew nearer we saw that they were two armed German soldiers marching on either side of a civilian. As they passed us in the road I thought to myself, 'that poor fellow has been arrested'. It was no one I had met before. He was about thirty-five years old, dark-haired, clean shaven, tall, with piercing eyes looking straight ahead from his lean, powerful-looking face. When the trio had passed, my companion and I exchanged glances; we both knew we must be careful or we would be marched off under escort like that. We wandered slowly on in silence and were only a short distance from the office when a man briskly overtook us. As he walked past, I realised that it was the same fellow whom we had seen under armed escort ten minutes before. I looked round and saw that the two Germans were following about fifty yards behind. This could only mean one thing: the man in civvies was a German and most certainly up to no good. The German soldiers passed us. One was a sergeant carrying a sub-machine gun, the other a private with a rifle. The man in front turned right at the next junction and the soldiers did likewise, trailing him up the street.

We turned left towards the office twenty yards away. Lefeure entered the building first and, as I followed, I took a quick glance round in each direction as a precautionary measure; I had become well used to doing this during the past few months. Glancing back the way we had come, I was surprised to see the tall dark-haired fellow again coming towards me on the same side of the street. He had apparently made a mistake in turning right, and was now retracing his steps. His 'escort' was walking on the other side of the road.

I followed Lefeure into the building, and as the staircase was opposite the door I mounted about ten steps to the first bend and then stopped in order that I might get a glance at the Gestapo man as he passed the open door. I hoped I would never have occasion to encounter him again but, just in case I thought, it would be as well to memorise his face. The footsteps reached the doorway. Suddenly my heart beat wildly and I felt a chill down my spine – the man was coming into the building. Lefeure had already reached the first landing and knocked on a door. I

The entrance to Robert Lhuerre's office in Bar-le-Duc

leapt up the remaining few stairs just as Robert

answered the knock. Before either of them could speak, I grabbed Robert's arm and pulled him to the banister. We looked down at the man standing on the ground floor, and I hissed 'Gestapo' in Robert's ear. We hesitated; perhaps he had only come to make a few normal inquiries at the flour distribution centre. But, while we watched, the sergeant came through the doorway holding his weapon at the ready. The civilian spoke to him, then drew an automatic from his breast pocket and led the way up the stairs. We had walked right into the building just as the Gestapo arrived to arrest Robert.

Robert said 'Upstairs!' and I raced along the landing, up the second flight of stairs, along the next landing, then up the top flight. I prayed that Robert knew a way onto the roof so that we could escape among the chimney pots, get into an adjacent building and then down through another skylight.

I flew up the stairs two at a time, fear giving me almost superhuman energy and strength. On the top landing I paused so that Robert could take the lead and show the way to some skylight by which we could climb on to the roof. I glanced round, but realised that only one pair of feet had been racing up the stairs behind me, and they belonged to young Lefeure – Robert had gone back into the office on the first landing.

I could hear heavy feet walking about on the floor and stairs below. German soldiers were pouring into the building now. I ran along the corridor and dived through a doorway at the end, much to the amazement of some clerks who were working there. I quietly withdrew and tried another door. This was a store room containing a few bundles of dusty papers. We entered and shut the door behind us. The colour had completely drained from my companion's face; he was trembling like a leaf, and so was I. My heart pounding as if it were going to burst. Heavy hobnailed German boots came up the top flight of stairs. Desperately we looked round the room. The one small window had a sheer fifty-foot drop to the street below; looking up, I saw the roof was well out of reach. There was no exit and we were stuck like a couple of rats in a trap.

The footsteps were coming along the corridor now. There was only one thing left – my knife, the same one that had killed cattle at Revigny. I slid it from its leather sheath with a trembling hand. Within a few seconds from now, either I or the Nazis outside the door would be writhing on the floor.

Just then, a shout in German came from down below, and a voice right outside the door replied. Apparently, it had been an order recalling the soldier. He retraced his steps and descended.

A wave of relief passed over me. We stood in silence, hardly daring to breathe as the sound of heavy boots descended the stairs and left the building. All was quiet. We looked out of the window and were horrified to see a little procession moving down the street away from the building There was poor Robert being led away handcuffed and escorted by half a dozen Nazis.

No one will ever know why he went back to the office on the first floor after sending us upstairs. Perhaps he stayed behind so that we would have a chance to get away. Maybe he tried to warn his cousin, who also worked in the office, and whom the Germans were leading away handcuffed as well. Robert had been very worried when I had last seen him two nights before; he knew the time had practically come when he must leave Bar-le-Duc and go into hiding. If only he had decided to leave there and then! Now it was too late; his life was doomed.

The gallant Robert Lhuerre

The only thing I could do was to get out of the building and warn all my acquaintances in Bar-le-Duc as soon as possible. We cautiously opened the door, tip-toed along the corridor and slowly descended the stairs right to the ground floor without meeting a soul.

Stepping out once more into the bright sunshine, I decided that first of all I would go to the house of the man known as Jules since this was the nearest. I knew the town thoroughly, but in the excitement of the moment I set off round a block of buildings by a route which was actually about fifty yards longer than the one I would have used at any other time.

I had just turned the corner when I saw a grim-faced figure hurrying along the footpath towards me – it was none other than Jules himself. He was not cool, stern and serious as I had seen him a few days previously; instead he looked more nervous and frightened than myself. When I stopped him it did not improve matters. I quickly told him that Robert had been arrested. "Where are you going to now?" he asked. "I was on my way to your house to warn you," I replied. "Oh, my God!" he said. "Don't go there! I've been tipped off at work on the railway that the Gestapo are in the house waiting for me, and I'm getting away as far as I can." I asked him what was best for me to do, and he said, 'Do you know the chemist up the road?'

This confirmed my suspicions regarding the identity of M.X, so I nodded my head, and Jules continued, "You'd better tell him what's happened". Then, with a very hasty goodbye, he hurried off.

As I walked along, still accompanied by Lefeure, towards the chemist's, I suddenly realised how lucky I was that I had accidentally started on the slightly longer route to Jules' house. Had I taken the usual one I would have walked right into the Gestapo trap.

At the chemist's shop I walked past the open door a couple of times and saw that one of the white-coated figures was definitely M.X. I told Lefeure I had spotted the man we had to see but he had not seen us, so the only thing to do was to make our presence known by going into the shop to buy something. Lefeure got some money out of his pocket and we both went in. Unfortunately, one of the other assistants offered to serve us, and M.X kept on working behind the counter without even looking up. So, while Lefeure bought something equivalent to a packet of aspirins, I coughed fairly loudly until M.X looked up. His eyes widened as he recognised me, but he immediately looked down again and carried on working quite normally.

We left the shop and after five minutes or so M.X came out of the doorway, this time without his white smock. He casually looked either way and then pretended to examine the display in the window. When I knew he had seen me, I turned and walked away; he followed and caught me up. As we walked side by side I quickly told him what had happened during the morning.

"You must get out of town as soon as possible," he said. "Revigny is the best place." Then he spoke to Lefeure, who said he lived locally and could get home. He asked Lefeure if he could borrow a bicycle nearby for me. Lefeure nodded and showed me the

way to a house near Notre Dame. Here lived Jean Pornot, one of the
lads whose silhouette I had seen at midnight at the farm.

At the house Lefeure told Jean that Robert Lhuerre had been
arrested. Jean realised how serious things were and lent me his
bicycle without asking who I was or where I was going. This was
probably a good thing, because a few hours later this poor lad was
arrested and brutally interrogated.

As we parted, M.X told me to get to Revigny as soon as
possible, and once there to tell Louis to double all precautions and
look elsewhere for a hide-out.

I pedalled away, keeping my eyes peeled ahead and at each side
of the road lest I should run into a check-point. Every now and then I
looked behind me to see if I was being followed. Only one vehicle
passed me all the way, a saloon car. I saw it when it was half a mile
behind me, so round the next bend I ran off the road and went
several yards into a wood. I lay in the bushes with the bicycle until
the car went by and the sound of the engine had died out in the
distance. I returned to the road again and off I went. It was probably
some harmless person driving along the road, but I could not afford
to take any chances now.

While I was hurrying along to Revigny, young Lefeure went in
the opposite direction to the farm. He had only been there a few
minutes when the family saw some cars full of Germans coming up
the cart track. The young lad ran out of the house and across the
fields. It was lucky for me that I was not hiding on the farm for, after
checking everybody's identity card, they made a thorough search of
the house and outbuildings. Finally they asked a few questions, and
when they left they took away some photographs of the son. He was
not seen again in that district until after the war.

CHAPTER NINETEEN

Return to Revigny

At last I reached the town of Revigny, and decided to make a short detour in order to approach Louis' house from the rear. I went to the bottom of the orchard, put the bicycle over the hedge, and then got through after it. Laying the machine in the long grass, I walked quietly past the fruit trees into the small wood and headed towards the garden.

Before walking up the garden, I studied the house from a distance, worried lest the Gestapo had got there before me. There was not a soul in sight; everything seemed peaceful.

I slowly walked nearer, opened the gate without a sound and stepped into the courtyard. Then I noticed that all the doors and shutters were closed. I tried the main door – it was locked. There seemed to be something unusual about the place, so I stealthily withdrew and retraced my steps back through the garden to the wood.

I decided to see if Louis and Jean were at Mme Marie's. I climbed over the fence into the copse and walked cautiously through the trees until I emerged at the fence at the bottom of Marie's garden. There was not a soul in sight; the bungalow was locked, but smoke came from the chimney. I tip-toed round the chicken-run to the barn. The door was open and the rabbits and goats seemed to have been fed that morning. Could it mean that Marie and Louis and Jean had been warned of a Gestapo raid? Had they evacuated and was someone from the village feeding their livestock? But, this did not explain why the kitchen fire was lit.

Before leaving, I scratched 'Denys' with a stick in the dry earth in front of the barn door, but then on second thoughts I rubbed it out again. I went back to Louis' garden and made up my mind that the best thing I could do was to get on the bicycle again and set off in a south-westerly direction towards the Normandy front, begging or stealing food on the way.

I decided to have just one more look round the courtyard and the house to see if I could get any clue as to what had happened and where Louis and Jean had gone to. As I stole across the courtyard, I heard strange voices coming from upstairs and then the sound of footsteps coming down to the front door. I dodged into the bushes in the centre of the courtyard. Through the leaves I could just see the door. I heard it being unlocked, and then waited tensely to see who would come out. It was Louis himself. What a relief! He locked the door again behind him, and then as he walked round the bushes on his way to the workshop I stepped out and said quietly, "Hello, Louis." He jumped with fright, then threw his arms around me, kissing me on both cheeks with tears in his eyes. "I knew you'd come back here, Denys, if you couldn't get home," he said, adding, "Come inside and meet some new friends."

I followed him into the house and to the upstairs kitchen. This door was also locked, but when Louis called, Jean came and opened it. He also was surprised and delighted to see me.

The place seemed full of young men. I looked round; there were maps of the Normandy coast pinned on the walls; a couple of automatics were lying on the table, and some modern rifles stood in a corner.

The newcomers were introduced to me. There was Charles, dressed in a check shirt and a pair of football shorts; I recognised him as being the GMR I had seen in uniform a few weeks previously, when he had come to ask Louis to get him away to England to join the Free French Air Force. Bob, now similarly dressed, had been with Charles. When D-Day had come a couple of days earlier, they had deserted, complete with their uniforms, rifles, an automatic and as many rounds of ammunition as they could carry. They had also persuaded two of their companions to do the same. There was a rather refined looking, fair-haired young fellow called Jean Vallette who had been studying as an architect at the beginning of the war; when the time came for him to be conscripted for work in Germany he had volunteered for service in the GMR so that he would be able to stay in France.

The final introduction was to a thick-set dark-haired young fellow named René. He had once been forced to work in Germany, but had been lucky enough to join the GMR and return to France. The four of them came from the South and spoke with a different accent from Louis and Jean Chenu, but I had no difficulty in understanding them. I told them all of the lucky escape I had had that morning, and of how the Gestapo were very busy in Bar-le-Duc, and warned Louis that he could expect a raid at any time now.

During all the time we had been talking, two other men had been washing the dishes from the last meal and had not been introduced. I asked who they were and received the reply, "Only Russians." I went over and shook hands with them and said in French, "The three of us are a long way from home." They seemed very pleased that I had spoken to them and grinned broadly. They spoke a kind of broken French and told me that their names were Arkadi and Nikolai. Arkadi was very swarthy, with hairy arms and a broad, typically Russian face. He was a sergeant electrician in what I gathered was the equivalent of the Royal Corps of Signals. The second fellow had Mongolian features, a sallow complexion and dark, bright eyes. He had been a private in an artillery regiment. They had been in a prison camp for a year in Germany and then dispatched to France in a working party. After a few months they had escaped from their guards and had been at liberty, evading capture like myself, since last summer. The French boys looked upon them as being just ignorant Russian peasants, and when the time drew near the pair of them set to work peeling the potatoes and preparing the next meal. During my brief conversation with them I found them to be interesting and intelligent.

Nikolai (holding the baby goat) and 'Denis Lebenec'

I suggested to Louis that if we were to form ourselves into an efficient little fighting force there must be some organisation. First, I made out a duty rota for each day's work to be done by different pairs of men, the Russians together, Charles and Bob, Jean and René,

Jean Chenu and myself, leaving Louis out of it as he had other things to attend to out of the house. The duties included chopping wood, lighting fires, peeling potatoes, cooking, and washing dishes. Next came a dawn-to-dusk guard rota. During the day every man was awake and beside his own particular weapon, but during the night there was to be a one-man guard, changed every hour.

After supper that night we sat talking and smoking until eleven o'clock, and then everyone retired to bed except myself; I was doing the first hour of guard duty. The bedrooms all led from one to the other, and the doors were left open so that the man who was patrolling could walk up and down the length of the house, looking out of each window in turn.

In the first room slept Louis in the single bed and Jean in the double bed which I would share with him at midnight. I walked quietly, bare-footed, through to the next room, where Arkadi and Nikolai were. There were not enough beds for everyone, so they lay on the floor with a blanket over them.

In the end room slept the four deserters. I paced silently up and down, spending a few minutes at each window in turn and occasionally fingering the revolver in my pocket, until it was midnight by Charles' luminous wristwatch lying by his bed. Then I woke the next man up for duty and slid into bed next to Jean.

I hardly slept that night. I kept thinking of the events that had taken place during the day, wondering what had happened to Robert so far; wondering how long my luck was going to hold out before I'd be caught; wondering if I'd ever see England again.

Looking through the darkness I could dimly see the figure at the window on guard. Sometimes I would doze for a short period and wake up to see a different silhouette at the window as a new guard took up his shift.

When the grey dawn broke I could make out Arkadi standing at the window. I wondered where his thoughts would be while he did his hour's guard. He had had no news of his family for nearly three years. Perhaps his village had been completely destroyed during the fighting; perhaps all his people were dead, they would almost certainly believe him to be dead. When he had been captured he had been wounded in both legs. A bullet had passed right through one thigh and was embedded in the other. Many wounded men who could not walk were shot on the spot by the Germans, but Arkadi's friends had picked him up and half-carried, half-dragged him for fifteen days, during which time they covered 200km, before he received any medical treatment.

Arkadi told me that at the end of this time he was very ill and his legs in a bad state, but the treatment he received in the German hospital was very good and in a few months he was able to walk again. He showed me the scars of the bullet wounds and the operation.

I was glad when the time came for me to get up and a new day started. We all crowded round the little radio that Louis had brought from Mme Marie's and listened to the news bulletin. We made pencil marks on the map of the Normandy front, moved pins about and discussed the situation amongst ourselves. The news was good: the Allies had got a good foothold on the coast; in Italy, the Boche were being slowly but surely pushed back, and in Russia they were suffering heavy casualties.

The two Russians smiled and jabbered away to each other as they looked at the maps. At last it looked as though Germany would eventually be beaten; previously we could only hope that it would happen and dared not think what would happen otherwise.

My four new French friends were continually asking me questions about England and my life in the RAF. What it was like bombing Germany? What were my impressions as I baled out over France in the darkness? Charles and I had many things in common, but I soon found that his flying knowledge was very limited. He had successfully passed a pilot's course in the French Air Force, but throughout his career he had flown less hours than I had when I was in Canada as a pupil pilot before being re-mustered to bomb-aimer.

They did not have very much civilian clothing between them, which accounted for the popularity of football shorts. It was essential that we made very little noise in the house, so most of us walked round in bare feet all the time.

For the first couple of days we did not move out of the house, but this was too good to last. Obviously, a group of young men could not remain silently creeping around in one house indefinitely, so we decided that we would each take a little exercise by going across the courtyard into the workshop occasionally, one at a time.

This was satisfactory for one day, and we took it in turns to go across and walk round the machines and benches – hiding, of course, if anyone came to the door. The following day, however, the men got impatient waiting for their turn to stretch their legs, and soon everybody seemed to be wandering round the courtyard and workshop. If the doorbell rang, everyone dashed back into the house. I considered this very imprudent. Furthermore, the conversations before had been carried on in whispers; now they were being carried out in a normal voice. In fact, occasionally a shout was being given from one room to another. Surely this would arouse the suspicions of anybody who was passing along the road outside the courtyard wall, especially as everyone in the village knew that four Frenchmen had deserted.

I had a long talk with Louis and reminded him of M.X's grim warning that his house was almost sure to be raided. Louis had previously mentioned a deserted farm in a very isolated spot about ten miles away, and I suggested that we should make a reconnaissance there and see if it would be suitable as a hideout for the nine of us. The following afternoon, Louis and I set off together on bicycles. The others envied us, but it was not possible for the ex-GMRs to venture outside the courtyard in daylight in case they were recognised by someone who had previously seen them on duty in uniform. The Russians could not leave because their features and accents would betray them, and Jean had to stay behind to answer the door when anyone made an inquiry regarding the woodworking business.

It was a glorious day as we pedalled along the hot, dusty road, leaving Revigny behind us in a direction I had never taken before. We went through Brabant-le-Roi, a small village with its chickens pecking in the roadway, white washed houses jumbled together with their shuttered windows, then out into the open country again. A few miles farther on, we came to another village, Laheycourt. Here we called at the baker's, and while we sipped glasses of wine in a back room, Louis explained to the son, who was an old friend, the position we were in at Revigny.

For the past few days, Jean had been going to the local baker and with the use of forged bread coupons had been able to obtain sufficient bread to feed the nine of us. This could not continue without arousing suspicion, for all the village knew that the two brothers lived alone and surely would not eat such a large amount as Jean had bought each day. The young baker was eager to help and promised to let us have as much bread as he could possibly spare. He was also able to direct us to the deserted farm and thought it would be an excellent hideout. After the usual quietly spoken toasts to

France, the Resistance and victory, we thanked him for his generosity and co-operation and continued on our way.

For five miles we rode, with the fields on either side and not a single house in sight, then reached a point where the road forked. Here we saw a cart track leading off to a belt of trees. We took this track, as the baker had told us; it was so overgrown with long grass that we had to wheel our bicycles down it.

Shortly we found ourselves on the shores of a lake. The water shimmering in the sun made it a marvellous sight, and we stayed at the water's edge for a few minutes admiring the peaceful scene. We could see no sign of a farm – nothing but water and trees – but the end of the lake curved round out of sight in a boomerang shape. The path skirted the rushes at the side of the lake for two hundred yards, and then led into the thick forest.

We pushed slowly along an avenue cut in the trees. It was wide enough for a horse and cart, but overgrown with grass and weeds which came up to our thighs. On either side was a solid wall of trees and bushes; we felt miles away from civilisation and wondered where on earth this farm could be.

At the end of a mile we were both perspiring freely, and as we rounded a bend a clearing ahead was indeed a welcome sight. We stepped out into the bright sunshine once more and looked around.

At last we had reached our objective. We had arrived at the other end of the boomerang-shaped lake, and there in front of us stood the farm. Between the thick wood and the edge of the lake was about six acres of pastureland, and the farmhouse stood there alone, silent and deserted, miles from the nearest neighbour. All the windows were shuttered, and we walked right round the building and found a well at the back. If the water in it was clean one of our problems would be solved; it looked reasonably clear, and the occupant of the farm many years previously must have used it.

We next examined the interior of the farm. At one end of the building were the living quarters, then a shippen (or cowshed) and a barn with large double doors at one side. We decided to explore the living quarters first, so we got in by the back door which was fastened with wire wrapped round a couple of rusty nails. By the light coming through the cracks and spaces in the shutters we could see we were in a large kitchen, with a big open fireplace at one end and a sandstone sink at the other. There were a couple of milking-stools and a roughly made table.

"It looks as if someone has been here recently," said Louis. In the next room we found a few fishing nets, and in the third a trestle table and some firewood.

As we mounted the creaking staircase, there was a flutter of wings and I got a glimpse of an owl leaving through what had once been the roof. The upper storey consisted of one long room. There were very few slates on the roof and the floor was covered with several inches of solid bird droppings. We walked gingerly over this, realising the boards beneath must be in a very bad condition. In one corner we found a nest; the eggs were still warm and it must have been the parent bird we had frightened away.

We realised that this farm would make an ideal place for us to hide in. We could live downstairs and keep a look-out upstairs. One corner of the house was only a few feet from the dense bushes, and we could possibly dig a tunnel underground for this distance to form an emergency exit by which we could leave in a desperate crisis, even if the building were covered with machine guns. Once in the forest, it would take thousands of troops to search for us.

The Germans had been known to search woods by going through from one end to the other holding hands in a huge chain. This required about a thousand men per mile, and this particular forest was ten miles long and almost as wide. The Nazis certainly could not spare ten thousand men at this critical stage of the war. So long as we kept a cool head and had a knowledge of the layout of the forest we could evade capture for as long as we had sufficient food to keep us alive.

There was a water supply and we could get bread from Laheycourt; Louis' goat could live here and supply us with milk or, better still, we could probably rustle a cow and fetch it through the woods alive. We could get poultry, eggs, and fish out of the lake with the aid of the nets in the house. Everything seemed ideal. Louis expressed his approval, and we decided to move in as early as possible.

We cautiously descended the rickety staircase and left the house the way we had entered. The shippen and barn were still unexplored, so we tried the shippen door. It seemed fastened on the inside. Louis stepped back a couple of paces and then charged at it with his shoulder. It gave way but only burst half-open, as if something were behind it. My inquisitive friend popped his head round the door and then suddenly jumped back with fright. We had thought that we were miles from the nearest human being, but there was someone behind the door!

We were so taken by surprise that we just stood there, frozen to the spot. There was a movement, and then a dirty, unshaven, terror-stricken form came round the corner. He was more frightened than we were and came towards us with his hands together as if in prayer, begging for mercy in almost incomprehensible French. He was a Russian, and when he saw we were in civilian clothes and were not armed, he slid round the corner of the doorway and ran for the woods as fast as he could.

We heard a rustle of hay inside the building and a second figure came racing out and dashed towards the woods like a hare. They must have been escaped prisoners of war. The poor fellows looked half starved, but it was too late to do anything for them even if we had called them, for I am sure they would not have returned. They must have heard us moving about at the end of the building and imagined they were going to be caught. No wonder they were frightened, for any escaped Russians who were recaptured received very brutal treatment and were very often shot.

Entering the building cautiously, we found a pile of hay which had served them as a bed. In the barn was an old horse trap and a few other farm implements. There were large holes in the roof and everything was covered with bird droppings. Our inspection now completed, we set off back down the track through the trees, past the edge of the lake, duly arriving on the main road once more. We pedalled along the hot, dusty road in silence until at last we were within sight of Revigny.

All the boys gathered round as we described the condition and position of the farm. Everyone was looking forward to swimming in the lake, climbing the trees and having a much healthier and safer existence than at the moment, tip-toeing round the house all day.

Before moving, we would have to get a fairly good supply of food to take with us. The meat we had preserved a few weeks previously was not going to last as long as we anticipated. Our potato stock was already low and our flour was finished.

We knew of a farmer in the district who was thought to be sympathetic to the Germans, so we decided to pay him a visit that night and relieve him of some of his goods. Louis was to gain entrance by means of a downstairs window, Charles and Bob were to follow him through, their faces covered with handkerchiefs, and carrying a flashlight in one hand and an automatic in the other; they were to proceed immediately upstairs to the bedrooms and find the farmer and his wife. This pair would wake to find a flashlight almost blinding their eyes and see a pair of gun barrels pointing straight at them. After being warned that no harm would come to them as long as they kept quiet, they were to be tied up and warned to make no attempt to get away or raise an alarm until daylight.

Meanwhile, Louis would have opened the back door, and the two Jeans would go inside and help him to remove all foodstuffs they could lay their hands on. Armed with the Mauser, and accompanied by Arkadi and Nikolai, I would search the outhouses and fill sacks with as much poultry as possible. The ninth man, René, was to keep a look-out on the road near by and give warning of any approaching danger.

When each man knew his duties we started to make our own individual arrangements. I put on my black beret and dark brown pullover, just as I had done for previous expeditions, emptied my pockets, blackened my hands and face with charcoal, ensured my gun was in good order and put ammunition in my most handy pocket. I moved my sheath knife round to a position on my belt where I could draw it in an instant, selected a good sack from the pile that lay on the floor, rolled it up and stuck it down my belt. I was then ready for the evening's work.

The Russians had also made preparations. This was by no means the first time they had done this sort of thing either; they had been living in France longer than I had. The ex-GMRs were rather excited, René pale and nervous; this was something new to them. Earlier, Bob had been thrilled at the idea of doing an armed hold-up, but now he was saying nothing and feeling a little doubtful.

It was midnight. Everyone's hands and faces were blackened, all pockets emptied of incriminating evidence which might be lost during the expedition, then off we went.

We found the courtyard pitch-dark after the bright light in the kitchen, but our eyes gradually became accustomed to it. Louis and Charles formed the advance party, then a hundred yards behind followed Louis' brother Jean, René, Bob and Jean Vallette. Arkadi and Nikolai and I were the rearguard a hundred yards farther back still. Since we had first met, the three of us had been the very best of friends and now that we were out on an expedition together, we were brought even closer. We went down the yard, through the copse, into the orchard, then through the hedge into the fields.

We would glide silently forward for a short distance and then crouch behind a tree or hedge and listen intently a couple of minutes or so for any sound coming from behind, then creep on once more. Occasionally, we would hear the party in front tread on a dead twig or a footfall on a piece of hard ground.

We hardly whispered all the way. Silently we held barbed wire apart for each other to crawl through; sometimes I held Arkadi's warm, powerful hand as we helped each other over a ditch, or perhaps gripped Nikolai's thin, sinewy fingers as I led him through a gap in a hedge. At other times, the three of us held hands as we trod gingerly over uncertain ground, where you could not tell what you were stepping into – a bog, or a ditch or something equally unpleasant.

When we arrived at the farm René had taken up his look-out position and Louis was deciding which windows and shutters would be easiest to open. There seemed to be no dog about the place, which was unusual for a farm but quite a relief to me; the poor thing would have had to be silenced and I would have hated to see an animal killed for doing its duty.

Louis made his choice, and in a few minutes the shutter and then the window swung open. Seeing that everything was going according to plan, my two accomplices and I started exploring the outhouses. Our sense of smell guided us to where the poultry were sleeping, and the door was opened without much delay. While I stayed outside so that I could have a good idea of what was going on at the farmhouse, my pals got to work. Nikolai, holding the flashlight, shone it straight into a hen's face, then Arkadi would reach forward, wring its neck and drop it dead into the sack before it had a chance to utter a sound.

I had seen Louis' silhouette come out of the back door, having worked his way through the house successfully, when suddenly the stillness of the night was broken by the terrified scream of a woman. This was something unexpected. We thought the farmer and his wife would be too frightened to breathe when they were 'held up'; instead, the woman was screaming, "Don't kill me; don't kill me."

To make matters worse, the man and wife were sleeping in separate rooms. The woman was hysterically screaming for her husband, and I could hear Bob trying to control her, first threatening to shoot her, then trying to persuade her gently to be quiet since he did not want to kill her unless it was absolutely essential. Eventually, Charles led the farmer into the room with his hands above his head and an automatic prodding into his back. With her husband beside her, the woman calmed down except for sobbing and wailing.

There were houses nearby and the occupants would most certainly have heard some of the noise, so it was essential that we made our getaway as quickly as possible before someone gave the alarm to the Germans in the barracks at the edge of the town.Nikolai swung over his shoulder the bag of freshly killed poultry, some of which were still kicking; I picked up a large ham which Louis had brought out of the house, and Arkadi took a sack of flour.

I quickly counted the eight figures in the darkness to make sure that everyone had left the house, then we headed across the fields as quickly as possible in the direction we had come.

As before, my two colleagues and I found ourselves in the rearguard, and while the others forged ahead we crouched in a ditch a hundred yards from the farm, listening. We heard footsteps running along the road nearby but no one was following us, so we pressed on in pursuit of our friends in front. We passed all the landmarks we had seen in the starlight earlier in the night, until finally we were once more walking up the garden path to Louis' house which we looked upon as home.

Once inside we examined our haul. It had certainly been a good night's work. There was ham, butter, pork, cheese and lots of other valuable foodstuffs, including a huge earthenware jar containing cooking fat which was perhaps the most valuable prize.

Suddenly, Jean Vallette made the disturbing revelation that he had lost his sheath knife during the expedition and that it had his initials on the handle. Louis and I were annoyed about this and lost no time in telling him what we thought of him.

Throughout the rest of the night the usual hourly guard was maintained. Although we had successfully made our attack and returned safely, we did not know whether dogs would be employed by the Germans to follow up our scent.

The following day, Louis went through the village and found that the main topic of conversation was the happenings during the night. Grossly exaggerated stories had already circulated concerning the doings of a murderous gang of bandits in the district. Some villagers sympathised with the farmer and his wife; others said that it was the best thing that could happen to a pair of collaborators.

During his travels, Louis met a local gendarme with whom he had been friendly. While they were talking about the raid, he told Louis that a knife had been found in the house bearing the initials J.V. They hoped this would lead to the owner, and he asked Louis if he could make any useful suggestions. Louis said he could not think of any possible owner for the moment, but assured the gendarme that he would bear it in mind and let him know if he found out anything.

CHAPTER TWENTY

Monsieur Colombo

During the next four days we hardly dared move about the house. Everyone in the village was wondering where the gang of robbers was hiding out, and if someone passing by happened to hear men's voices other than Jean's and Louis' coming over the courtyard wall or from the house, their suspicions would be aroused immediately.

A set of chessmen and a pack of cards helped the hours to pass by. We had little tournaments on the chessboard among the six Frenchmen and myself, the Russians just watching, but they used to mutter in Russian to one another. One day, a particular tournament had resulted in Charles and me becoming the finalists. After all the practice we had been getting, our standard was quite good. In the afternoon we fought out the battle of wits for the championship, which lasted two hours until finally I was victorious.

Nikolai had stood behind my chair throughout the game, and seemed intensely interested, so I asked him if he would care to try his hand. He nodded his head enthusiastically and took Charlie's' place opposite me. I asked if he understood the rules. He said he did and that the same game was played in Russia.

The game commenced. I didn't want to take his men too quickly and too brutally, so my first few moves did not consist of any definite attack; I just carelessly and haphazardly responded to his various moves. Suddenly he put my king in check and the only way out meant the sacrifice of my queen. This was indeed bad, and a few moves later the game was over, with Nikolai grinning victoriously from ear to ear over his Mongolian face.

I laughed and congratulated him, thinking it was nothing more than 'beginner's luck.' However, the same thing happened for four games, and I realised that I had definitely met my master.

Nikolai told me then that at home chess was played in all the cafés and that when he was a schoolboy he had played a great deal: in fact, he had once played ten games simultaneously against other boys his own age and won every one. No wonder he had beaten me so easily! This was not the first time these two supposedly 'ignorant

Russian peasants' had surprised the household. The more I got to
know about them the greater the respect I had for them.

One day Arkadi started a conversation with me about England
and began to say all sorts of words that I simply couldn't understand.
He seemed amazed when I shook my head, and started all over
again, giving a long jumble of words that didn't mean a thing to me.
He tried saying the same things again, varying his pronunciation to
see if I could understand. Listening as he spoke very slowly and
deliberately in his broken French, I managed to make out that
somehow these words he kept repeating were connected with
England, Italy, a pair of scales, and yet the whole thing was
something he had seen in Russia.

Nikolai came to us and joined in the conversation. First he
repeated a lot of words in a similar manner to his countryman, and
he, too, seemed certain I should be able to understand. I gradually
gathered that he was talking about some historical play he had seen
in Russia which concerned England and Italy, and suddenly the
whole thing became clear. I said "Shakespeare" and realised that
they had been pronouncing it in a dozen different ways for me and I
couldn't recognise it. The rest was easy. Arkadi had been saying
names such as Antonio, Shylock and so on, and we soon agreed
upon a sort of mutual pronunciation. He had seen several of
Shakespeare's plays, including 'The Merchant of Venice' and 'As
You Like It', and various others acted in Russian theatres.

As the days passed, the boys became more restless and once
more everyone started darting over the courtyard into the workshop
and even occasionally walking into the garden in daylight. This was
dangerous and I kept urging Louis to make the evacuation to the
farm by the lake, but always there seemed to be some reason for
putting it off. This time he said it was too soon after the robbery of
the farm, and that each night extra patrols were on the roads waiting
for us to strike again. The police knew now that the knife which was
found belonged to a certain Jean Vallette, who was one of the four
GMRs who had deserted a couple of weeks previously, and a
detailed description of them had been circulated.

Some form of exercise was essential to keep us fit, so Louis and
I fitted a trapeze in the wood at the bottom of the garden and after
dusk we all used to go down there; the lucky ones wore galoshes, the
others went in bare feet. We used to swing from the two iron hoops

upside down, by two feet, by one foot and in every conceivable position we could think of, each trying to do something more spectacular than the rest. These strenuous exercises would carry on in the moonlight until we were all tired out and then we would retire to bed, leaving only the solitary guard awake.

One afternoon, the bell rang at the courtyard door, and everyone quickly concealed themselves. I took up my customary position with a rifle at a bedroom window overlooking the courtyard. Louis tip-toed across to the iron door and peeped through the little spyhole we had drilled for that purpose several months previously. He was apparently satisfied that it was a friend outside and turned the key in the lock. In walked a short, round-faced fellow whom I had not seen before; Louis greeted him warmly and led him into the house.

Arkadi and Nikolai were at my side and excitedly told me that the stranger was a great friend of theirs, a M.Colombo, who had helped them and whose quick action a few weeks previously had prevented them from being captured.

Louis called us all from the kitchen and we were introduced. M.Colombo appeared to be a 'hail fellow well met', jovial, easy-going sort of man. He thrust his hands into his pockets and gave us each a packet of cigarettes. Charles' eyes nearly popped out of his head to see so many, for our own stolen supply had given out and he had been craving for a smoke all day. These cigarettes were obviously black-market stuff; when the boys reached to their pockets to pay for them, he laughed and would not accept anything.

In the neighbourhood, this fellow had the reputation of profiting by his association with the occupying army – which indeed he did. On the outbreak of war he was a scrap-metal dealer and his sole ambition in life was to make as much money as possible by any reasonable means possible, irrespective of whose side he worked on. His first stroke of luck came when the RAF decided to build an aerodrome quite near his village in 1940. He put himself and his lorry at their disposal, and according to local gossip very soon built up a very good side-line selling RAF blankets, food and so on. Then came the disastrous German breakthrough, and the RAF had to evacuate at very short notice. Before leaving, they destroyed a lot of equipment they could not take with them, but much was left behind undamaged. Hardly was the last Britisher out of sight than Colombo rolled up with his vehicle and took as much as he could lay his hands on before the rapidly advancing Germans arrived.

There was a store of petrol and he collected every single tin drum and barrel he could lay his hands on, filled them up and hid them in various parts of the district. When he had taken as much as he could hide, he set fire to the rest. Unfortunately, a woman who had a grudge against him informed the Germans that it was he who had set fire to the RAF petrol dump. He was arrested and interrogated, and pleaded that he knew nothing about it whatever. The Germans accused him of lying, and he was marched outside. His hands were tied behind his back and he was placed in front of a tree. Half a dozen soldiers were lined up as a firing squad, and orders barked at them until they were holding their rifles to their shoulders, pointing directly at him ready for the word 'fire'.

He told me how his whole body trembled at that moment, and sweat poured out him. He was thinking desperately, but his trembling lips could not utter a single word. Everything had happened so quickly and so unexpectedly; he was peacefully at home a few hours previously and now he was going to be shot. If he confessed he had set fire to the dump he would be shot just the same and he had already unsuccessfully pleaded innocence.

Just as he was expecting the hot bullets to burn into him, an order was given and the soldiers lowered their rifles. The whole affair had been a bluff. The Germans expected him to confess his guilt and plead for mercy when he saw the firing squad, but being so frightened he was utterly speechless and the Germans had taken him to be innocent and allowed him to return home.

Shortly after this, he offered the services of himself and his lorry to the Germans, and since then had done absolutely everything possible to earn favour in their eyes. So now, after four years, he had become on very good terms with the local commanders and at the same time was growing increasingly prosperous. He was the black-market king for many miles around, owning several vehicles and living in a large country house. He had also worked himself into the position of chief gamekeeper of the woods around. The Commandant would perhaps ring him up and say that a party of a dozen or more officers would be coming for a shoot at the weekend, instructing him to make the necessary preparations. He would discover the whereabouts of the wild boar and decide the best way for the hunters to make their sweep, then arrange for the employment of several local men as beaters. These hunting expeditions always ended up in a glorious celebration at

M.Colombo's house, and he would spend the night laughing and drinking with the very men that the rest of the population dreaded. They knew of his black-market activities but turned a blind eye in that direction, receiving in return bottles of whisky, rolls of silk for their wives, and anything else that was in short supply. He was so well known in the headquarters at Bar-le-Duc that when he approached the entrance the guards would recognise him and stand to attention while he walked straight through to the Commander's private office. He was very much hated by the patriotic French people for miles around, and one dark night someone had actually shot at him in his car.

I don't know how he originally came to be acquainted with Nikolai and Arkadi, but I know that when the pair of them were living together with my old friend Raymond in a deserted wood-cutter's cabin in the middle of a wood, Colombo knew they were there, and had from time to time visited them with food.

One evening, the German Commander rang up M.Colombo saying that he had received a report of men living in a certain wood not very far from his house, and that the area was going to be surrounded and a search made the following morning. Knowing of M.Colombo's expert knowledge of the woods, the officer suggested that his assistance would be most valuable and asked him to join in the operation. M.Colombo's active brain responded to the situation and he straightway accepted the invitation, saying he would be only too pleased to help, whereupon it was agreed that a car should call at the house for him at 7am the following morning. It was already dusk, and darkness would fall before he could find his way to the three fugitives in the wood, so he got up at dawn the following day and made his way hurriedly through the dewy grass among the trees. His unexpected arrival at the cabin took the boys by surprise, but they soon realised the urgency of his situation. There was not a minute to waste and they followed swiftly and silently behind him as he led the way out of what was certain to have been a death trap. They reached the edge of the wood. There was no one in sight; the soldiers had not arrived yet. The four figures half-ran, half-stumbled across the fields, over ditches and through hedges until finally they were at the rear of M.Colombo's house. He opened the door of an outhouse, ushered them inside, and locked it behind them. Running into the house through the back door, he had hardly recovered his breath before the German car pulled up outside the front door.

The search went on all day, but needless to say it was unsuccessful. All that was found was a derelict hut, and straw which seemed to have been slept on recently. Finally defeat was acknowledged and the soldiers withdrawn. Before returning to Bar-le-Duc, however, the officers called at M.Colombo's and several bottles of champagne were opened.

Our three friends in the outhouse listened with relief as they heard the last of the German cars disappear. Shortly after, M.Colombo's footsteps approached, a key was turned and he opened the door. It was decided that the Russians should go to Revigny in the back of M.Colombo's van and hide out at Louis', while Raymond preferred to work his way through the countryside back to his own village where he knew he could hide successfully amongst friends.

All this occurred while I was away in Bar-le-Duc with Robert, and this was how I came to find Nikolai and Arkadi living at Louis' the day I returned to Revigny after Robert had been arrested.

We all stood round M.Colombo laughing and joking, only too pleased to see a fresh face and hear a new voice and opinions from the outside world. Before leaving, he promised to call again the following week with more cigarettes and some foodstuffs for us.

CHAPTER TWENTY-ONE

The New Recruit

The days slowly dragged. We listened regularly to each news bulletin in French from the BBC and carefully plotted the Allies' position on our maps. Then came the personal messages. Patiently, we listened for a phrase about a certain goldfish to be spoken by the announcer; this would mean that our much-needed supply of arms and ammunition would be parachuted down that same night a few miles away. Each day more and more aircraft were passing overhead; the air raid sirens were sounding day and night now.

Rail traffic was almost at a standstill: the RAF and USAAF were picking every strategic point they could find and hammering it. One day, a long train of oil tank wagons was standing just outside Revigny station. A bridge farther on was damaged, so the train was obliged to stay where it was for the day. The air-raid sirens went in the usual manner and twelve Mustangs appeared on the horizon. We had seen dozens of other similar formations going over on previous days to some predetermined objectives, but this time they all turned steeply round and circled the town.

"They've seen the train!" I shouted to the boys. We all jumped for joy and, casting care aside for the moment in the excitement, we all ran out of the house into the garden. Standing amid the gooseberry and blackcurrant bushes, we could just see the wagons about three hundred yards away.

Three times the aircraft circled the town; the French folk believed this was done deliberately to give the citizens a chance to get away from the railway. This was a pleasant thought, although I personally believed the circuits were being made while the pilots had a good look at their quarry and made certain that no enemy fighters were liable to drop on their tails once they went down to the attack. On the last circuit they were all in line astern. Round they came right over our heads, then suddenly the leader dropped his wing and peeled off in a dive. Down and down he came; at about a couple of hundred feet we saw two little bombs come away from the aircraft. The pilot flattened out and the bombs carried on downwards; when they hit, the second aircraft was already making his dive, and behind him came the third. Six of the aircraft dropped pairs of bombs, then it seemed to be a 'free for all'. They all came down, machine-guns and cannons roaring, pouring lead into the target. On the last wagon there were the usual couple of machine guns manned by the Germans. We heard these fire a few bursts, then finish.

In the bushes our nine heads bobbed up and down excitedly; bits of shrapnel and occasional ricocheting bullets whizzed dangerously near, but we all felt like shouting with joy. Huge clouds of thick black smoke rolled upwards from the blazing oil tanks. The attack had been a great success; the twelve Mustangs gained height and re-formed and headed back towards England. It was not until they had been out of sight for a couple of minutes that two Fw 190s came tearing across the sky. Sadly for them, they were far too late; the damage had been done and the raiders were well on their way to safety.

Arkadi and Nikolai found the days of waiting long, particularly Nikolai; he kept thinking of the home he hadn't seen for over three years, and wondered if it was still standing. Often, we would sit on a bench in the workshop and he would talk to me about home. He was an only child, and due to the early death of his father he had looked upon himself as the man of the house, and cared for his mother and grandmother since he was thirteen years of age. He was very fond of his grandmother, and as he recalled little incidents connected with her, his eyes would water, and he would look at me and say, "I hope you don't think me silly talking like this, but I don't know if I'll ever see my dear old grandmother alive again." She was a very old lady and would not live long if she was subjected to bombing and evacuation.

Each day I kept suggesting to Louis that it was time we moved out of the house to the farm by the lake; I could see he was not taking M.X's warning as seriously as the situation warranted. We had heard news from Bar-le-Duc about Robert and the other young fellows who were arrested at the same time. Little bits of information had filtered out of the prison, and it was known that the three boys I had seen in the moonlight (one being the lad who lent me his bicycle to get out of Bar-le-Duc) had been handcuffed to a radiator in the Chief's office and beaten up personally by 'The Butcher' – the fellow I had seen coming up the stairs on the fateful morning when Robert was caught.

Robert was known to be still in the prison and the last news we had heard was that he was lying in his cell in great pain. His hands had been tied behind his back ever since his arrest three weeks before.

One morning we awoke to the sound of powerful engines and the metallic rattle of tank tracks in the streets as an armoured division moved into the town. We peeped through the shuttered windows and saw that the street was full of enemy vehicles and men. Harsh German voices were rasping out orders above the din. Louis went out to the courtyard door to find what all the commotion was about. A couple of minutes later he came running back into the house.

"This armoured column is on its way to the Normandy front," he said. "They've been on the move all night, and now they are going to hide all the vehicles amongst the houses during daylight as a precaution against air attack, then move off again at dusk."

He went out to the street again and, just as he opened the courtyard door, a German officer approached, pushing Louis aside. He stepped into the courtyard, glanced round, and then told Louis to get the big double doors open. He had propped several wooden beams against the gates and it took Louis all his time to move them. As soon as they were open a huge armour-plated troop carrier rolled in. It seemed to be half-lorry, half-tank; in front were four large rubber-tyred wheels, and behind a pair of caterpillar tracks.

Looking downward through the shutters from the upper rooms, we could see that it was equipped with wireless and machine guns and could probably carry about fifteen or twenty men. Over the top a sort of wire-netting cover could be drawn, probably to prevent hand grenades being thrown inside. The vehicle was manoeuvred against the side of the house, and then the crew of three started breaking branches off the trees in the courtyard until they had sufficient to cover their vehicle completely.

The same thing was taking place throughout the whole village, until every vehicle was camouflaged. Even if a low-flying aircraft did perceive them, the town would have to be absolutely flattened by a heavy bomber force in order to inflict much damage.

Throughout the day the Germans spent most of the time sleeping and did not attempt to enter the house. We tip-toed silently round the rooms in our bare feet or stood behind the shuttered windows with revolvers in our hands, ready to shoot our way out if the Germans decided to billet any soldiers in the building.

The sirens sounded and the Allied aircraft flew overhead: there was not a single German in sight, and the planes flew straight on without giving the quiet, peaceful-looking town a second thought.

I knew that in a few days' time the machine in the courtyard would be in action killing my own countrymen, and I longed to do something to immobilise it. I discussed the matter with the men; the enemy were practically sitting on our own doorstep, surely we were not going to let them just go off unhindered. Looking through a kink in the shutters, I spotted the petrol filler cap and remembered a hint I had heard a few years before, when England was in danger of invasion. If a small amount of sugar was dropped in the petrol it would eventually ruin the engine.

I got some sugar and determined to slip it in to the fuel tank somehow as soon as darkness fell. However, as soon as it became dusk the whole town came alive with activity. Branches were taken off the vehicles, engines started, orders were shouted and within a quarter of an hour every tank, gun, ammunition car and machine of the division had left the town and was on its way towards Normandy. Apparently, they would travel all night and then conceal themselves again when daylight came.

We were relieved to see the troop carrier leave the yard, but annoyed to see it disappear up the road without having had the opportunity to interfere with it. During that night we mounted guard in the usual manner until it was time to get up and start another day.

The Chenu's house at Revigny-sur-Ornain, refuge to evaders of all nationalities

We were always hungry, for our meals consisted almost every day of just one slice of bread, a couple of boiled potatoes and lots of cupfuls of water to fill us up.

The games of chess continued daily, Nikolai proving his superiority beyond all doubt. We each spent turns over in the workshop, making daggers and spears out of bayonets and knuckle-dusters out of pieces of solid oak. The fruit in the garden was becoming ripe now, and Arkadi used to make tea out of the blackcurrants. Some nights, when we went out all muffled up and with blackened faces, we returned with sacks full of cherries stolen from orchards in the district.

We had acquired some small cheeses which were allocated in little pieces to each man with some meals. The last to be eaten were absolutely heaving with maggots, so I used to mash my small ration up with my potatoes before eating it.

Hardly a day passed now without the air raid warnings being sounded, and we were seeing more and more Allied aircraft overhead. We saw lots of them with the undersides of their wings painted black and white, and soon saw that the Germans lost no time in disguising their aircraft to appear exactly the same. Another thing we noticed was that lots of Red Cross trains loaded with wounded were passing along the railway lines coming back from the Normandy front. Our Allied pilots had deep respect for these trains, with their huge red crosses painted on roofs and sides; it is a pity they did not know, as we did, that these same coaches were being used to take hundreds of fully armed unwounded men to the front on their return journeys.

A couple of nights later the alarm was sounded, and the little town vibrated to the roar of four-engined bombers in the darkness overhead. The aircraft seemed to be circling round and round, but this time the bombers were not alone. I had become so accustomed to Fw 190 night fighters flying around Revigny that I could easily distinguish the sound of their engines as they hunted the sky above for their prey.

Occasional streaks of tracer bullets crossed the sky as fighter and bomber snarled at each other with machine-guns blazing. Duels to the death were taking place in the sky above our heads. He who struck first and hardest would survive. Unfortunately, the bombers could only hit with ·303 machine guns against their attacker's heavier armaments. Furthermore, the bomber crews had already been staring into the blackness on the alert for several hours. I could all too easily imagine the Bomber Command boys peering through the perspex of their aircraft with bloodshot eyes which were longing to close, being kept open only by the occasional swallowing of 'wakey-wakey' tablets. My own countrymen were so near and yet so far; only a few thousand feet away and yet they would soon be on their way home. If all went well they would be having their breakfast in the morning, but I would still be in Revigny. Many memories of my own Bomber Command operations came to me as I stood there.

During the following day, M.Colombo brought news to the house that a parachutist whose aircraft had been shot down the previous night was hiding on a farm a few miles away. We were all very pleased to hear this, myself in particular; I felt like jumping for joy. Louis lost no time in putting on his coat and beret and sticking an automatic in his pocket. Jumping into M.Colombo's van, he set off to bring in the new recruit.

I knew that the chances of his being an acquaintance of mine were very slight, but even so I started thinking of all the men I would like him to be. At the time I had landed in France there were several of my pals from schoolboy days who were undergoing training as aircrew, and I hoped this man would turn out to be one of them. I hardly left the window until Louis returned two hours later. Through the slits between the wooden shutters, I saw him enter the courtyard and beckon our new companion to follow him into the house. Louis burst into the room and shouted excitedly, *"Denis. Voilà l'Anglais!"* (here's the Englishman).

Behind him came the survivor of the previous night's air raid. I stepped forward and shook his hand, grinned and tried to say something. But I had spoken French for so many months that I could not summon up my English. I eventually stammered out: "I too am an *aviateur anglais*," and went on to tell him that I had been in France since the previous summer, then suddenly realised that I was speaking in French again. The boys standing round saw what was happening and they laughed and told me I'd better start learning English.

The newcomer was looking me up and down, obviously wondering who I was. I had said I was English and yet I could jabber away to the Frenchmen, and when I started to talk English I did nothing but hesitate and stammer. However, after half an hour in his presence I was able to sort myself out. The boys kept on bombarding me with questions such as: "Ask him his name", "How old is he?", "Does he think Hitler is nearly beaten?" and so on. I translated the questions as fast as I could and learnt that his name was Dick; that he was twenty-six, married, no children; and that he thought the war would soon be over.

While this was going on, Louis, Bob and Charles had been whispering to each other at the end of the room, and eventually called me over to them and said: "Will you ask him to prove to you that he is an Englishman?" The whole room went quiet; everyone looked towards the newcomer. He was very thin, with a pasty complexion and a receding jaw. "He looks too weak to be an airman," said Bob, imagining all airmen to be as keen on physical development as himself. I countered this remark by saying that brain is generally more useful than muscle in the air, but at the same time I recalled that all the hundreds of aircrew members I had been associated with were fairly robust, athletic specimens. I added the remark that if this stranger were anything but English, he would not get out of the building alive.

The silence that followed was embarrassing, particularly for Dick, for he saw that everyone was studying him from head to foot. I started the conversation again by asking about everyday things that happened in England, and the very fact that he was willing to talk of them removed most of my suspicion. I asked where he had been stationed, and he mentioned various training aerodromes. When I asked him where he was operating from, he must have recalled the 'gen' received during intelligence lectures about disclosing nothing more than number, rank and name and perhaps he was still doubting my own fidelity. Anyhow, he just said vaguely: "Somewhere in Lincolnshire."

"Ever been in Scunthorpe?" I asked. He said he knew it quite well, and I soon learnt that riotous pub crawls were still being carried on nightly by aircrews from the neighbouring squadrons. After mentioning all the popular pubs we could remember between us, I said: "Ever heard of Elsham Wolds?"

"I was once stationed there," he admitted cautiously.

"So was I," I said.

In a few minutes, all suspicions of false identity had been dispersed from both our minds and I was listening eagerly to all the latest squadron news.

Shortly after we had gone to bed that evening, the air-raid warning sounded. Louis and I sat up and looked across at each other, wondering if perhaps the bombers were coming for yet a third time to try to locate the railway installations at Revigny. During the afternoon an ammunition train had come into the sidings. The news soon spread round the streets, and people started speculating regarding the possibility of an RAF visit that evening.

We all stood at the window, listening. Soon we heard the drone of the bombers approaching; the sound came nearer and nearer. They were heading straight towards us, and the ammunition train was only a few hundred yards away from the back of the house. We decided the time had come to evacuate as quickly as possible. From the bedside I grabbed my Mauser and stuck it down my belt, then felt in the dark for something to put over my shoulders. Running down the stairs, I made my way to the front door. The darkness in the courtyard was inky black, and I caught hold of Dick's hand to lead him quickly through the gate into the roadway outside. By now the aircraft were overhead, and suddenly white flares started dropping and the whole of the little town became lit up. Everyone was running from their houses with the same idea as ourselves, regardless of the curfew.

As we ran, the air overhead seemed absolutely filled with aircraft; they were only flying at about 1,000ft and the whole town seemed to tremble with the roar of the engines. Louis knew of a dried-up canal which he thought would be the most suitable place to shelter, and led the way across the fields. Everyone was running in the same direction, men, women, children. I suddenly became aware of a uniformed figure running at my side. I turned and saw it was a German soldier, probably from the nearby barracks. It was then I realised for the first time that I was haring along in the bright light of dozens of flares. There was nothing to do but keep running; there were several other Germans crossing the fields, but they were all too intent on getting away from the railway to worry about anything else.

Bright green PFF target-indicating markers were floating down. This made me run even faster, knowing that in a few seconds the bombs would be falling. Sure enough, just as I reached the edge of the canal the horrible whistling sound came as the first bomb load dropped downwards.

Glancing round as I went down the grassy side into the canal, I saw the most amazing sight. The first bomb, possibly weighing 4,000lb, had dropped right on the ammunition train and in the enormous sheet of orange flame I could actually see the wagons blown about fifty feet into the air. Down I went into the trench, helped on my way by the blast, and lay on the bottom. I panted for breath and tried to keep as flat as possible, wishing I could burrow into the ground like a rabbit. By my side lay Dick; probably some of his old messmates were circling overhead. On either side of us lay various people, and about five yards away I could hear the guttural voices of the Germans muttering and cursing to one another.

Bomb after bomb came screaming down to earth, and the ground shook at every explosion. The ammunition train was blazing away from end to end, and wagons were exploding every minute. The light from the flares and the glow from the ground fires were so bright that occasionally I could see the aircraft silhouetted above their target.

The aircraft were all making their bombing runs from the south, which meant they carried on right over our heads. I knew all too well that a bomb aimer had only to make a small error of judgement – perhaps a miscalculation of wind direction or speed, or place a wrong airspeed or altitude setting on his bomb sights – to make for a few seconds' delay in releasing the bombs. The result would inevitably be that they would land right in the trench.

Once I had overcome the initial fear created by the first few dozen bombs, my curiosity overcame my better judgement, and I ventured to peep over the top of the canal bank and watch the display of pyrotechnics. Each time an aircraft made its run over the target I lay there perspiring, listening to the screech of the bombs, imagining that each time the whistling had lasted slightly too long and the missiles had overshot their target and would land right into the middle of my back. Then came the deafening explosion, the ground would shake and I knew another had missed us. Every minute seemed a lifetime as hundreds of tons of explosives rained down upon us. The women and children were praying aloud for the bombardment to cease. As I lay there, it made memories of air raids I had seen in England seem like child's play although I had crawled out of the wreckage of my own home in 1941.

Gradually the roar of engines overhead died down, and eventually the last aircraft was on its homeward journey. Explosions still continued from the railway sidings as the ammunition train burnt, but it was essential that we should get back to the house as soon as possible before the rest of the neighbours. We did not want them to see a group of young men entering the house.

We crossed the field to the road and were soon once more in the courtyard. Just as we entered the house, a terrific explosion shook all the shutters and we heard pieces of earth falling in the garden and on the roof. It was apparently a delayed-action bomb that had gone off in the field behind the house.

We lay on the beds resting, but the explosions of delayed bombs kept shaking us every half-hour. The idea was obviously to keep repair workers away from the railway as long as possible.

In the morning we went to the bottom of the garden in twos and threes to watch the explosions. A pall of smoke hung over the twisted masses of steel that had been railway lines only a few hours previously. Then suddenly the ground would heave and up would come a fountain of earth; then came the deafening bang as the noise of the explosion reached our ears, followed by a rushing sound something like a waterfall as all the rubble poured back to earth.

An RAF delayed action bomb exploding at Revigny

This went on throughout the day and following night, but when we awoke the next morning all was quiet and peaceful – the silence being broken only by the town crier in the distance as he walked through the streets with his message. Finally, he reached the corner of the road not far from the house, and I could see him from the bedroom windows. He carried a form of mechanical drum round his shoulder, and as he turned a handle a series of sticks beat out a roll to attract the attention of all the citizens. Then, holding a piece of paper before him, he began calling out a message. Louis went out onto the road to listen and came back with the information that every man in the village had to report to the Town Hall carrying a spade to work on the damaged railway, and the two brothers had no alternative but to obey.

Destruction after an Allied air-raid on the railway yards at Revigny   (photo Parisse)

The terrible price paid to attack this small, strategic target at Revigny was 41 Lancasters and 231 airmen's lives. ('Massacre Over The Marne' by Clutton-Brock, Patrick Stephens, 1994).

CHAPTER TWENTY-TWO

The Seven Saboteurs

At midday the brothers returned, neither of them having moved a spadeful of earth in a useful direction if they could avoid it. They told us that the damage at the junction was unimaginable; the whole area was covered with immense craters which would require hundreds of tons of earth to refill. Already, squads of German Pioneer Corps were hard at work, together with groups of French prisoners. The prisoners were serving sentences for various offences committed since the German occupation. They received very brutal treatment, and their only chance of regaining their freedom was to dig up a certain number of delayed-action bombs. Often, a bomb would explode before the required number had been excavated, but even so the unfortunate victims were better off dead than alive in captivity.

An unexploded RAF 2000lb bomb at Revigny

While Louis had been out he had learned, through his contact with members of his widespread network of prospective partisans, the exact position of an aircraft which had come down in the course of the raid. It so happened that the wreckage was very close to the site we had chosen for a possible landing ground, and the place where we were waiting for our arms to be parachuted. But the most interesting item of news was that a survivor was believed to have reached a house a couple of miles away and was hiding there.

Immediately after dinner, Louis contacted M.Colombo on the telephone and, without disclosing the nature of the business, asked him to visit Revigny with his van later in the afternoon.

At three o'clock the courtyard gate bell rang, and as usual I watched the entrance through the shuttered windows of the house with a rifle in my hand while Louis went outside to investigate. Peeping first through the hole in the iron door, he ascertained whether our visitor was friend or foe and then turned his key in the lock. In walked our jovial friend M.Colombo. He had brought a few packets of cigarettes, which he passed round into eager hands, and then we began considering the possibility of collecting the alleged survivor of the latest air crash. Louis slipped on his coat, stuck an automatic in his pocket, and in a few minutes was bounding away along the dusty road with M.Colombo in quest of yet another recruit to our little band of outlaws.

M.Colombo had brought us news that about twenty Russian escapees had grouped together in a forest not very many miles away, forming a Maquis unit. It was decided that if all went well and Colombo returned with the new airman, he should take Arkadi and Nikolai straightway in the van to a certain village where an acquaintance could be contacted. This acquaintance knew the exact whereabouts of the other Russians in the forest, and our two friends could join their countrymen. It seemed a pity to lose two good colleagues, but orders had come from higher authority, and reached us through the mysterious M.X, that the two Chenu brothers, myself, and the four deserters were to form a group of seven saboteurs. We would soon receive supplies of explosives, together with orders regarding when and how to attack various objectives in the region.

By now I spoke the language fluently, complete with slang words, grammatical errors and accent, as if I had lived in that part of the country all my life. I was flattered to find that I was no longer classed as an *aviateur anglais*, a 'passenger' who had to be fed and kept out of sight. Instead, I had become a man with a far more intimate knowledge of underground activities than the majority of Resistance workers, and the time was drawing close when I would be taking an active part in attacking the German communications.

I was in the workshop when I heard M.Colombo's charcoal-burning vehicle come to a standstill. Peeping across the courtyard through the cobweb-covered windows hanging heavy with sawdust, I heard the lock being turned, then the iron door opened.

Louis stepped out into the courtyard, glanced round to ensure that everything was in order, then beckoned to someone behind him to follow. It was then that I had my first view of Flight-Sergeant Fred White of the Royal Australian Air Force. He had fair curly hair, and his pale face wore a worried, nervous expression. He did not understand a word of French and was no doubt wondering where he was being led to by the black-haired, dirty-faced Louis, who had about a week's growth on his chin. I followed them across the courtyard into the house, and in the kitchen Dick and I lost no time introducing ourselves and endeavouring to put his mind at ease.

I soon realised that the poor fellow seemed to be in a sort of daze; his thoughts appeared to be far away all the time. We asked him what had happened a couple of nights before. He said he was a rear gunner and had been at the squadron only a couple of weeks. His crew were not supposed to be on flying duties that night, but he was just entering the camp cinema when someone called his name out. He was told that due to illness he would be required to replace the gunner in another crew which was taking off on operations in a couple of hours' time. He bustled around getting his four machine-guns, ammunition, parachute and flying kit, attended the final briefing and eventually took up his position in the rear turret, ready to set off on his first night operation with a crew of complete strangers.

Soon they had left the English coast behind, crossed the North Sea, and every turn of the four propellers took them deeper into enemy territory. Once the coastal defences had been crossed, the flight to the target was comparatively calm and Fred sat there rotating his turret back and forth and his guns up and down, unceasingly searching the night sky for the black speck which might be an oncoming enemy fighter.

The target was reached, and he could hear the bomb aimer and the pilot talking over the intercom as they moved into position to make the bombing run. Suddenly the whole sky seemed to be alight as tracer bullets and cannon shells tore their way through the aircraft. Fred, blinded by the light, searched frantically for the night fighter, pulling his triggers at the same time. By now, the aircraft was a sheet of flame; he heard someone say, "Bale out". He struggled out of his gun turret and started to make his way up the flaming fuselage to the exit – then everything went black.

The next thing he remembered was opening his eyes and finding it was daylight. The birds were singing and he was lying on the grass. He was still wearing his flying kit and harness, and a parachute lay in a crumpled heap beside him. He tried to reconstruct his thoughts; he remembered moving towards the exit but had no recollection of having pulled his rip cord.

He moved and found he ached in every joint; at first he thought he had a broken leg, but eventually found it was only a very badly bruised thigh. He managed to stand, gather up his parachute and hide it under some bushes. Looking along the cart track, he saw a few yards away the tail unit of his aircraft complete with turret. The aircraft had actually broken into two pieces before hitting the ground.

Fred looked round in all directions but was unaware that only three hundred yards away, behind some trees lay the remainder of the aircraft, together with the mangled corpses of some of the less fortunate members of the crew. He staggered along for a couple of miles until he reached a farm house, where some kind people bathed his cuts and bruises, gave him food, and then put some blankets down for him to sleep on, out of sight in a garden shed.

Dick listened quietly to Fred's story, and then I translated it for the benefit of the others. M.Colombo could not stay long, so we all bade goodbye to Nikolai and Arkadi, and after exchanging wishes of "Good luck", they went off to join the Russian Maquis.

CHAPTER TWENTY-THREE

Visit to Loupey-le-Château

During the next couple of days I realised what meagre rations we were living on. Since I had first parachuted down in France I had become used to a diet considerably less than I had enjoyed at the squadron in England. Our daily food usually consisted of two or three boiled potatoes, a piece of black bread and nothing else. I was now quite accustomed to walking away from a table feeling hungry, but to Dick and Fred it was something that they had never experienced in their lives before. I looked at myself in the mirror in Louis' bedroom; my face did look a bit thin. I was actually about three stones lighter than on the night I baled out.

Rumours passed round from mouth to mouth about Resistance activities believed to be taking place in Louis' house. Even in a little village called Laheycourt, several miles away, it was whispered that a certain carpenter in Revigny was known to help Allied airmen to return to England. Consequently, when the village priest entered his church one morning and found himself confronted by two men in RAF battledress who could speak only about six words of French between them, he ushered them into a hiding-place and sent a message to the carpenter.

Once more, Louis summoned the help of M.Colombo, and for a third time within a week stuck an automatic in his pocket and set off in quest of Allied airmen. This time they returned with Bill Johnson of Liverpool and Sgt. 'Ginger' Brown of Dover, who had been the flight engineer and bomb aimer respectively in the same aircraft as Fred. From them we heard their story of the attack; of how the sky was suddenly full of tracer, and then the aircraft caught fire. Ginger had just gone through the forward escape hatch and Bill was following him when suddenly an explosion blew him through.

They could give us no more news of the remainder of the crew, but we knew that the local inhabitants had pieced together three bodies from the wreckage – despite the German orders to the contrary

– had dug graves, erected wooden crosses and decorated them with flowers. Local rumour had it that the Germans had captured one wounded airman alive, but no one knew where they had taken him.

Bill Johnson, with John 'Ginger' Brown and one of their French helpers

Now that there were four new faces in the house, the next few days did not seem to drag as slowly as before. There was so much to talk about; I learnt about the films that had been shown since my absence, and listened to the latest tunes sung or whistled softly for my benefit. I, in turn, had lots to tell them about. I explained the procedure for an emergency exit, showing them the secret trap door, and giving them a rough idea of the layout of the countryside and which direction to take in the event of a visit from the Gestapo.

Of course, everyone's question was, "How can we get back home?" I knew very well that the position was hopeless. I told them that organisations for repatriation of airmen had once existed in the district, but that the Gestapo had gained the upper hand and that I myself had been stranded in this particular house for a long time already. I also told them that they were lucky to be in this house and that as long as there was any food within ten miles of the place, the six Frenchmen and I would lay our hands on it and they would get a fair share.

The meals we ate were meagre, but even the handfuls of potatoes we shared each day were by no means easy to obtain. I took them into one of the little-used rooms and showed them our store of stolen potatoes. There was a sack and a half left, and this had to supply eleven of us for an indefinite number of weeks. When they saw the German eagle and swastika markings, together with other military signs, on the sides of the sacks, they realised that even potatoes were not easily come by. The only thing we had in abundance was fruit. There were apple and blackcurrant trees in Louis' garden, and even when these became bare it was a comparatively simple task for a couple of us to slink out after midnight with an empty sack.

One day M.Colombo called in again to see us, and this time he had brought with him a friend whom we Englishmen promptly nicknamed 'Specs'. He was a plump, bespectacled, prosperous-looking, middle-aged fellow, and from the conversations that were carried on I soon gathered that he conducted some sort of business that required his co-operation with the enemy, but somehow he had learned of the presence of three wounded airmen laid up in a wood in his district. To render them any help put himself in a very precarious position indeed. He had come to tell Louis that the unfortunate three had now been hidden inside his home for the last couple of days, although he had been entertaining German visitors within the same building.

Louis agreed that they should be brought to Revigny to live with us for the time being. At this point I again brought up the subject of us moving to a safe place as soon as possible. Everyone agreed that it was very imprudent for us all to live in a house right on the edge of the town, and I felt sure the suspicions of the neighbours must have been aroused already. On various occasions they must have seen strange faces bobbing about amongst the bushes in the orchard, and everyone knew that the two orphan brothers were supposed to live alone.

I told M.Colombo about the deserted farm by the lake and pointed out all the advantages to be gained by evacuating there. He knew the place quite well and agreed, but spoke of an even better hideout. It was a woodcutter's or charcoal burner's cabin in the centre of a forest; Colombo had accidentally found it about five years previously when he was hunting wild boar. Even then, it was completely overgrown, but he remembered that the building was more or less intact and amongst the undergrowth nearby he located a well. This, he claimed, would suit our purpose perfectly.

I stressed the urgency of making a move away from Revigny as soon as possible, especially if three more men were to join our ranks. So it was decided that Jean Chenu and I should cycle to Colombo's the following day and he would take us into the forest.

Jean and I had both visited the farm by the lake, and if we saw the other prospective hideout we would be able to decide which was the more suitable of the two. It was also arranged that during the same day 'Specs' should bring along the three new recruits, and he also promised to give us some flour which we now badly needed.

Fred, Dick, Bill and Ginger had been living with us about a fortnight now and Ginger Brown had proved himself to be the bright spark of the company. It only needed the slightest opening and

John Brown (Ginger)

he would crack a joke which would have all of us English-speaking personnel in peals of laughter. Then the French boys would turn to me for a translation, but in most cases the humour did not stand up to translation and explanation. Very often, wisecracks would be passed about the French boys, particularly about René (known as 'Ta-Ta'). He did not understand a word of English and used to be very offended and annoyed, thinking everyone was insulting him.

Quite often I would see him standing in front of the stove in the kitchen, his black curly hair falling over his eyes, several weeks' growth on his chin, his hairy, brown, greasy body naked except for a pair of football shorts. He would be covered with dust and soot from the stove from his head to between his toes, holding a spoon in one of his huge hands stirring the potatoes.

All might be peaceful, then Ginger would walk into the kitchen.

"What's cookin', good lookin'?" he'd say, to which Ta-Ta's invariable reply would be "Yees, pleese."

"You're just a big, daft, hairy ape," Ginger would continue. "Yees, pleese," Ta-Ta would say again, and by now all the airmen would be doubled up, suppressing their laughter lest it be heard outside. Whereupon Ta-Ta would fling down the spoon in a temper and come to me, calling Ginger all the names under the sun for making a fool of him. Ginger's assistant in all these items of entertainment was usually Bill. He too was feeling more at ease at Revigny, but it was clear that most of the time his thoughts were back in Liverpool where he had left a five-week-old son and a wife who would believe herself to be a widow.

Gradually a change was coming over poor Fred the Australian. He seemed to have been in a coma for the first week; sometimes he did not reply when I spoke to him; his eyes would be gazing into space, and when he did speak it was mostly about those fatal few seconds when the night fighters were firing. Because the attack had come mostly from the rear, he had believed that it was all his fault and wondered if the other two thought so too. As the days went by, however, his injured thigh improved, and when he realised that Ginger and Bill bore him no malice whatsoever he seemed happier. But it was obvious that he had certainly received a terrific 'shake-up' both mentally and physically on 19 July.

Louis normally got up at eight o'clock and went round to Mme Marie's for a cup of coffee and a piece of bread, but the rest of us stayed in bed (the lucky ones) or on the floor much longer. If you did not leave your blanket before midday you did not feel so hungry – and in any case there was very little to do except peel a few potatoes, give your rifle another polish and then tip-toe about the house peeping through the slits in the shutters. I used to get up about eleven o'clock because I could always hear the poor goat and her kid bleating for something to eat. Their diet consisted mainly of leaves, grass and weeds but each morning I used to take three handfuls of grain from a sack. One I gave to the duck and the two hens, which still spent a miserable existence scratching round the courtyard and catching flies and other insects which were abundant around the primitive lavatory. The rest I put into a little coffee grinder and turned the handle round and round for about ten minutes until I had a bowlful of roughly ground wheat. I added water and potato peelings, mixed it up and took it down the courtyard to the goats. Very often I would be on the verge of giving them the bowlful of mixture and then change my mind and eat half of it myself, apologise to the goats, stroke them on the head, and give them a handful of hay in compensation. I was always hungry first thing in the morning but usually had nothing but drinks of water before midday. Any bread left over from the previous day had always been carefully measured before being put away by Ta-Ta, and he created a terrible uproar if he found someone had cut an inch off the loaf during the night.

One morning, however, I got up to feed the goats and caught Ta-Ta red-handed. There he was in the kitchen with a knife in one hand and a slice of black bread in the other. To make matters worse, on the table lay a thin slice of our precious cheese.

He looked at me, blushed, and stammered out: "The rest of the boys can't be as hungry as I am or they wouldn't still be asleep." I told him I thought it was a very dirty trick, but we settled the matter quietly and agreeably by eating half each.

The morning following the visit from 'Specs' and Colombo, I got up earlier than usual and shook Jean Chenu out of bed. I fed the goats and three birds, washed and shaved as well as possible without soap, put on my best clothes, ensured that my false identity card was in a handy pocket together with my worker's certificate and finally Louis' taxation card belonging to the bicycle.

Just in case I ran into any real trouble, I slipped the loaded Mauser into my inside pocket. We bade Louis goodbye at the gate and set off in the morning sunshine at 10am. This gave us ample time to cycle the fifteen kilometres and arrive at M.Colombo's before midday.

Pedalling along at an easy rate, we soon left the little town of Revigny behind and took the road to Bar-le-Duc that I knew so well. The trees on either side were laden with fruit and we picked a couple of apples, eating them as we rode. Going through the first little village on our route, I glanced cautiously at the wall near the post office on the left. Yes, the notice that Louis had pointed out to me once was still there. It read that any person concealing, feeding, or helping Allied airmen, parachutists or saboteurs in any way would be sentenced to death. On the other side of the village we left the main Bar-le-Duc highway and cut across the countryside along a minor road.

For several kilometres the scenery consisted of nothing but fields and woods on either side. We pedalled along the dusty road until eventually we saw the village ahead.

Loupey-le-Château was a typical French village, with church, a school, and a collection of houses round about. We rode into the centre of the community and Jean asked one of the inhabitants where we could find M.Colombo. He pointed to the largest house in the village and said, "You'll find him there."

The door was opened by one of M.Colombo's young daughters, who called to her father that some visitors wished to see him. M.Colombo shook hands in his usual robust manner and ushered us into his sitting-room. First he insisted that we each took a cigar, saying they were his favourite brand and had been specially smuggled across the Belgian frontier. Then he disappeared, to return a couple of minutes later carrying glasses and a bottle of champagne. We toasted each other's health, then 'La Victoire and finally 'La France et l'Angleterre'.

I heard a telephone ring in an adjoining room and then Mme Colombo's head appeared round the door to tell her husband he was wanted. As he left the room, he called back over his shoulder to tell us to finish the bottle of champagne between us and that there were plenty more where that came from.

Mme Colombo stayed behind, refilling our glasses; she was a plump, motherly, middle-aged lady and talked with us about the weather and other everyday topics, apparently unconcerned and resigned to her husband's latest venture – that of actually inviting an Allied airman to the house. I'd met other people who were a bundle of nerves the moment I was in their presence, and who would have locked their doors and been dashing to and fro to the windows every few minutes to see if anyone was approaching.

M.Colombo finished his conversation and re-entered the room. "I'm expecting visitors, and I doubt if I will be able to go to the wood with you until much later in the afternoon," he said, and asked us if we minded having dinner and then waiting a couple of hours. Of course, we had no objection and told him so.

He quickly told his wife to prepare four extra dinners and then said he would show us round the village.

I soon realised he was a sort of dictator amongst the villagers. As we walked down the street he called out orders to three or four different men who happened to be standing round. "Oui, M.Colombo," they all replied, and set off to carry out his instructions.

In one of the side streets lay several railway lines. M.Colombo, or Paul, as we were now more affectionately calling him, said they weighed several tons, and he would sell them as soon as he thought the price of scrap iron had reached its peak. From here we went round to the back door of a small cottage; there was an evil stench about the place, and I noticed a vile-looking liquid was coming under the door. Paul undid a large padlock and swung open the door, and I saw that the two ground floors of the place were full almost to the ceiling with slimy-looking animal skins. They represented dozens of cattle that had passed through his hands into the black market. He quoted the present-day prices of a cow hide, and a quick, rough calculation told me that before me lay hides to the value of many hundreds of pounds.

We wandered farther up the street to another house, where we followed our host round to the back and saw heaps of aircraft wreckage. He was under contract to the Germans for the purpose of collecting wrecked aircraft and taking them to the smelting works, but it was obvious that many lorry loads had failed to reach their correct destination. He showed me about half a dozen large, all-metal aircraft propellers; some were more or less intact, but others were twisted and bent as if by some giant's hands. I gazed at them and wondered what tales each one of them could tell if only it could speak. I wondered how many of the airmen they used to carry were similarly twisted and torn, and how many of them were fortunate enough to be running round like myself. I was jerked out of my daydreams by Paul's voice telling me what excellent aluminium cooking pans he was able to have manufactured from the propellers, and that these particular ones were due for their transformation next week.

Our next place of call was a large barn. The little entrepreneur swung back the big wooden doors, letting in the sunshine, and I saw six or seven cars in a row. Each one had timber under its axles and all the wheels had been removed. Paul explained that after the Germans had overrun the country they started commandeering French vehicles right and left. The owners knew very well that they would never see their cars again, and the better the quality and condition of the vehicle the greater was its chance of being taken. Consequently, owners had been only too pleased to sell their vehicles at absolutely give-away prices to Colombo before it was too late. He had driven each in turn to the barn and then removed the wheels to another hideout several miles away. He then took a hammer and smashed headlights and in some cases windscreens.

Shortly afterwards, the Germans searched throughout the region for good-quality cars. They called at Loupey-le-Château and must have been informed that M.Colombo had some cars stored in the barn, for they demanded to see them. He took them inside, but one glance was sufficient; they told him they only had use for cars in first-class condition, and left to carry on their search elsewhere.

As soon as the war was over, he intended replacing the wheels, fitting new glass, and then selling all except one of them. He showed me the one he was keeping. It was an American type of car. He rubbed some dust off the body with his fingers and showed me the condition underneath, and it certainly looked perfect. He told me that with some petrol in the tank and a battery fitted it would be the best car for many miles around. We heard voices in an adjoining building, and following Paul through a doorway found that the men who had been spoken to in the street were busy cutting up the remains of what must have been two cows. They were wrapping up each limb in a clean sack and putting it in a position where a lorry was obviously due to be run inside the barn and loaded.

Paul gave a few words of supervision, then led the way back to his house. We found that the other two guests had arrived during our absence. One was a middle-aged German who, I learnt, was in some way connected with the administrative affairs of the occupation. He was apparently not satisfied with his ordinary salary and preferred to supplement it with large-scale black market dealings, taking advantage of his position by employing German military vehicles and drivers to transport his merchandise. He was accompanied by an attractive, well-dressed young woman, who looked as though she also was profiting well from the illegal dealings of her companion.

Dinner was served, and the five of us took our seats at the well-spread table. Shortage of foodstuffs had long since ceased to exist in our host's house. Jean and I lost no time in taking advantage of the opportunity of filling ourselves with everything on the menu, from double helpings of roast chicken to the final glasses of champagne so liberally poured out by Mme Colombo.

When the box of cigars was handed round at the end of the meal, Jean and I withdrew from the table leaving the two businessmen to discuss their facts and figures. We wandered round the village in order to ease the strain on our overladen stomachs, unused to such rich feasts.

When we returned to the house there was a huge German army lorry outside the front door. Inside the cab, a soldier was dozing over the wheel, and against the wall leaned another 'Fritz', complete with rifle slung over his shoulder.

The amount of liquor I had consumed during the last couple of hours had given me extra confidence, and prudence had been replaced by a desire to do something daring, risky and cheeky. As I entered the doorway, I drew a cigarette from my pocket and, tapping the Nazi on the shoulder, said, *"T'as le feu, s'il te plait?"* The fellow fumbled in his pockets and then produced a lighter. He made three or four attempts to ignite it, cussed quietly in German, shook it downwards, and then succeeded in producing a flame.

I had intended asking him what was his home town in Germany and questioning him about the bombing, the Allied invasion and so on. But as I leaned towards him to light my cigarette, my eyes came to within a few inches of the rifle; it had a sobering effect, and I realised I must not let the champagne take charge of my tongue. Not only was my own life at stake, but also that of many French friends as well, so I just took a couple of puffs to ensure I had a light, then quietly muttered *"Merci bien"* and continued into the house.

Paul spoke to us alone in the front room, and said he did not think he could possibly take us to the wood that afternoon. The lorry had to be loaded with meat, etc, for dispatch to Paris, and he had much other business to attend to as well. He suggested that we return to Revigny and he would call and see us again later in the week. We had no alternative but to thank him for the good dinner wish him goodbye and mount our bicycles once more to pedal back along the dusty road.

CHAPTER TWENTY-FOUR

A Job on the Railway

When we arrived at Revigny we found that the three new members to the band had arrived. There was Redmond Banville, a Canadian pilot, together with Nick Nickolson, a Flight Engineer from Knaresborough and Ken Hoyle, a mid-upper gunner. All were survivors from the same crew. Their whole aircraft was a sheet of flames before they had a chance to bale out and each man's hands and arms had been badly burned in his life-or-death struggle along the stricken aircraft to reach the escape hatch. The rest of the crew were believed to have been killed by the initial burst of bullets and cannon fire.

For a month the trio had been living in a kind of dugout in a wood where their wounds had been treated daily by a young medical student. This young man had been living in the woods for a long time, ever since he had been ordered to report for forced labour in Germany. His father was a doctor in a nearby village, and each week he left food and medical supplies at a prearranged place at the edge of the wood where his son would collect them after dark. In addition to their misfortunes, Nick and Ken had both contracted bronchitis as they lay in their damp hideout suffering from shock and burns. But for the unceasing attention of the medical student they might both have passed away.

The Frenchmen were full of the news that at long last a message had been received about sabotaging the railway lines. While Jean and I had been absent, a heavy and lengthy bundle wrapped with sacking and string had been put in Louis' possession by some mysterious messenger of the underground. It contained several huge spanners of the type used by linesmen on the railway and half-a-dozen crowbars.

Louis unfolded his map of the district and we carefully examined the proposed route which we had planned and the best place for a derailment. Louis had been informed by the mysterious bush-telegraph system of the underground that a goods train heavily laden with supplies was due to pass that particular point in the early hours of the following morning on its way to the Normandy front.

It was decided that the expedition should set forth as soon as night fell, so that the distance to the prearranged point could be covered, a rail loosened and the return journey made before dawn broke. It would be hard going over several kilometres of fields; all roads would have to be avoided. Time was going to be a very important factor and there would not be a minute to spare. The initial procedure was going to be the same as on previous sorties into the night. All pockets were to be emptied, only dark-coloured clothing to be worn, hands and face to be blackened with charcoal, etc. As we waited impatiently for darkness to fall, we started discussing the procedure if our plans should go wrong. If we encountered an enemy patrol or if we found it impossible to return to the shelter of the house before daylight we would have to disperse ourselves in ones and twos throughout the countryside. Then the question arose about the *aviateurs*; if our plans went wrong, someone would have to help them to get away from the house as soon as possible. We all knew that if any of us were captured alive we would be tortured until we revealed our headquarters, and none of us was foolish enough to say that we would not give way once we were subjected to intense pain.

Someone would definitely have to stay behind on this occasion and I was the obvious choice. I was very disappointed, but there was no alternative. Fred, Dick, Bill, Ginger, Red, Nick and Ken just could not be left alone in a house without the slightest idea of which way to run in the event of a Gestapo raid. I helped the French boys with their last-minute preparations, then shook their hands and wished the best of luck to each in turn as he tip-toed out of the house and slunk away into the darkness.

I did not sleep at all that night; my heart missed a beat every time I heard the slightest noise. Had a car pulled up outside the house, or someone rung the doorbell, I would have led the boys through the secret escape door and shown them the way to the nearest woods as fast as possible. I spent most of the night standing by an open window straining my ears, half expecting to hear the distant crack of rifle fire. The time passed much more slowly for me than it did for those who were straining feverishly on the spanners trying to undo the securing bolts on the railway line.

A slight noise in the corner of the courtyard brought me up with a jerk from my solitary brooding, reminding me that I was still in enemy territory and my life was in danger every minute. My muscles tensed, a chilly shiver ran down my spine as I strained my ears for further sounds. Again came the same rustling sound, like someone pushing their way through the bushes; and then I realised how jumpy my nerves were getting – it was only Ninette the goat, pawing the straw to make her bed more comfortable.

By now the first grey streaks of dawn were showing along the horizon and I knew that if all had gone according to plan, the French boys would arrive back at any minute now. The cool, still night air was suddenly vibrating with the barks of a dog a quarter of a mile away. This was a good sign, for I knew the boys planned to pass quite close to a farm which lay in that direction, and good farm dogs always seemed to sense when someone was sneaking around at night.

A few minutes later my anxious vigil was relieved by the padding of galoshes along the garden path, then in the misty light of the summer dawn I saw the six footsore figures slinking softly across the courtyard towards me.

They told me that the task of loosening a rail had proved to be much harder than they had anticipated, but after much sweating and straining they had succeeded. While they swilled the charcoal off their blackened faces, I cut slices of bread and poured out glasses of wine. Everyone was too tired to talk much, and within half an hour they were all sprawled out on the floor fast asleep, the two beds in the house having been now allocated to the three most recent members because of their burns and poor state of health.

Later in the day, Revigny was buzzing with the news that a train had been derailed. By making cautious inquiries Louis learnt that eleven German soldiers who had formed the guard on the train had been taken to hospital, and the most up-to-date rumours said two had already died.

This was good news; the expedition had been a success and the only cause for anxiety now was the possibility of reprisals being taken by the Nazis. Up to that time, no massacres or atrocities had been carried out in the district, but we all knew the sort of reprisals that had been inflicted in other parts of occupied territory during the past few years. For a couple of days a dreadful fear hung over the town, but it gradually lifted as people realised that the Germans were apparently too busy fighting their losing battle and trying to check the Allied advance to take any steps to find out who was responsible for the derailment.

This was an incredible stroke of luck and seemed too good to be true. Having tasted success the boys were keener than ever to carry out more operations.

CHAPTER TWENTY-FIVE

Night Excursion

B y now the Germans were cutting off the supply of electricity for several hours each day, and it was feared they might stop it altogether. This was very serious from our point of view because we would not receive BBC messages, and M.X had assured us our arms allocation would definitely be parachuted down within the next few days.

One morning, Louis came running into the house very excited. He had just learned that one of our colleagues in Bar-le-Duc had heard the long-awaited message earlier in the day when our own radio was silent through want of electricity. This was wonderful news; it meant that our much-needed supply of arms was to be parachuted down at last.

We knew the procedure off by heart. As soon as darkness fell, we would make our way to the prearranged dropping ground and then listen in silence for the sound of a lone aircraft; when we heard this we were to shine three red lights upwards, held in a straight line, at 100-metre intervals. I myself was to stand 100 metres from the end of the red line, and, as the aircraft circled, I was to flash a letter S with a white light. We were warned to keep a sharp look-out not only for any patrolling Nazis but for the heavy metal canisters as they came floating down in the darkness; a hit from one of those could easily prove fatal.

Each canister would bear the same number. If, for example, we found they bore the mark 'No.15,' we would know then that we must search for fifteen canisters. As each one was found it was to be carried to a hiding place in a nearby wood to await further transportation at a later date concealed in a load of hay.

Together with the arms and ammunition, we knew we would also find some cigarettes, tinned foodstuffs, clothes, and money; we had been told that a rate of pay had been established – ten francs per day for members of the Maquis living in the forests and thirty francs for members of sabotage squads like ourselves.

Louis suggested that I picked one of the airmen to accompany me in the party, thus making a total of eight men, so that we could work in pairs carrying the heavy containers. This seemed to be a good idea, so I said to the boys in English, "A consignment of arms is being dropped tonight a few kilometres from here; the six Frenchmen and I are going out to collect them and hide them in a wood." Everybody seemed interested, and I continued, "We would like an additional helper. Which one of you wants to come?" There was a complete silence, and everybody started glancing awkwardly at one another. Red Banville and his two surviving members of the crew were in no fit condition for the job, so the choice lay between Dick, Fred, Ginger and Bill.

I had thought that after being cooped up in the house for so long, they would all have been eager to get a bit of exercise and fresh night air. I explained that the route to be taken was straight across the fields. The dropping ground had been specially decided on many months before. Apart from a farmer living in an isolated farm nearby and acquainted with our activities, there were no other in habitants within three or four miles. The nearest country road did not come within a mile of the place and in my opinion there was very little danger attached to the expedition.

Still no one seemed eager to volunteer. During the past week they had watched the columns of Nazi soldiers in their green uniforms tramping up and down the streets each day, within a few feet of their eyes as they peered through the space in the wooden shutters. In fact, by now they could each whistle the popular German marching songs from memory. I explained that all these men slept in their barracks at night with the exception of a few sentries and occasional patrols in the streets, but my colleagues were not easy to convince. Again there was silence, each looking embarrassed and hoping that one of the others would volunteer. The Frenchmen stood quietly by, trying to puzzle out the meaning of the English conversation, and studying the expressions on the four faces, knowing very well that night after night they themselves took far greater risks to obtain food to keep these airmen alive.

At last, Bill Johnson suggested that as obviously no one was really keen to venture out of the house the four of them should draw from a pack of cards. The greasy, much-thumbed pack was produced. I gave it a thorough shuffling, then put it down in the middle of the table, saying, "Ace low, highest to go."

The atmosphere was tense. Ginger and Bill each took a cut and each showed a low card. Then Fred tried, and threw a queen on the table. Dick seemed to have been hesitating, but once he had seen the queen he cut, knowing that in the complete pack there were only four cards which could possibly beat the unfortunate Fred.

We all watched as the face was turned over. It was a king! Fred gave a loud sigh of relief at his narrow shave, and the worried expression on his face gave way to a slight smile. But a more dramatic moment was yet to come. Dick threw the king on the table and said "I'm not going anyhow, irrespective of what card I have drawn."

I seethed with embarrassment and struggled to control my temper before the French men. We all lived in considerable fear, despite our joking and bravado, and realised that the poor fellow before us had recently survived one horrendous ordeal serving his country, but now he pathetically muttered about being a married man. Even if he had been persuaded to change his mind I wouldn't have let him join the party; we would never know when a man of that character would let us down again.

Fred the Australian then stepped forward. He said that rather than let the Frenchmen think that all of us had a yellow streak down our backs, he wished to volunteer although he admitted that he hardly spoke a word of French and was absolutely terrified at the idea of leaving the house. Ginger said that he also would like to accompany Fred if possible. I explained this to Louis; he agreed that the party should be made up to nine, and suggested that most of us should try and snatch a few hours' sleep during the afternoon in preparation for the strenuous evening's work ahead.

Fred White

At 11pm we were all wandering uneasily about

the house, waiting for the night to grow darker. We had all inspected our arms, such as they were, at least a dozen times, and were longing to get on with the job ahead, instead of quietly waiting and thinking all the time of things that could go wrong and weighing up their disastrous consequences.

Louis and I, who were just as impatient as any of them, finally decided that the zero hour had come. With a few final words to the five who were staying behind, we slunk out into the darkness of the courtyard. Silently we tip-toed through the gate into the garden; that afternoon Jean had put a drop of oil on the hinges to stop a slight squeak we had noticed a few nights previously. Down the garden path we went in single file, through the little copse and then the orchard. Another gate was silently opened and we stepped into the outer world.

From here onwards every step was unknown to Fred and Ginger. They kept closer to me, and I remembered the first few nights I had roamed round the outskirts of Revigny with the two Chenu brothers.

Following the ditch through the fields, we reached the main road without incident. After lying in the grass for a few minutes to make absolutely certain that the road was deserted, we tip-toed quietly across. Once in the fields again we made our way along as swiftly as possible, crawling through hedges and under and over barbed wire, jumping over ditches, and hoping that the blackness we saw on the other side would turn out to be solid ground.

The little River de Nausonge ran directly across our path but there was a small footbridge, too insignificant for even the Germans to consider worth guarding, which we crossed. We then turned left to skirt round the village of Brabant-le-Roi, where its handful of population was sleeping peacefully. After completing a semi-circle we stepped on to the country road leading out of the village due north. For a couple of miles we walked briskly along the grass verge, black silent figures in single file intent on our purpose and prepared to dispose of any person who was likely to interfere with us. We had been keeping up a pretty stiff pace since we left Revigny, but the night air was refreshing and kept us plodding along. Suddenly, someone in front stopped. We all pulled up and listened. A long way in the distance we could hear a motor vehicle, the still night air carrying the sound across the flat country from perhaps a mile or two ahead.

Within a few seconds we had all scrambled or jumped through a low hedge and were lying in a cornfield. Nearer and nearer came the sound until, after what had seemed an incredibly long few minutes, a single lorry passed by. It was now after midnight, and the occupants were bound to be enemy troops. However, the few minutes' breather on the cool earth refreshed us, and we returned to the road feeling better.

Fred and Ginger kept asking in whispers, "How much farther do we go?" At last we left the road to take a cart track leading off at right angles and I was able to tell them we had only one more mile to reach our destination.

Our eyes were well accustomed to the darkness now, and the moon had pushed its way through the clouds so we could see the surrounding trees and fields quite clearly. I asked Fred if he had any idea where he was. "This stony cart track seems very similar to the one where I woke up and found myself in France," he said. "It is the same," I told him, and knew that farther along we would come to the actual place where the Lancaster's tail unit and Fred's turret had landed in the hedge. Louis and I had been along there previously to see if there was any ammunition lying around and perhaps a Browning machine gun still intact, but found the Germans had removed them before us. We came to the broken hedge and found a few pieces of aluminium and perspex lying about; the rest had all been taken for salvage. Fred recognised the place and showed us exactly where he had hit the ground a few yards away. He pointed out a group of bushes where he had hidden his parachute so we had a quick search for it, but without success owing to the dark shadows of the trees overhead.

Leaving the track, we crossed a field to where the remainder of the aircraft had fallen. This also had been carted away. The only remaining evidence that here some British airmen had died was a huge burnt patch on the ground, with odd pieces of metal scattered about, and bunches of 'window' strips (the small black and silver pieces of paper the RAF used to confuse enemy radar). We each rooted about for anything that might be useful, but I was hoping against hope that no one would find a finger or an ear and pick it up. Fred and Ginger had not spoken for a long time, but I knew the sort of memories that would be running through their minds and I spoke to Louis about it, whereupon we all moved a few hundred yards away from there.

We were now actually on the dropping ground and could do

nothing but lie on the grass and wait for the sound of the aircraft which we hoped would have crossed the Channel by now and be somewhere over France, bringing us the precious cargo.

I lay there with Ginger and Fred on either side, all of us straining our ears for the noise of an aircraft, but there was not a sound to break the silence of the night. Once I dozed off to sleep and woke up to feel myself frozen, and had to walk round for a few minutes to restore my circulation.

The hours went by until we saw the first faint streaks of dawn, and still we had not heard any aircraft. For months now there had been aircraft – either enemy or Allied, in fact, usually both – flying over every night, but on this occasion the silence was uncanny. We had the choice of either waiting longer, hiding in the wood till daylight came and then making our way back the following night, or setting off immediately on a quick journey back the way we had come before the countryside started stirring. We decided that as the light was much better now and we had memorised the route, the best thing to do was to start off as soon as possible rather than spend the day completely without food. Once we reached Revigny again, we would at least be able to have a slice of black bread and then a few boiled potatoes at midday.

The thought of being exposed to the ever-increasing daylight spurred us on to a good pace across the fields and over the fences and ditches we had encountered a few hours previously in the darkness. On and on we ran until we were circling round the village of Brabant-le-Roi, where we could hear the cocks already crowing.

Then came a mishap. Running down a slippery grassy embankment, Ginger fell heavily, and rolled over, holding his ankle in pain. It had healed only recently after being badly wrenched when he landed by parachute, and now it was injured again. We were fighting against time and every minute made our position more precarious. After about two minutes' rest on the ground, he had to be pulled up on to his feet and assisted along as quickly as possible. Any words of sympathy would have to wait until we were back in the shelter of the house. Ginger bravely put his foot down and kept on going, otherwise we would never have got back in time. When at last we came wearily up the garden path and into the courtyard once more it was bright daylight, and glancing at the church clock I saw it was already 5.30am. It would soon be Reveille in the nearby barracks, and shortly the farmers would start their daily work in the fields, welcoming the rising summer sun that we had been so eager to avoid.

We each lay down in our places on the floor, feeling tired and disappointed after a strenuous night's exercise. I soon dropped off to sleep, wondering what had happened to the aircraft which had not reached its objective.

The few hours in which I slept seemed to flash by like minutes before a hand shook my shoulder. I sat up, instantly wide awake, feeling annoyed – not for being awakened, but with myself for having slept so soundly that some person had actually entered the room without my knowledge.

I looked up from my sitting position on the floor into Louis' face. "I've got some meat for dinner, Denys. Will you come and prepare it?"

Since receiving a few lessons from our slaughtering expert, Raymond, I had taken over any butchery duties which arose in his absence. Louis had apparently been round the town already and laid his hands on something or other, so I buckled my belt and followed him to the kitchen, wondering what sort of a luxury was going to be on today's menu. For the past few weeks meat had been merely a memory.

There, on the kitchen table, was a huge horse's head, the tongue protruding between the lips and the lids fallen halfway across the sightless eyeballs. Man's best friend, who had probably pulled carts since before I was born, was going to serve his human master for the last time. That pair of blood-caked ears would flicker no more to catch the barks of command from the man behind the plough.

No one can realise the size of a horse's head until confronted face to face with a specimen on a table. It would have to be divided into four pieces and each cooked separately in a bucket. There were only old horses left in France today, as the Germans had commandeered all the strong healthy ones. I remember riding a bicycle through a village a few months previously where a horse had dropped dead in the shafts while trying to pull a load up a gradient. The population were already standing in a queue with plates and baskets awaiting the arrival of the veterinary surgeon who would make a quick examination and certify if the unfortunate beast was fit for human consumption or not. I understood that this was merely a formality and the chances of the meat being declared unfit were remote. Getting to work straight away with my sheath knife, which always had a razor-like edge ready to meet such circumstances, I found the task to be more tedious than I expected.

The rest of the boys soon woke up and made their way to the kitchen to get a drink of water and perhaps a piece of black bread which would take the place of breakfast. Bill was the first one to look through the kitchen door. "What the hell have you got there?" he said, eyeing the raw-looking object which by now was completely stripped except for the ears, which I had found useful handles during the operation, and the pair of blood-stained eyeballs looking pathetically in different directions.

"It's a cow's head," I lied, hoping it would seem more savoury under that title. Bill watched me in silence for a couple of minutes, then disappeared to tell his 'side-kick', Brown, all about it.

In a few moments he returned and Brown's ginger-coloured head followed him through the doorway. I carried on with the job under silent observation, slicing off the cheeks and proceeding to remove the lower jaw. Eventually, Ginger could contain his curiosity no longer, "Where are the horns?" he asked suspiciously.

"I've never seen a cow with big front teeth like that," said Bill, and the pair of them walked off to discuss the matter with the rest of the gang.

The task of dividing the skull into quarters was far easier said than done, but after wrestling with the bony, blood-stained object for half an hour and bringing into use two wood chisels, an axe and a hacksaw, I finally succeeded. The brain was removed and then fried; the rest, boiled with potatoes, making an excellent soup. The following day chunks of bony skull were boiled again, and once more we enjoyed a savoury soup. However, when they were boiled for a third time, someone said the soup was ninety-nine per cent potato water, and hoped that another horse would die soon. So we decided to change the menu back once more to mashed potatoes, a slice of bread and a glass of cold water. We tightened our belts and wondered if we would ever get another good English dinner again.

By now, the country side was in a state of air-raid alert almost continually day and night. Wave upon wave of bombers droned overhead, with very little fighter opposition. The Nazis were definitely fighting a losing battle and taking terrific punishment; the Allies would win, but so much could happen to our little community in the meantime.

A large house further up the road past Mme Marie's little bungalow had now become an emergency hospital full of wounded Germans. A nurse saw Mme Marie working in her garden one day, called her to the hedge, and gave her a large paper bag full of some kind of macaroni. I suppose the Germans did not like the stuff; anyhow, Marie passed the packet on to Louis.

It so happened that the same morning M.Colombo passed through the village, and when Louis answered his knock at the courtyard gate he had a little pig thrust into his hands. M.Colombo was in a hurry and he just said the little *sanglier* had been killed by a German shooting-party the previous day, bade a hasty farewell and drove off.

As Louis came back towards the house, eleven pairs of hungry eyes peered through the shutters, wondering what on earth he'd got this time. The pig was only a few weeks old, and unlike the plump, curly-tailed little farmyard porker who has nothing to do but eat and sleep, this little fellow had to run round the forest with his mother, helping to find acorns and chestnuts and to dig up edible roots with his snout and tiny trotters. He must have been continually alert for the approach of his great enemy, the man with the gun, the slightest sound or smell of whom would send him tearing through the undergrowth with the rest of the family at absolute top speed, crashing recklessly through bushes and brambles in a flight for their lives. Consequently, the little porker, when stretched out on the kitchen table, did not look much bigger than a large rabbit and did not carry an ounce of fat or superfluous flesh on him. His hard, bony little body was covered with a tough, leathery skin and coarse black bristles.

Our midday meal surpassed even the super-excellence of the horse's head broth; we ate the entire pig regardless of the morrow, together with most of the German macaroni. When the bones had been picked clean, we threw them out of the window to the two hens and the duck which still scratched around the courtyard. This trio would have been eaten long ago had it not been for the appearance of an occasional hen's egg in the nesting boxes, and on much rarer occasions, a duck egg amongst the straw on the floor.

Louis thought that only one hen was laying, but it so happened that about once a week there were two eggs laid the same day. The jubilant clucks of the second hen were cut short as she was hustled across the courtyard away from the shed. The egg eventually found its way into a downstairs room, where Fred, Bill, Ginger, Nick and myself all slept on the floor. A saucer was kept there; a deft crack on the edge, and then into the saucer went the egg, and a few seconds later 'down the hatch' it went, raw, just like an oyster, and the shell was disposed of in the garden as soon as possible.

This was a very deceitful thing to do, but an empty stomach has no conscience.

CHAPTER TWENTY-SIX

A Prisoner Returns

L ife was made considerably more bearable by the occasional packet of cigarettes which reached our hands from M.Colombo, but one day our nostrils twitched at a smoky smell in the kitchen which seemed somehow different to the Gauloises and Caporal to which we had tried to accustom ourselves. Louis sat by the stove drawing at a cigarette, inhaling deeply and contentedly, and blowing the blue smoke towards the ceiling. I saw by the familiar twinkle in his eye that he had something up his sleeve. It did not take Bill long to realise that Louis was smoking a real Virginia tobacco of a popular English brand. "Where's he got that from?" asked several English voices at once. But Louis stubbornly revelled in his secret and refused to part with it. My first thoughts were that they had been originally in an arms container, perhaps parachuted into a neighbouring region. I asked him, but he just shook his head, grinned, and went out, leaving us completely baffled.

The appearance of an English cigarette in the house was indeed a mystery. The Englishmen looked at each other with expressionless faces. Most of them had landed in France with an odd four or five in their pockets, but these had all been smoked in the excitement of their first couple of days' evasion. After a short absence, Louis returned; through the shuttered windows we saw him pause in the courtyard, strike a match, and then walk triumphantly into the house with yet another cigarette between his lips. Not wishing to carry the joke too far, lest everyone's curiosity turned to anger, he took a few draws, and then passed it round to each in turn until the stump was too small to hold. But he still he kept the secret of its origin.

Louis, Jean and I had lived almost as three brothers for several months now, sharing our hardships and anxieties as they came along. I could see that Louis, although joking outwardly about the cigarettes, was inwardly concealing some form of trouble. Ever since we met, there had been constant danger of capture by the Gestapo, the difficulties of obtaining food and so on, but today I felt sure Louis was keeping something from us apart from these things that was worrying him intensely.

My suspicions were confirmed later in the day, when Jean returned from his daily quest for bread. He had found the whole town murmuring with the news that Robert Stef – Marie Stef's husband – had returned from Germany. After four years as prisoner of war, he had now been repatriated for medical reasons. The entire population were soon expressing their sympathy, knowing that any prisoner looked upon as unfit by the Nazis was usually a very sick man indeed. At first, everyone thought how happy the poor fellow must feel to be back in Revigny again and to see his wife and two children after such an absence, but the village scandalmongers had different ideas. They were already making speculations as to what would happen in the little bungalow at the edge of the town.

Life had not been easy for Marie, a young woman caring for two small children while at the same time producing an income from a market garden throughout her husband's absence. She worked long hours, tending all the produce under the lines of wooden frames that supported glass panels, each of which had to be raised or lowered with wooden blocks in accordance with temperature changes during the day. All this as well as watering, weeding, picking and plucking.

What aroused the interest of the local gossipmongers was, however, the regularity of young male visitors into her home. Obviously they knew the young joiner and his teenage brother, for they had been born in the village. Who, however, was the fair-haired fellow who spent time gardening and feeding the livestock? Where did he come from? Where did he sleep at night? All so very intriguing for those with sordid minds.

The poor prisoner in Germany had received an anonymous letter bringing this matter to his attention, and, just before his release, had written to his wife demanding an explanation.Of course she could not possibly tell him that the two nearby brothers were devoting their lives against the enemy's occupying army, and greatly appreciated every meal she prepared for them. Nor that the worker in the garden who always kept in the background was in reality a British *terrorflieger* who also enjoyed her hospitality. We had hoped that some day, when the whole of France was in a state of triumph, the husband would return safely and all could be explained.

However, circumstances had changed unexpectedly and the delicate situation was rapidly reaching its climax. The following morning, before the rest of us got out of our blankets, Louis went round to have his usual bowl of coffee with Marie. When he returned an hour later, Jean and I asked him outright. "We know Robert Stef's come home, why the hell don't you stay away from the place instead of asking for trouble?" we asked.

Louis said Robert was glad someone had helped his wife during his absence, and they were the best of friends. He also told us that Marie wanted me to go round to the bungalow that evening to be introduced to her husband. It hardly seemed possible to me that the eternal triangle could be smoothed over so easily, but of course I had no objection to accepting Marie's invitation to meet her husband. After being shut up in the house day after day, pacing silently in and out of the rooms bare-footed, seeing the same faces every meal-time, one longs for a change of scenery, so I could hardly wait for darkness to fall.

I had a soapless shave, brushed my shoes vigorously to make them shine without using any polish, wet my long hair at the kitchen pump then combed it back. One of the boys said I would be able to have plaits down my back in a couple more weeks.

At last darkness fell and Louis and I were able to glide silently out into the courtyard and make our way through the garden and trees into the neighbouring garden, and finally over the last fence to drop on the soft soil of Marie's garden. We tip-toed up to the bungalow and listened at the shuttered windows for a minute to make sure she and her husband were alone, then tapped lightly on the door. We heard the light switched off with a click, the door opened. "Is that you, Louis?" whispered Marie in the darkness. "Yes, Denys and I," he replied.

We stepped inside. Louis closed the door behind us and turned the key, and then Marie switched on the light again. There at the table sat her husband. Straight away his sunken eyes and hollow cheeks reminded me of the youth I had met in Sampigny who had escaped from Germany last Christmas. We exchanged greetings and he passed a packet of twenty Players across the table. Louis looked at me and winked – this was where he got his English cigarettes from. Robert explained he had saved them from occasional Red Cross parcels he had received.

Within a few minutes, the principal topic of conversation became the Allied bombing offensive. Robert asked what raids I had taken part in, the question I had been asked in every household I had visited so far. I knew that the French population had suffered considerable losses during air attacks on fortresses, railways, bridges, and other military installations in France; that the Germans used this fact unceasingly for propaganda every day through the press and almost every hour on the radio. Consequently, I always made a point of emphasising that I had never dropped a bomb on *la pauvre France*, but had had the pleasure of releasing many tons over Germany and Italy. This reply always brought pleasure to the eyes of the French, but the man to whom I was speaking tonight had suffered the misfortune of being about five miles below me on some of the occasions when I and a few hundred other bomb aimers had peered down our bomb sights and pressed the release buttons.

As we talked, vivid memories came back to him. He told me of hundreds of tons of bombs screaming down, buildings blowing up and collapsing all around, and then when daylight came he had seen the mangled bodies of the victims piled high on lorries going through the streets. He had smelt the stench of death from decaying bodies under the ruins, and had watched the Germans spraying the streets with disinfectant to try and keep down disease.

I could see the look of terror in his eyes; his lips were quivering, and his fingers could hardly hold the cigarette. I wondered more than ever how the German population held out after such terrific onslaughts.

"Do you know that fifty RAF officers escaped from a prison camp?" he asked suddenly.

"Yes," I replied.

"Do you know they all got captured?"

"Yes," I nodded.

"Do you know what happened to them?"

I nodded silently. One evening a few months previously, with my ear against Marie's little radio set and the announcer's voice toned down to almost a whisper, I heard the tragic BBC announcement that fifty RAF officers, recaptured after a mass escape from Stalag Luft III, had been murdered by the Gestapo.

I rather pitied Marie's poor, nerve-shattered husband, and tried to hold a light-hearted conversation welcoming him back to France, but he kept referring to conditions in Germany.

"Did you know about the concentration camps?" he asked.

My answer was, obviously, yes. There were notices around saying that any man helping an Allied airman would be shot, whereas any woman doing so would be sent to a concentration camp in Germany. The man before me began to endorse the rumours I'd already heard via the French railway workers that thousands and thousands of people were being gassed and then burnt in huge ovens within these camps. However, although I lived in fear of arrest and

AVIS

Toute personne du sexe masculin qui aiderait, directement ou indirectement, les équipages d'avions énemis descendus en parachute, ou ayant fait un atterrissage forcé, favoriserait leur fuite, les cacherait ou leur viendrait en aide de quelque façon que ce soit sera fusillée sur le champ.

Les femmes qui se rendraient coupables du même delit seront envoyées dans des camps de concentration situes en Allemagne.

Les personnes qui s'empareront d'equipages constraints à atterrir à leur capture, recevront une prime pouvant aller jusqu'à 10,000 francs. Dans certains cas particuliers, cette récompense sera encore augmentée.

Paris 22 Septembre 1941.

Le Militarbefehlshaber en France
Signé : von STULPNAGEL
Général d'Infanterie

A notice to the French people from the occupying Forces. In brief, it reads:

Any men who aid, directly or indirectly, enemy aircrew who have parachuted or force landed; or help them to escape or hide them, will be shot on the spot.

Any women who are guilty of the same crimes will be transported to concentration camps in Germany.

Those people who assist in the capture of enemy aircrew will receive a reward of up to 10,000 francs. In certain cases, this reward may be increased.

interrogation for the Resistance information I had accumulated, all the enemy troops I had seen wandering around Bar-le-Duc and in Revigny seemed well-behaved, just human beings in a foreign uniform. Maybe the horror stories were exaggerations.

We talked and smoked regardless of time, and it was well after midnight before Louis and I put on our berets and said *"Bonsoir"*. Switching the lights out, we opened the door quietly, and while we stood there in silence for a few moments, listening, Robert put some cigarettes into my hand. All was quiet, so we slipped out into the night, over the garden fence and back again the way we had travelled many times before.

Louis gave a low whistle as we approached the house so that a trigger-happy sentry would not put a bullet through us. The door was duly opened by Jean, and we tip-toed inside. I made my way over the sleeping bodies on the floor until I found Fred, the Australian with whom I shared a blanket.

As I wriggled down, making myself comfortable beside him, he awoke and sleepily mumbled, "Hello, Den, did you get any ciggies?"

"Half a dozen," I whispered.

"Good show," said he, and dropped off contentedly to sleep again.

CHAPTER TWENTY-SEVEN

Point of Departure

The following day I redoubled my arguments that we should move away from Revigny as soon as possible to live at the derelict farm by the lake. Louis continued his frequent visits to Marie's bungalow, and very soon he and I – who had been such good friends for many months now – were at loggerheads and quarrelling broke out every day. I pointed out time and time again all the reasons why a move was essential. Obviously fourteen young men could not remain indefinitely living in one house at the edge of the town without arousing suspicions. Many precautions were being relaxed; conversations were no longer being carried out in a low voice; some of the boys even wandered about the house whistling, ignoring the possibility of being overheard by passing pedestrians on the main road which ran along the side of the courtyard wall.

The sun shone brilliantly; the fruit was ripe in the gardens and the temptation was too great for those who had been cooped up in the house so long, especially as most of them did not fully realise the dangerous position they were in. If any stranger had happened to look over the hedge at the bottom of the garden some sunny afternoon, he might have seen half a dozen fellows sunbathing among the currant bushes. Had he approached the hedge unobserved and a few words of RAF slang reached his ears the news would have spread round the whole town within a few hours.

Eventually, Louis arranged with M. 'Specs' that, to relieve the situation, some of the airmen should go back into hiding in his district several kilometres away. This was a good idea, and the sooner it could be carried out the better, but still Louis was making no move towards a complete evacuation.

"You're like a mouse contentedly nibbling the cheese in a trap," I told him one afternoon. "The only difference being that you're a bigger fool because you know the trap is liable to snap closed any minute."

For an hour we shouted unpleasant things at each other like a couple of politicians in the *Chambre des Députés*. "If you're not moving, then I'll set off on my own," I concluded, and stamped out of the room.

The English boys knew that this time it was something more than my daily arguments with Louis and wanted to know what it was all about. I told them that I was tired of waiting for him to make his mind up and was going to leave the house at dusk to strike out on my own towards the derelict farm. M. 'Specs' was due to call the following day in his van to take some of them away with him, and I felt confident that Louis would decide to follow me up to the farm with the rest of the gang a few days later.

As I sorted out my one or two possessions in readiness for my trek, Fred came over and said he would like to come along with me. This was just what I had hoped, because I knew only too well the value of having a good companion on such an occasion as this. We agreed on the spot that we would set off and stick together through fire and water till we reached Allied lines.

We persuaded Ta-Ta, who had taken command of the kitchen, to part with half a loaf of black bread and a chunk of cheese, which we rolled up in our blanket together with what few possessions we had between us, and were ready to go.

Since Fred had been hiding at Revigny, the town had been in an almost continual state of air-raid alert day and night. The railway sidings had frequently been bombed and strafed. Each time this happened the Germans and civilian population would all run out into the open fields as fast as they could go, having more faith in being away from the target than staying behind in the cellars and air-raid shelters.

During the daylight attacks we were obliged to stay in the house, listening to the deafening explosions which almost shook the old place down. Then came the roar of the cannons and the machine-guns and the sound of bullets zipping through the air as they ricocheted round the empty town. Fred felt sure that a mistake would be made one day and the whole town flattened; he considered himself lucky to be still alive when he landed in France and said he would rather take the risk of getting a Nazi bullet than be a victim of an Allied air attack.

When darkness fell we shook hands with each of the Frenchmen in turn and they wished us *"Bonne chance."* Finally I stood before Louis. "We will head for the farm first," I told him. "If you haven't joined us there within seven days we'll set off across country in the direction of Normandy."

Revigny after an Allied air-raid, August 1944   (photo Parisse)

"It's already past curfew time and you'll be shot at sight if you go out now," Louis argued, trying desperately to persuade us not to leave. He soon realised, however, that we were both determined and knew we were capable of travelling silently through the night and avoiding German patrols.

As we shook hands, I said, "Although we have a slight difference of opinion at the moment, Louis, I will never forget all you have done for me, and if we're both alive at the end of this wretched war, I'll come back to Revigny and celebrate with champagne and we'll laugh and joke about all the dangers we have faced together." He kissed me on both cheeks with tears in his eyes, and in a husky voice whispered, "*Bonne chance, Denys, mon cher ami.*"

Before leaving Revigny, I wanted to say goodbye to Marie and her husband. It was not yet dark enough to cut across the main road, so we could afford to make our way round the back and spend a quarter of an hour at the bungalow. As we climbed over the fence into the smallholding, I could see Robert Stef in the half-light having a final glance round his garden and seeing the chickens were fastened up before retiring. He was startled when he saw two dark figures approaching quietly across the soft soil.

"Good evening, Robert," I said softly to put his fears at rest. "It's only Denys and a friend."

We walked into the barn where I had spent so many hours feeding the rabbits and Ninette the goat. I explained briefly that Louis and I had had an argument and I was leaving together with the Australian, my companion. The three of us entered the bungalow and I thanked Marie for everything she had done for me. I told her I hoped to come back after the war and find the market garden flourishing and everyone living happily.

While we talked, a little voice called my name from the bedroom; it was young Claude. I tip-toed in, patted his forehead and told him to go off to sleep again quietly so that he wouldn't waken his little sister. Ever since I first arrived at Revigny, the little fellow had known I was an English airman, and it must have been a great temptation to him to boast about his acquaintanceship amongst his playmates, but he knew that if the German soldiers found out who I was they would come along and shoot his mother for helping me.

After the usual handshakes and exchange of good wishes, Fred and I stepped out into the garden again. It was quite dark now, and as our eyes were not yet accustomed to it. I had to lead Fred by the hand in between the garden frames and rows of vegetables which I had cultivated earlier in the year. As we passed the barn where we had stood talking to Robert earlier, little did we think that a few weeks later the poor fellow would pass away.

Soon we had left Revigny behind and were stepping out briskly across the fields, wondering excitedly what the future had in store for us. We passed along as speedily as possible under barbed-wire fences, over ditches and through hawthorn hedges. Within the first half-hour our eyes adapted themselves to the darkness and we were able to go along at a steady jog-trot. After two or three miles, we were well clear of all signs of habitation and decided to approach the country road which I had ridden along when cycling to the farm previously. We paused a few moments behind a hedge to regain our breath and ensure that the road was absolutely deserted, then scrambled through.

Once on the firm surface and knowing we were definitely going in a straight line instead of continually having to check our bearings with the stars, we made better progress. Our only method of checking the time was by my RAF stop-watch, but this had no hour hand – only a needle, which made a complete circle in one minute, and a small hand which made a circuit in half an hour. Consequently we had to keep looking at the watch and remembering how many periods of half an hour had passed.

We soon realised that the journey would not be completed before daylight, and we would be obliged to lie in hiding until darkness fell again the following evening. As there was now no particular hurry we reduced our pace to a walk to conserve our energy, and hoped that this would make us less hungry later on.

While walking like this up a slight incline, we heard a motor vehicle approaching from behind. It so happened that there was a thick, high hedge on either side of this stretch of road, so we ran along for a hundred yards or so. We wanted to find a gateway or opening of some sort but we found none. The sound was coming nearer and nearer, and our first instinct was to dive into the hedge. However, we had learnt from experience how easy it was to get caught half-in and half-out of such hedges, almost unable to move, and that in the least bit of a panic one's clothes, hands, and face would get torn to ribbons. So we flung ourselves face-downwards on the grass verge and prayed that we would not be spotted.

The vehicle sounded as if it were heavily loaded and came up the gradient at little more than a walking pace. Nearer and nearer it came until the wheels were crunching the gravel only three feet away from our prostrate bodies. Suddenly the engine note died down, and for a horrible moment I thought we had been spotted, but a split second later the revs increased to a higher pitch and I realised that the driver had only been changing into a lower gear. I never actually saw the vehicle because it had disappeared into the darkness before I dared to raise my head again, but it sounded like a heavily laden army lorry – probably making its way to the front with supplies.

Soon we saw the first grey streaks of dawn, which warned us of approaching daylight. Wrapping a good supply of apples from roadside trees in our blanket, we left the road and headed across a field of cut wheat to a wood outlined in the misty morning half-light. We found it was only small, but it seemed fairly thick and dark inside; it would provide us with suitable shelter for a day. The thought of making a bed of dry leaves and going to sleep made us both suddenly realise how very tired we were. Although we had probably travelled only six or seven miles, we were sadly undernourished and did not really have the strength left to go much farther. At this pace it would certainly take us a long time to reach Allied lines some three hundred miles away, especially with the prospect of living on even shorter rations. We laid a few wheat sheaves on the ground for additional comfort, and a few moments after pulling our blanket over us we were both fast asleep. This was about the first time I had been able to go straight off to sleep for several weeks without spending a long time itching and scratching my legs, which were now showing signs of scabies.

A few hours later, we both awoke to hear the birds singing and the bright morning sun rays streaming through the trees. We exercised a bit to restore the circulation to our stiff and chilly limbs and then began to consider our plans for the immediate future.

We had eaten our piece of bread and cheese during the night, so now we rubbed heads of wheat in our hands, blew away the chaff and then chewed the remaining grain laboriously together with bites of apple, trying to imagine we were eating apple pie.

We now had two alternatives. We could stay in the wood till darkness fell and then break into some unfortunate person's house and obtain something more substantial than apple pie to help us to continue our journey through the night. Alternatively, we could approach some house now, before the countryside was properly awake. We could beg for some food, then come back into hiding.

After a brief consideration, our stomachs helped us to make the decision. So we set off towards a farm we could see about half a mile away. As we topped a grassy mound, we saw a cluster of houses forming a village with the usual church spire sticking up in the centre. I knew this would probably be Lehaycourt; the church we could see must be the one where Bill and Ginger had spent their first few hours in France before being helped by the priest, who ultimately passed them into Louis' hands.

Hearing shouts from nearby, we peered through a hedge and saw a farmhand a couple of fields away driving cattle towards a gate. Most farmers in the district seemed to bring their livestock into the safety of the shippens during the hours of darkness, but apparently these had been out to grass all night and were now being driven home to be milked. By speaking to this fellow we could find out what the position was at the farm without actually approaching any nearer, so we made our way quickly along the hedges to the point where the cows were leaving the field and entering a narrow lane.

The last cow made its way through with a red-faced young man of about twenty-five tapping its hindquarters with a light stick. As he turned to shut the gate behind him, Fred and I brushed our way through the hedge. "*Bonjour*," I said, and "*Bonjour*," he replied with an amazed expression on his face, wondering whatever we were doing in the fields at that early hour. I came straight to the point and asked him if he could help us to get some food.

"*Vous êtes Anglais?*" he asked. I nodded.

"*Aviateurs?*" I nodded again, and he smiled, saying he would be pleased to help us.

So far, so good, I thought. He told us that the farmer and his wife did not like the Germans and would be sure to help us.We walked along at the heels of the cattle towards the farm with hardly a word passing between us, but the grins and winks our new friend gave every few yards told us that he was certainly pleased to bring a couple of parachutists home with the milk. Once inside the shippen, we helped to slip the halters over the cows and then waited while Roger went into the house.

CHAPTER TWENTY-EIGHT

On the Farm

Soon Roger beckoned us to follow him. We had previously decided that, to avoid a lot of awkward questions, I would say that I had been in the same crew as Fred and that we had both been in France only a month. Fred's knowledge of French still consisted of only half a dozen words and I decided it would be better if I reduced my vocabulary considerably. This would mean reverting to the painfully slow business of listening to people repeating small phrases over and over again slowly, but I would gain the advantage when they spoke amongst one another, for they would imagine that if they jabbered away at a normal speed – especially in the local dialect – I would be unable to understand. Actually, I would be finding out their true feelings and whether or not we were really welcome in the house.

We followed Roger into a spotlessly clean kitchen, where the farmer's wife greeted us with a warm handshake. She was a plump, fair-haired lady who immediately reminded me of an aunt at home, and I am sure Fred and I could not have been received better had we been a couple of nephews.

This good lady did not start asking us where we had been, how we came to the farm, had anyone seen us approach, and so on. Instead, she turned to the farmhand and said, These poor lads look very hungry, and straight away set about preparing a meal.

As we sat at the table with our mouths watering at the delicious smell of frying eggs, I saw that the kitchen clock said 7am. Apparently the farmer himself had already started his day's work, but the news of our arrival was travelling round the bedrooms above, and soon two sleepy-eyed, blond-haired and very English-looking little boys peeped into the kitchen. They each came forward and shook hands. One was Louis, about thirteen years old, and the other, Claude, was perhaps twelve months younger.

Soon their mother laid the eggs before us, together with two bowls of steaming hot coffee made with milk. She also gave us a loaf and about a pound of home-made butter to help ourselves to. This was the best meal we had had for many weeks, and we kept cutting off further slices of bread and spreading on butter, glancing at one another continually, each wondering if the other thought that having yet another slice was taking undue advantage of the hospitality we were receiving. Before the meal finished I had already offered thanks in broken French on behalf of the pair of us at least three times, and emphasised to the good lady that we wanted to work on the farm to repay our debt before leaving.

Through the kitchen window I could see that a river ran across the bottom of the farmyard. While I watched, a horse came splashing through while its master walked over a small footbridge. Roger approached them and, taking hold of the horse, he started to speak to the newcomer. There was little doubt what passed between them, for straight away the other man strode quickly up the yard towards the house.

Although it was so early in the morning, he was already stripped to the waist and his chestnut-coloured skin rippled with muscles. This was the farmer himself. "Two English boys," his wife said, whereupon he stepped forward and shook our hands warmly.

Fred nudged me and asked me to tell him how grateful we were for the grub his wife had dished up and that we wished to repay him in work.

M. Louvet turned to his wife, and in a brief conversation between them I realised that we had arrived at the farm just at harvest time. All available hands would be working almost every hour of daylight to get the crops in, and our services would come in very useful.

Camille Louvet was a man of action, and before the kitchen clock said seven-thirty Fred and I were sitting on a cart and heading for the fields. Soon, we were loading sheaves of wheat in the morning sunshine, and with a good breakfast inside us were thinking we were the luckiest pair in the world. As Roger led the cartload away, young Claude walked through the gateway leading an empty cart, and so it went on throughout the morning. After each load, M.Louvet would grin at us and say, "*Ça va?*"

"*Oui, ça va bien, merci*" I always replied, but actually we felt ready to drop. Our hands were becoming blistered with the unaccustomed use of the pitch-fork and our bodies were very much out of condition. Each sheaf felt heavier than its predecessor, but just when we thought we were reaching the limit of our strength an empty cart came in and our bronzed, untiring benefactor said, "This will be the last one before dinner."

New power came to our arms at the thought of something to eat and we eagerly hurled up the wheat until the wagon was piled high, flung the ropes over to secure the load and then climbed up aloft. The horse plodded wearily back to the farm, making a short detour to avoid splashing through the river with a heavy load.Once more in the kitchen, we met the people who had been busily unloading each wagon as it came in and storing the crop in the barn. There was M.Louvet's younger brother, who lived with them but was in daily fear of arrest as he had never registered for service, and almost all other young men of his age group were already in Germany. There was an older man and his wife, who were friends of the family and helping them for the harvest.

The table was being laid by a hard-working little twenty-year-old servant girl, whose duties extended beyond the house to the farm and included milking the cows, feeding poultry and harvesting. Toddling round the table was little four-year-old Bernard, and sitting on her mother's knee was a lovely little baby girl with blue eyes and fair curly hair. Her parents had every reason to be very proud of her, because if she had not come into the world her father would still have been in Germany. He had been taken prisoner of war in 1939, but

Camille Louvet at Laheycourt

after a few months was released from a prison camp and put to work on the land. At this time the Germans were allowing satisfactory workers who were fathers of four or more children to return to work near their homes in France, but Camille only had three sons. However, in 1942 he was lucky enough to receive fourteen days' leave to visit his wife and family, and in 1943 applied successfully for repatriation as he had now become the father of a baby daughter.

Since then he had been working exceptionally hard to restore the farm to its pre-war prosperity after its decline during his absence, when his wife had been trying to manage it and bring up the family as well. Judging by the happy, healthy faces on either side, and the well-stocked table before us, it looked as though he was succeeding.

After a glorious dinner, we were handed cigarettes and a glass of rum. Then we relaxed for about half an hour before returning to work.

We worked loading wheat all afternoon until about five o'clock, when we returned to the farm for a glass of wine and a large chunk of bread and butter and cheese, then back to the fields till nine o'clock, when once again M.Louvet said "Last load" and our weary, aching arms made their final effort.

The farm was known as the *Ferme du Moulin* and had originally been a flour mill. Round the side of the house, the river was trapped to form a weir and the remains of the waterwheel and large grinding-stones still lay there. The water was deep enough to swim in, and as soon as the last load was stacked in the barn we all went round there and stripped off to plunge our dusty, sweaty bodies into the lovely cool water. We each had a brisk rub-down with a towel, shook the hay-seeds and chaff out of our clothes, dressed and then trooped into the kitchen. Mme Louvet was the only one who had not been harvesting but she had been busy preparing a supper. Judging by the size of the casserole of beans, cabbage and potatoes, she knew what sort of appetites we would all have. The steaming plates were put in front of us. We all set off to a good start but Fred and I soon took the lead and had wiped our plates clean with chunks of bread and had them refilled long before the rest had finished the course. M.Louvet passed round the cigarettes again, served us with home-made whisky, and complimented the household on the good day's work.

It was almost dark now, so I expressed my deep appreciation for the meals they had given us and said that Fred and I had better start moving off across country again. But apparently our good friends had different ideas, for Mme Louvet opened a door leading from the kitchen and revealed a room on the ground floor with a double bed ready made up with snow-white sheets for us. She pointed out that in the event of any trouble we could easily jump out of the window into the orchard and get away.

This was almost too wonderful to be true, and we certainly needed no second invitation to stay. Fred was so impressed with the hospitality and genuine, warm-hearted attitude of these people that, although he didn't understand a word they spoke, he said, "I wish to hell there was no such thing as a war, and I could work with these folk and eat good grub on this farm in peace for ever and ever."

I was still maintaining my pretence of having been shot down with Fred a month ago and giving the impression of a very limited knowledge of their language. Now everyone was talking about what could be done for Fred and me; needless to say I was listening eagerly to every suggestion that came forward. Here again, Mme Louvet had already got things moving. She had been to see someone during the day who, she said, would help us to get home and she said that he would be along to speak to us as soon as it got a little darker.

This was welcome news, and I appreciated the effort, but I knew very well that all organisations for repatriating Allied airmen were at a complete standstill throughout the country.However, I listened intently as they spoke amongst themselves on the subject, but my heart suddenly stood still as I heard the name of the expected visitor mentioned – it was Serge. That was the name of a man I had been warned to avoid at all costs. Surely Fred and I had not walked into trouble so soon, just when things seemed so comfortable! But as I listened to the conversation at table my fears were confirmed; the visitor who was due any minute was none other than the man I had heard described as a gangster and black-market racketeer, now suspected of being used as a bait by the Gestapo to trap unwary underground workers. He had himself engaged in Resistance work in the earlier part of the war until one day he was arrested with several others and taken away to a concentration camp. The other men were never heard of again, but within a few weeks of his arrest Serge mysteriously returned home, looking very much the worse for his experience but nevertheless an apparently free man. The local Resistance men could think of no possible explanation for this, and knew that the Gestapo would not be so generous unless there was something to be gained by it. Consequently, they surmised that Serge had broken down under 'treatment' and had saved his life by returning to his home to act as a stool pigeon.

Word of his return passed round the countryside quickly, and all Resistance workers endeavoured to steer clear of him. M.Louvet, who did not know of these suspicions, had visited him that afternoon to tell him of an Englishman and an Australian who had arrived at the farm.

There was a knock at the back door, and since I knew it was too late now to avoid meeting the notorious Serge, I had no alternative but to keep my wits about me and above all to keep up the pretence that I had been in France for only a month.

The door was opened and in walked a gaunt, dark complexioned, round-shouldered fellow whom I judged to be middle-aged. He bade M.and Mme Louvet good evening, and then came over and shook hands with Fred and me and gave us each a packet of cigarettes. His eyes were sunk deep into the sockets of his bony, hollow-cheeked face.

"*La Gestapo*" he said, pointing to the scars where the dark skin was drawn taut across his prominent cheek bones. "Do they speak French?" he asked, turning to M.Louvet. "The Englishman understands if you speak slowly," he replied.

Serge then proceeded to tell us how he was tortured by the Germans, his dark brown eyes showing terror and agony as he opened his mouth wide to show how an electrical device was forced inside. When switched on, this gave intense pain – as if all his teeth were being extracted at once without anaesthetic. He now had no teeth whatsoever and said they had dropped out since his return to France. I translated everything to Fred. This was the first time he had become acquainted with evidence of Gestapo methods, and there was certainly no doubt that this man had undergone some very brutal treatment. Every couple of minutes, he had to stop speaking and pause while we watched him gasping and wheezing for breath.

He unbuttoned his jacket. "Look how my heart beats," he said, and I would swear I could actually see the movements under his jersey. I put my hand there and could feel the heavy abnormal rhythm.Twelve months later I learnt that our friend Serge had passed away at the age of thirty-six as the direct result of his maltreatment.

The important point of that memorable meeting with him was, "Could he help us to get back to England?" He shrugged his shoulders and confirmed the knowledge that I already possessed – that there was no easy or speedy way whatsoever out of this part of France.

He considered the position carefully for a couple of minutes and then said there was just one slight possibility left, and that was through a certain organisation with which a young man in Revigny was alleged to have connections. Before he continued any further I knew very well he was referring to Louis and that all possibility of repatriation from that source had ceased to exist months ago.

I was tempted to speak out and say I had understood every word they had spoken amongst themselves, and that I had already spent a long time as the non-paying guest of the young man at Revigny. But, I remembered the warning about Serge and although I did not distrust him, I decided to keep my mouth shut. The less people knew of my journeyings and the length of my sojourn in France the better would be my chances of reaching England alive.

When Serge stepped quietly through the back door into the darkness again, everyone prepared for bed. Mme Louvet led my Australian pal and me into the room she had prepared, and wished us a good night's rest.

We looked at the snow-white sheets and felt ashamed to get into bed lest we should soil them. Ever since Fred had arrived at Louis' house, the pair of us had shared a blanket on the floor. As soap was non-existent, both our bodies had developed scabies and the warmest places became breeding nests for tiny little insects which we used to pick off ourselves daily.

Hardly had we shut our eyes than it was morning and the day's work on the farm had already started. While we sat in the kitchen eating our *petit déjeuner*, Andrée, the young servant girl, came in with buckets full of fresh milk.The weather was glorious, and as Fred and I worked in the fields stripped to the waist, with the sun streaming on to our perspiring backs, we felt as though every minute of it was doing us the world of good.After dinner, two newcomers arrived to spend a working holiday at the farm. They were both relatives of the family – an elderly uncle and Madeleine, a pretty, fair-complexioned nineteen-year-old niece. Her eyes widened as she was told who the two young men were, quietly sitting in the kitchen, and she seemed almost too shy to shake hands. While her uncle helped in the fields and barns, she assisted Mme Louvet to prepare the huge and delicious meals which we ravenous harvesters devoured.

On the fourth day, Fred and I were busy throwing sheaves of wheat off a cart to Andrée, who was high up near the roof of the barn laying them in position. She was a very hard worker, but at the least excuse she would not hesitate to romp and wrestle in the hay with us. Suddenly, a shout from the courtyard warned that a car was approaching. All the laughter and singing died instantly. Remembering our precarious position, Fred and I dived to the back of the barn and buried ourselves out of sight in the hay, while the remainder of the workers threw our two pitchforks to one side and spread themselves out to fill the vacant links in the broken chain. When the car drove into the courtyard a few seconds later, the wheat was being passed from the cart to the top of the barn with a rhythm one would think had been established over a couple of hours.Lying with the hay prickling my bare back and stomach, I could hear Fred muttering softly nearby; he had thrown himself down on a dried thistle.

The motor-car stopped; I heard the doors slam and tensely listened to the voices, scarcely daring to breathe lest the dusty hay brought about an attack of sneezing. A few seconds passed, and then Mme Louvet entered the barn and called, "Denys, Fred."

We stood up and shook the seeds from our hair. The new arrivals were none other than Louis and M.Colombo. Everyone stopped working and looked on with amazement when Louis threw his arms round us as if we were long-lost brothers. Apparently a message from Mme Louvet had reached Revigny that two airmen were hiding at the farm, whereupon Louis had contacted Colombo and the pair of them had come along to collect *les aviateurs*.

We soon learnt that our friends at Revigny had not yet moved to the derelict farm by the lake, but the various airmen had all been hidden in safe localities a few miles away. Otherwise, there had been no fresh developments in the local Resistance movement, so it was decided that Fred and I should remain on the farm and then rejoin the partisans when open fighting actually broke out.

Throughout the following fortnight, my Australian friend and I were extremely happy. We worked hard in the blazing sun all day, sustained by the nourishing meals Mme Louvet and Madeleine prepared, finishing each day with a refreshing plunge into the cool, clear water of the mill stream.

Sundays were always strictly observed as days of rest, only the essential work of feeding and milking being carried out. Fred and I joined the younger generation in the afternoon, splashing in and out of the stream and playing hide-and-seek round the barns while M.and Mme Louvet looked on contentedly from the chairs set out in the courtyard. After supper, the kitchen floor was cleared for singing and dancing to the strain of an old gramophone until midnight, when all the merry harvesters made their way to bed – to wake up on the Monday morning refreshed and ready for the hard week's work ahead.

Sometimes, we almost forgot the daily danger in which we lived. There were no military objectives in the vicinity, so the Allied bombers which were almost continually droning overhead did not trouble us. Often, we would pause for a few seconds listening to the heavy crump of bombs in the distance, or to watch a group of Mustangs go streaking across the fields at low level looking for something worth destroying, but there was not even a railway line at the little village. At the moment it seemed as though we were living apart from all the horrors of modern warfare which were raging on either side.

Day by day the Allies moved nearer and nearer. The sleepy little village became a depot for wounded Germans, and ambulances were drawn under cover of the trees at the side of the farm. Several times the soldiers came into the farm for eggs and milk, but Madame's reply was invariably "The hens are not laying," or "The cows are dry." When these interviews were taking place, Fred and I remained in hiding. Our discovery would have meant death for the happy country folk who were protecting us.

News reached us one day that a detachment of British paratroops had landed in a forest thirty kilometres away. The man who brought this news had a large old car with its engine modified to run on charcoal. He was closely associated with a group of Maquis operating in the same forest, and told us that he knew how to make his way through the Germans (who were now preparing to make a stand in the district) and get us there the following day.

Fred and I considered the matter carefully. Although we had become very fond of our friends at the farm, we decided it was our duty to offer our services and local knowledge to the paratroops.True to his word, our new friend arrived the following day with his big car. Hasty farewells were spoken, lips pressed to tear-moistened cheeks, dry throats whispered goodbye and good luck, and we set off towards the rumbling of the distant artillery.

CHAPTER TWENTY-NINE

In the Forest

The main road was packed with retreating Germans on bicycles, motor-cycles, in trucks and any conveyance they could find. Some of them were tattered and torn, with dirty, unshaven faces, and their one thought was to retreat towards Germany. They had no time to pay any attention to the old saloon chugging along at a steady fifteen to twenty miles per hour in the opposite direction.Our driver was keeping to the lanes and minor roads as much as possible to reduce our chance of being machine-gunned by the RAF, but even so we were obliged to halt for several minutes on some occasions when the traffic became congested at crossroads.My colleague and I looked at the mass of enemy troops around us and then into the blue summer sky from which our own countrymen might swoop at any minute and blow us to pieces.

The British-American army was getting nearer and nearer; in a few weeks we might be on our way home, but before then we were bound to undergo days more dangerous than we had so far experienced. Supposing the Jerries made a successful stand, held the Allies at bay and the very forest in which we intended sheltering became a no-man's-land and got shelled and bombed by both sides!

We entered the small town of Sermaize-les-Bains which had been totally devastated in the 1914-18 War, then ransacked and looted when the German army came through again in 1940. One street bore the commemorative name 'Rue du 6 septembre 1914'. I though it rather ironic that I should parachute into France during another horrible conflict precisely 29 years later.

The first part of our journey had been completed without mishap. Our chauffeur ushered us quickly through a doorway and we found ourselves amongst a group of Resistance men.Everyone was very tense and nervous; the Allies were not far away and each underground worker was ready for the order to fight in the open. The town was on the northern edge of the *Forêt de Trois Fontaines*, which was thirty-six square miles of dense woodland. The leader of the group told us that we could stay the night in the house and enter the forest the following morning. There were several groups of

Maquis operating from inside and a few other Allied airmen amongst them. Our new friends did not know the exact whereabouts of the contingent of paratroops, but once we were inside with the Maquis we would be put in contact with them.

The following morning we woke to hear the gunfire sounding nearer; the enemy were being pushed farther and farther back towards Germany in an endless stream of traffic through the town.

We were taken by a guide a couple of miles into the forest to a clearing where a group of young men lounged about in the sunshine. We soon found that they were all airmen – three Americans, five Australians, and six Englishmen – most of whom had been shot down during the air battles which had taken place overhead during the past couple of weeks. Two of the Americans, however, had been evading capture for as long as myself, having made their way on foot from Belgium.

I asked where the paratroops could be found and learnt to my disappointment that instead of being several hundred strong, they were only a handful of Special Air Service men. Some of the airmen had already offered their services, but been told they would only be an encumbrance. The following night these SAS men left the forest to carry out sabotage against predetermined objectives farther afield.

The beaten German army, as it withdrew across France, was in a very ugly frame of mind. We had already heard of incidents quite nearby where hand grenades had been thrown from passing vehicles amongst groups of children playing in the streets. The most appalling accounts of atrocities had been circulating, just when we were getting so very near our long-awaited moment of liberation, which increased our anxiety.

We had spent several nights in the forest when a young Frenchman staggered through the bushes into the clearing. His face was terror-stricken and his whole body trembling. He was the sole survivor of the Maquis camp which Fred and I were originally supposed to have joined. Somehow, the Germans had found out the position, completely encircled it, then closed in, shooting every man as he tried to escape.

We realised immediately that it was unsafe for us to remain in the same position any longer and decided to disperse in twos and threes. Unfortunately for me, my constitution – which had kept me in perfect health for eleven months – had almost reached the end of its tether. I was suffering from malnutrition, the scabies had now become septic and my fingers and wrists became a mass of yellow discharge. Large abscesses had broken out on my body and I could hardly walk.

One of the RAF boys was Flight Sergeant Paddy Leary, an Irish rear gunner. He told us that a few weeks previously he had been treated for a sprained ankle by a doctor in a house at the edge of the forest. Studying a map, we found that the village was only six miles away. So, wishing the rest of the boys good luck, Fred and I set off with our compass slowly and painfully through the trees. A few hours later, we cautiously emerged from the bushes and stepped into the open to establish our exact position. Seeing a few landmarks we soon managed to locate Pargny-sur-Saulx, the village we wanted. An elderly woman was approaching along a cart track, so I stopped her and asked whether there were many Germans in the village and how near were the Allies.

She looked first at me from head to toe, then at Fred, and finally said, "You poor boys, you're hungry and tired." "She could not have spoken a truer word!" I said to Fred, imagining that she had guessed our identity. She continued the conversation, and I suddenly realised with horror that she thought we were two German deserters!

Fred still understood only a few words of French, so I turned to him and explained the situation, using something resembling a Scottish accent in an imitation of the German I had heard the Nazis using so often in the streets of Revigny and Bar-le-Duc.

The woman asked us if we were trying to get back home to Germany, or if we wanted to get taken prisoner by the Americans! I told her we both preferred the latter, as we had suffered too much bombing along the roads already. She agreed that it was terrible, and promised to return in half an hour with some food.

This was the first collaborator I had had the misfortune to stumble across since my descent into France. Needless to say, my Aussie pal and I did not wait to enjoy her generosity.

We boldly approached the village, located the house where we hoped to receive assistance, and knocked on the door. The householder, a man whose name was Adolphe, quickly beckoned us inside. He was a keen Resistance worker and enjoyed telling us that the Americans were on the outskirts of Vitry-le-François, only twenty-five kilometres away. We explained how we knew where to find him, and asked if he could contact the doctor on our behalf as he had done for the previous English guests.

Adolphe Bertrand was only too pleased to help us and spoke highly of Doctor Henri Fritsch who lived in the small town of Sermaize-les-Bains where Fred and I had slept before entering the *Forêt de Trois Fontaines* a few night previously. Although only four miles away down a straight road, we had walked much further through the trees from the clearing where we had left Paddy and the others.

The doctor was an outstanding personality, already well known as having been a gallant young officer in the First World War, having won the *Croix de Guerre* (three citations) and the Cross of *Chevalier* of the *Légion d'Honneur*. Later on, people were to learn of the allied airmen he had helped, and that he was a member of the BOA *(Bureau des Opérations Aériennes)*. He went under the code name 'Frédéric' and had participated in several parachute drops of arms and equipment.

When Adolphe pedalled away to contact the Doctor, Fred and I had a good wash and enjoyed a meal prepared by Mme Bertrand and her daughter. We felt very much better, especially when Adolphe returned to tell us that the Doctor – who normally toured the villages on a motor-cycle – would come to see us tomorrow and that we could stay where we were for the night.

CHAPTER THIRTY

The Four Villages

The following day we waited and waited for our visitor, peeping cautiously through the curtains at every man who passed along the road. Fred seemed to find the minutes passing very slowly; he too had contracted scabies, almost certainly through sharing the same blanket with myself for several weeks. We both felt like a pair of filthy animals and worried lest we should pass the infection on to our host and his spotlessly clean wife and daughter.

From the rear of the house we could look across the field and watch the flow of retreating Germans along the main highway. Nearby was a railway line, and Adolphe pointed out the twisted shapes of wrecked and burnt-out wagons – all that remained of an ammunition train which RAF fighter-bombers had attacked a few days previously. Unfortunately, several window panes in the house had been broken by the detonations. The edge of the woodland was only a few yards away from the house, so we lay in the long grass, peeping through the trees from time to time for our much-needed motor-cyclist.

There were various explosions, some being the demolition of bridges by the retreating army, but we also wondered about Allied and German shells passing overhead in opposite directions. We cringed lower to the ground when the pitter-patter through the leaves could be a stray bullet. We were two young men, trained in modern warfare but unarmed, hiding right in the front line, frightened and feeling ill, longing to be back home.

Adolphe arrived with no news of our motorcyclist, but with some food. He spoke of the distant sound of machine guns that seemed to come from the far side of the forest and of the pall of smoke in the sky which we could not see from our refuge. We wondered if a spearhead of the Allied army had already fought its way south of the forest and was now heading north towards Bar-le-Duc. There had been sounds of battle from down the road, at Sermaize-les-Bains. Had Fred and I actually been 'liberated', but left still hiding in the trees?

Later in the afternoon Adolphe again came to see us. This time he was trembling and brought horrifying news. Some German military vehicles had been passing through the small town square of Sermaize-les-Bains when, for some reason, they had paused. The terrified inhabitants took shelter as the German soldiers threw hand grenades into the shops and houses. Fires started and twenty people were badly injured; the German vehicles prepared to drive on. Just then, our motor-cyclist rode into the town. He stopped and quickly started administering first aid, but a soldier in the last departing lorry saw him and he was shot in the head, making a final death toll of thirteen inhabitants.

Sermaize-les-Bains, August 1944

Fred and I listened to this in silence. At home in England we had read of this sort of happening on the Russian front and imagined that a certain amount of exaggeration would have to be allowed for. Now we were almost face to face with the ghastly truth, and did not know if during the next few days we also might become victims of similar atrocities.

This disgusting atrocity was by no means an isolated incident. The machine-gunning we had heard during the day had been the sound of dozens of innocent men and boys being brutally murdered while four tiny villages alongside the forest were being burnt down. One of the RAF men from the forest was at the time hiding in the cellars of a house which was burnt down. Incredibly, mid-upper gunner Sgt.

Albert De Bruin – an Englishman with a French name – survived.

In the centre of the little community of Robert Espagne, with less than a thousand inhabitants, several German vehicles came to a standstill. The soldiers dismounted, burst into the houses and dragged the menfolk out into the streets, shouting *"Arbeit! Arbeit!"* and indicating that the men were required to do some digging. Fortunately, most of the men were working in the fields at the time, bringing in the last of the harvest. Nevertheless, in a short time an unhappy group of fifty old men and young lads were being driven down the street towards the railway station.

Every house was being ransacked, mattresses torn open, heaped on the ground floors and set alight. One after another the houses burst into flames and women and girls ran out screaming for mercy. *"Nicht Pitié"* was the only reply. A man made a dash towards his burning home and was shot in the back. The prisoners were too well covered to stand the slightest chance of escape. They were lined up in threes at the side of the railway while their homes were burning to the ground.

One woman approached the officer in charge and asked if she could give a small package of food to her husband before they took him away. The soldiers all laughed and said "Your husband won't need any food where he is going." Whereupon they counted the prisoners and then started counting their ammunition.

"How many are there?" called one soldier. "About fifty, I think," came the reply. "Have you got enough cartridges?" continued the first one, as he counted his own, watched by fifty pairs of petrified eyes.

Just then, a captain arrived. Standing on a lorry, he gave orders for three machine guns to be placed in position, one in front and the others at either side of the potential victims. The women realised their intentions and pleaded for mercy, trying to awake a little pity in the captain's brutal heart. They tried to make him understand the injustice to humanity he was going to commit if he carried out the massacre.

"One officer and three men have been killed by partisans near here, and this village, together with several others, is going to pay the penalty for the crime," he said. Then, turning to the men, he added, "We've no more time to waste; the Americans will be here tomorrow."

A deathly silence fell as the gunners took aim; women watched a few yards away as their husbands and sons stood hand-in-hand waiting for death, rooted to the spot with fear. An order was barked, and the three machine guns began mowing down the defenceless group. Fifty Frenchmen had paid the penalty for an ambush carried out by a handful of British SAS troops.

Aftermath. Some of the 52 men and boys machine-gunned at Robert Espagne

The barbarians reboarded their vehicles, which were by now full of radio sets and other valuables looted from the blazing village, and set off towards the north. A short while later the village of Beurey, only a mile away, was also in flames, and machine guns were heard again. Fortunately, most of the inhabitants had fled into the forest; they had seen evidence of the inhumanity of the soldiers only a couple of days previously.

For quite a while the Luftwaffe had occupied the Château Salleron, a fine building on the outskirts of the village, without causing any trouble to the population. This day, however, a contingent of soldiers had approached the Château, possibly with the idea of using it as a billet. The Luftwaffe apparently had different ideas; they quarrelled, a brawl broke out and shots were fired. Nazis were killing Nazis. The Luftwaffe withdrew, leaving several dead comrades behind.

A few miles away, another little village, Couvonges, had received a visit from a detachment of the 29th RI (3rd DI) under command of a Lieutenant Fritsch, i/c 10th Company, and was now in flames. A house-to-house search had been made, and twenty-four more innocent victims fell to Nazi bullets. Two old farmers, M.Vignon and M.Petitprêtre, aged eighty-eight and seventy-eight respectively, were too ill and weak to walk to their own execution, so they were burnt alive in their beds. A fourth village, Mogneville, was also the scene of similar brutalities. It is a cruel coincidence that the German officer bore the same surname as the gallant French doctor.

Aftermath. The scene where 26 men and boys (from a total male population of 44) were shot at Couvonges

> Extrait de la déposition faite devant la Chambre civique de la Cour
> de Justice de Strasbourg par **M. Joseph Schmitt**, alsacien enrôlé dans
> la Wehrmacht et faisant partie de l'unité qui opéra le 29 août 1944
> à Couvonges :
>
> « ... J'eus connaissance de l'ordre de fusiller les hommes de Couvonges
> le 29 août 1944 entre midi 30 et 13 heures.
>
> J'en informai le Maire environ dix minutes après, au moment même
> où les soldats boches commençaient à cerner les maisons et à rassembler
> les hommes...
>
> Vers 13 heures est venu un second ordre de fusiller aussi les femmes
> de Couvonges ainsi que les habitants de Robert-Espagne. Je devais porter
> cet ordre aux Commandants de Compagnie ; au lieu de le faire, je l'ai
> déchiré... »
>
> LIBÉRATION SANGLANTE
de quatre villages

An excerpt from LIBERATION SANGLANTE de quatre villages Meusiens – The bloody
liberation of the four Meusian villages – published in May 1946 to aid the families of the
victims.
It is an extract from the evidence given by Joseph Schmitt (from Alsace) to the Court of
Justice in Strasbourg. Schmitt was enrolled in the Wehrmacht, and was part of the unit in
Couvonges on 29 August 1944.

> *"I had knowledge of the order to shoot the men of Couvonges on the 29th*
> *August 1944 between 12:30 and 13:00.*
>
> *I told the Mayor of this about 10 minutes later, at the exact moment that the*
> *boche (German) soldiers began to surround the houses and gather-up the*
> *men...*
>
> *At about 13:00 there came a second order, to shoot also the women of*
> *Couvonges as well as the inhabitants of Robert Espagne. I had to give this*
> *order to the Company Commanders; instead of doing that, I tore it up..."*

Adolphe pushed his way through the bushes in the evening, his
face white and his hands shaking. He said the Americans might be in
Pargny-sur-Saulx the following day, but such terrible things had
happened in the neighbourhood that he asked us if we would return
to his home, lock and barricade the doors and help him to defend his
wife and daughter with the aid of two shotguns he had been hiding
since the German occupation. We instantly agreed, and followed him
to his house just beyond the edge of the trees.

Sometimes during the previous twelve months I had had a
feeling of self-satisfaction at successfully evading capture for so

long. It had seemed quite a romantic situation and I thought of the pleasure I should get when I told friends of the exciting times I had played hide and seek behind the enemy lines. But now circumstances had changed. I was seeing warfare at its absolute worst, very far removed from the comparatively sporting air battles where it was a case of 'kill or be killed, and may the best man win.' There was certainly no thought of bravado in the two young airmen, one from England, the other from Australia, both in a pitiful physical state, who waited up all night clutching a shotgun, knowing their liberators were only a few miles away yet wondering if they would be alive to meet them.

Adolphe had sworn that if any Germans entered the house, it would be over his dead body. Fred had solemnly supported him with similar grim promises. During the night, Germans were moving on all sides of the house; hand grenades were thrown into the post office, cutting telephone communications, and all bridges were blown up – sure signs that evacuation was imminent.

CHAPTER THIRTY-ONE

Liberation

At dawn, the village was as silent as a graveyard, and the anxious faces peering through the Venetian blinds could not see a single Nazi in sight. The sun rose and birds began to sing. It was a glorious summer morning, but nobody left the houses; they were all watching and waiting. Fred and I peered through the windows across the field towards the main road. At last came the sight for which we had waited so long. Two mud-bespattered American tanks came nosing their way cautiously along the highway, expecting mines to explode beneath them or anti-tank guns to bellow from any building or clump of bushes ahead. A few seconds passed; people could not quite believe their own eyes. Then a door opened and someone began racing across the fields; soon the population were in hot pursuit, rushing towards the liberators.

The tanks were followed by a pair of armour-plated cars, a couple of ambulances and vehicles with bridge-building equipment. They paused for a few moments and I was able to get close enough to announce my identity. As one American leaned out to shake hands, he turned to a pal in the vehicle and said, "Say, Joe, here's an English flyer who was running around France before you enlisted!"

The liberating forces arrive in Revigny at the 'Place de l'Hotel de Ville', 31 August 1944

A lieutenant told Fred and me to lie low for a few more days because this was only a spearhead forcing its way through, and behind them were lots of pockets of enemy troops holding out. But the happiness of the population who had been under German occupation for so many years was too great to be restrained, and as soon as they had finished cheering the Americans on their way, they turned to Fred and me to carry us shoulder-high through the streets.Everyone seemed to produce a bottle of champagne: this was the most wonderful morning the village had ever known. My companion and I eventually found ourselves on the balcony of the town hall, with the entire population cheering frantically below. The *Marseillaise* was sung again and again. Poor Fred could still hardly understand a word of French, but every time a glass of champagne was thrust into his hand he emptied it.

We had seen no other American troops since the advance detachment the previous morning but learnt that a larger force had pushed its way round the other side of the forest, passing through Robert Espagne, Beurey, Couvonges and Mogneville less than twenty-four hours after the massacres had taken place.

We were asked to attend the funeral of the doctor and the twelve villagers whose lives he had tried to save. At Requiem Mass the thirteen coffins were put at the foot of the altar, and Fred and I occupied seats of honour with relatives and leading officials. In the cemetery we each filed past the graves, making the sign of the Cross with an olive branch.

The roadway was believed to be cleared of Germans right through to Revigny, and Adolphe found a man who was willing to take the risk of running us that far in his car. At Revigny we found our old friend Louis bubbling over with the excitement of the recent liberation; his brother Jean had jumped on to the first American tank to enter the town, and continued with it as guide towards Germany. The rest of the boys were busy in the woods round about, mopping up pockets of resisting Germans. Raymond and my Russian friend Arkadi had both been slightly wounded in the course of the fighting.

A doctor examined me and insisted that I be taken immediately to Bar-le-Duc Hospital for attention, instead of joining my colleagues in the revengeful annihilation of Nazis.It was almost midnight when we reached the hospital gates, and as I followed the black-flowing robes of the nun who was on night duty up the staircase to the men's ward, I became faint. I remember being guided to a chair, and the lady with the white coif round her face putting a lump of sugar between my lips, telling me to suck it slowly and breathe deeply.Soon I was fast asleep in a hospital bed, but awoke with a start in the early hours of the morning to the familiar sounds of machine-guns and hand grenades. A determined group of enemy troops had come out of the woods and were making a futile attempt to retake the town.

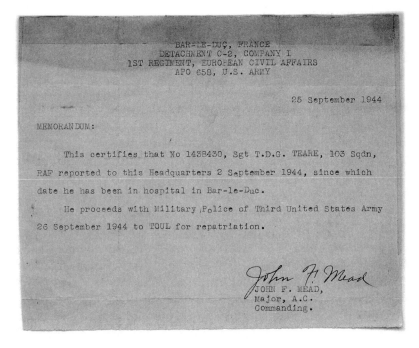

BAR-LE-DUC, FRANCE
DETACHMENT C-2, COMPANY I
1ST REGIMENT, EUROPEAN CIVIL AFFAIRS
APO 658, U.S. ARMY

25 September 1944

MEMORANDUM:

This certifies that No 1438430, Sgt T.D.G. TEARE, 103 Sqdn, RAF reported to this Headquarters 2 September 1944, since which date he has been in hospital in Bar-le-Duc.

He proceeds with Military Police of Third United States Army 26 September 1944 to TOUL for repatriation.

John F. Mead
JOHN F. MEAD,
Major, A.C.
Commanding.

Liberation for 'Denis Lebenec'

News that I was back in Bar-le-Duc soon travelled round the town. One of the first people to visit me was M.Althuser, the photographer who had created my false identity. He had been convicted of possessing forged food coupons and confined in the former girl's school that had been converted into the prison I had seen. The windows had been blocked up and the classrooms divided by brick partitions to make separate cells. Robert Lhuerre and Jean Pornot were both imprisoned here also. Robert Lhuerre had been here since the fateful day in June when the Gestapo raided as I was speaking to him, Jean Pornot was the lad who had lent me his bicycle to flee the town that same afternoon. As Jean Althuser had been convicted of a minor crime, and the Germans were not aware of his Resistance activities, they took advantage if his bi-lingual ability and made him a messenger within the establishment.

He told me that on 28 August he went to Robert's cell and told him that he was about to leave the prison. Robert replied "I think they are going to kill me", whereby Althuser said that he thought it could be a general evacuation. The final words he heard from Robert concerned whether or not he should take his overcoat with him. Whenever I had seen Robert, he had always been smart and well-groomed, so now, true to form, he climbed aboard the back of an army lorry wearing a tie and carrying a neatly folded overcoat. Jean Pornot, a Russian prisoner of war, and two other young Frenchmen were also aboard. The vehicle came to rest on the outskirts of the town, and as four of the men disembarked they were shot in the head. The fifth, one of the young Frenchman, made a desperate dash for the trees, but was shot down and then crushed to death by the vehicle.

Other prisoners were dispatched elsewhere with similar brutality, but by the following day only four soldiers remained on guard. The citizens of Bar-le-Duc stormed the building and released Jean Althuser and the forty surviving inmates.The population of the town was fifteen thousand, and in the course of that evening the German *Feldkommandant* ordered the Mayor to announce that if a single shot was fired during the night, the entire town would be burnt down.

Thus ended the final twenty-four hours that Bar-le-Duc suffered after four years of Nazi occupation. Before the next day was over, the first vehicles of the United States Third Army reached the outskirts of the town.

Another familiar figure approached from the end of the ward: the man with the sly smile and twinkle in his eyes who had helped me so much – none other than M.X. I now learnt that his real name was Jean Jeukens, the previous day he had been elected *'Président de la Délégation Spéciale'*, and later he became Mayor of Bar-le-Duc.

He said that I had led a charmed life whilst living in France and that he himself was astounded at the way I always seemed to walk out of trouble, just one step ahead of the Gestapo. I asked him the date; it was now 5 September 1944, exactly one year since I had left my aerodrome in Lincolnshire to bomb Mannheim.

I received tender care from the hospital doctor and his devoted nuns for almost a month. They even bestowed upon me the entitlement

Robert Lhuerre and Jean Pornot, 28th August 1944

The five prisoners executed by the retreating Nazi forces. This photograph was taken by Jean Althuser the day he was 'liberated'

of a wounded French soldier of a full bottle of red wine at my bedside each day.News reached the outlying villages and more familiar faces came to my bedside, wonderful people who I recognised so well but to whom I could not put a real name; previously it would have been wrong of me to ask. My existence had been wrapped in secrecy for twelve months, but now the fictitious Denis Lebenec had gone for ever. Now it was the original *aviateur anglais* who, although deeply aware of the disgusting cruelties that had been recently inflicted, sat up in bed laughing and

Jean Jeukens – Monsieur'X', as Mayor, celebrates the anniversary of the liberation with General Charles de Gaulle at Bar-le-Duc, 1946

joking with his friends. The area was liberated, and those who had survived had good reason for rejoicing.

Bill Johnson and Ginger Brown called at the hospital before leaving for England, and Bill kindly said that he would visit my parents in Liverpool. This indeed he did, giving them the first news that I was still alive.In the later weeks it had been good to have Fred White, my Australian colleague, alongside me. We stayed together until the US Military Police provided transport to Paris, where we boarded an aeroplane for England.

Skimming over the Channel in a Dakota, I realised how extremely lucky I had been. I owed my life to the loyalty, courage and kindness of so many everyday French people. These people had risked everything to protect me; I owed them a debt of gratitude which I would never forget.

A post-war Resistance celebration. In the foreground, left to right:
Jean Jeukens – Monsieur'X'; Mme Brion; Jules Brion; Jean Althuser

Epilogue

The war in Europe was by no means over when I was joyfully re-united with my parents in England, having – as far as they were concerned – come back from the dead. It was difficult to know what to say about my one-year's absence. I was obliged not to reveal the circumstances of my escape and evasion, and I carried a document stating that I could not be questioned about my time in enemy-occupied territory without the authorisation of the War Office.

---

103 SQUADRON
NO. 1. GROUP.
BOMBER COMMAND

FL/ SGT. TEARE. T.D.G.
Royal Air Force No. 1438430

RESTRICTED

WAR DEPARTMENT
The Adjutant General's Office, Washington

AG 383.6 (31 Jul 43) OB-S-B-M   6 August 1943   KLS/el-2B-939 Pentagon

SUBJECT : Amended Instructions Concerning Publicity in Connection with Escaped Prisoners of War, to include Evaders of Capture in Enemy or Enemy-Occupied Territory and Internees in Neutral Countries.

TO : The Commanding Generals,
      Army Ground :
      Army Air Forces :
    The Commander-in-Chief, Southwest Pacific Area :
    The Commanding Generals,
      Theaters of Operations :
      Defense Commands :
      Departments :
      Base Commands :
    The Commanding Officers,
      Base Commands :
    Director, Bureau of Public Relations.

1. Publication or communication to any unauthorized persons of experiences of escape or evasion from enemy-occupied territory, internment in a neutral country, or release from internment not only furnishes useful information to the enemy but also jeopardizes future escapes, evasions and releases.

2. Personnel will not, unless authorized by the Assistant Chief of Staff, G-2, War Department General Staff, publish in any form whatever or communicate either directly, or indirectly, to the press, radio or an unauthorized person any account of escape or evasion of capture from enemy or enemy-occupied territory, or internment in a neutral country either before or after repatriation. They will be held strictly responsible for all statements contained in communications to friends which may subsequently be published in the press or otherwise.

3. Evaders, escapees, or internees shall not be interrogated on the circumstances of their experiences in escape, evasion or internment except by the agency designated by the Assistant Chief of Staff, G-2, War Department General Staff, or the corresponding organization in overseas theaters of operations. In allied or neutral countries, American Military Attaches are authorized to interrogate on escape, evasion and internment matters.

4. Should the services of escaped prisoners of war, evaders, or internees be deemed necessary for lecturing and briefing such services will be under the direct supervision of the agency designated by the Assistant Chief of Staff, G-2, War Department General Staff, or the corresponding organization in overseas theaters of operations.

5. Commanding Officers will be responsible for instructing all evaders, escapees, and internees in the provisions of this directive which supersedes letter, AG 383.6 (5 Nov. 42) OB-S-B-M, 7 November 1942, subject : Instructions concerning Publicity in Connection with Escaped Prisoners of War and other previous instructions on this subject.

By order of the Secretary of War :

/s/ J. A. ULIO
J. A. ULIO
Major General,
The Adjutant General.

1. Information about your escape or your evasion from capture *would be useful to the enemy* and a danger to your friends. It is therefore *SECRET*.

2. *a*   You must therefore not disclose, except to the first Military Attache to whom you report, or to an officer designated by the Commanding General of the Theater of Operations, or by A. C. of S., G-2, W.D.
    (1) The names of those who helped you.
    (2) The method by which you escaped or evaded.
    (3) The route you followed.
    (4) Any other facts concerning your experience.
  b   You must be particularly on your guard with persons representing the press.
  c   You must give no account of your experiences in books, newspapers, periodicals or in broadcasts or in lectures.
  d   You must give no information to anyone, irrespective of nationality, in letters or in conversation, except as specifically directed in Par. 4.
  e   No lectures or reports are to be given to any unit without the permission of A. C. of S., G-2, W. D., or corresponding organization in the theater.

CERTIFICATE

I have read the above and certify that I will comply with it.
I understand that any information concerning my *escape* or *evasion* from capture is *SECRET* and must not be disclosed to anyone other than the agency designated by A. C. of S., G-2, War Department, the corresponding organization in overseas theaters of operations, or the Military Attache in a neutral country to whom I first report. I understand that disclosure to anyone else will make me liable to disciplinary action.

Name (Print) _____   Signed _____

Rank _____ A. S. N. _____   Dated _____

Unit _____   Witness _____

RESTRICTED

Don't tell anybody anything...

I reported to an RAF Convalescent Depot on Blackpool Promenade, known locally as 'cripple's corner'. Here the treatment for malnutrition and general debility included daily spoonfuls of cod-liver oil and malt, sun-ray lamps and lots of table tennis against the sick and wounded.

Three months later I was officially considered to be physically fit. However, I was still tormented with continual nightmares: always running away, although I knew the danger was over. I could not discuss this problem with anyone, and came to realise that there were so many things I actually did not want to forget. Not just the atrocities, which people were unlikely to believe, but also all the wonderful kindness I had received too. To ease my problems I wrote down the names of certain villages and their inhabitants in a small notebook, for my private reference only.

My activities in France excluded me from any further flying duties in Europe, and I was to receive 18 months rest before even being considered for warfare in the Pacific. I was posted to a disused airfield in Shropshire, in the position of doing very little as long as the CO didn't realise. This gave me full opportunity to scribble down all the details that were still so fresh in my mind. When I was eventually demobilised, I left the RAF carrying a very personal and very precious bundle of notebooks.

After five years of military service, I needed some adaption back into civilian life. I promptly declined the mundane position awaiting me at the Trustee Savings Bank, and instead went into training as a professional fire-fighter. That training was followed by three years service in the industrial town of Widnes. After that I made my livelihood as a self-employed man in a wide variety of enterprises.

Twenty-five years ago I moved to the Isle of Man – back to the land of my ancestors, to enjoy a semi-retirement of tranquillity, restoring a dilapidated farmhouse set in 30 acres of hillside. More recently I moved to a bungalow in the small port of

Jeanette Patural of Sampigny, now Madame Petrowski of Bar-le-Duc with the author. For over 50 years Jeanette has telephoned or posted birthday greetings on the 22nd December.

Ramsey. Throughout I have managed to maintain contact with my wartime compatriots, through holidays, reunions and visits. Even today, more than half a century after the end of the Second World War, I still look forward to the regular contacts from the children and grandchildren of the people who once knew an *aviateur anglais* called Denis Lebenec.

Paying tribute to the fallen in Revigny on the 50th anniversary of the Liberation. Denys Teare (left) and Louis Chenu

APPENDIX
Lancaster I ED751 'S for Sugar'

By the fateful night of 5 September 1943, the all-NCO crew of Lancaster 'S for Sugar' had already taken part in the four major raids on Hamburg and been to Berlin and the Ruhr Valley many times. They had also made a couple of long-distance raids to Italy, one of which involved climbing over the Alps and then descending for a low-level moonlight attack on the Pirelli factory at Milan. At this time, the average loss rate in Bomber Command was 4% per operation. Given that a 'tour' (the minimum duty a crew could undertake) consisted of thirty operations, it was certainly a most unhealthy occupation. Such were the odds that faced the aircrew of Bomber Command in 1943.

Bob Cant was the captain of 'S for Sugar'. He was a warrant officer and his crew was one of the most experienced on 103 Squadron. They were a crew of survivors, sometimes known to have said, "the shrapnel was so bloody thick up there, we could have got out and walked home on it!"

On the night of 5 September the crew of 'S for Sugar' were scheduled to fly in the first phase of the attack against Mannheim, bombing immediately behind the Pathfinder Force. They had been to Mannheim the previous month with the usual bomb load for that distance:

    1 x 4,000lb High capacity;
    3 x 1,000lb Medium capacity;
    48 x 30lb Incendiaries;
    540 x 4lb Incendiaries.

On that occasion there had been a vicious exchange of gun-fire with a German night fighter and Bob Parkinson in the rear turret duly registered a 'claim' of having damaged one Messerschmitt 110.

As 'S' for Sugar took-off from Elsham Wolds on the night of 5 September, the crew were:

    Bob Cant, the twenty-one year old pilot, from Mansfield;
    Bill Milburn, the mid-upper gunner, from Whitehaven;
    Eric Dickson, the flight engineer, from Cheltenham;
    George Thomas, the navigator, from Watford;
    Bob Parkinson, the rear gunner, from Wigan;

Syd Horton, the wireless operator, also from Wigan; and Denys Teare, the air bomber.

The crew of Lancaster S for Sugar:
Horton, Teare, Cant, Parkinson, Thomas, Milburn, Dickson

The trouble on this second visit to Mannheim started with heavy flak as they crossed the European coast. By the time they approached the target area only three engines were running; they were behind time and 5,000ft below the main force. The bombs were dropped on target, but another engine was lost on the homeward journey. When one of the two remaining engines caught fire, the aircraft began to go down. Bob Cant gave the order to bale out, then bravely held on to the controls for vital seconds whilst the crew baled-out from their respective escape hatches before abandoning the blazing aircraft himself. With all its crew gone, the crippled 'S for Sugar' swung round in a steep horseshoe, then plunged down and crashed in the forest of Koeurs, fifty miles south of Luxembourg, exploding on impact.

At Elsham Wolds on the morning of 6 September, there were seven unoccupied chairs at the breakfast table in the Sergeants' Mess and word was passed around that 'S' for Sugar had not got back. Once it was known that 'S' for Sugar had not landed somewhere in England, the Service Police entered the crew's Nissen huts to parcel-up and remove their personal possessions. Post Office workers soon delivered the ominous telegrams that would bring heartbreak to seven households. Within twenty-four hours a brand-new crew of volunteers moved into the hut, straight from their training stations, ready to fly on their first operation.

Meanwhile, the crew from 'S for Sugar' were scattered over the French countryside. These are their stories.

Bob Cant

Bob Cant landed safely and had just buried his parachute when a Frenchman appeared, who ushered him into a barn where he was concealed under the hay. Later in the day the door opened and he was joined by Bill Milburn – the mid-upper gunner. Helped by the local population

they moved from contact to contact. Dressed in civilian clothes, sometimes on bicycle and sometimes on foot, they made their way towards Switzerland. Eventually they were both smuggled safely across the border and were joined shortly afterwards by Eric Dickson, the flight engineer.

Eric Dickson, Bob Cant and Bill Milburn in Switzerland

Syd Horton and Bob Parkinson

Bob Parkinson and Syd Horton landed almost side-by-side in the moonlight. They walked as far as Bar-le-Duc, from where they were helped right across France (via Paris) to Quimper in Brittany. Hidden beneath the deck of a small fishing boat, they brazenly sailed out right beneath the vigilant harbour defences. After three days on the open sea they were jubilantly escorted into Falmouth by the Royal Navy. Both men were subsequently 'mentioned in dispatches'.

George Thomas landed safely, but then walked 150 miles before anyone dare shelter him in their home. He was then assisted across Paris and on to the long journey south towards the Spanish frontier. Two months later he reached the foothills of the Pyrenees and joined a small multi-national group of civilians trying to escape occupied Europe. A guide led them high into the mountain range, until a point was reached where he assured them that beyond a distant ridge they could walk downhill into neutral Spain. He then turned back to avoid German patrols. It was now November and a blizzard set in. Four days later, one person had died in the snow and the rest were trying to survive by eating frozen moss scraped from the rocks when a German patrol spotted them. George was taken back to Paris, accused of being a

George Thomas

spy and interrogated by the Gestapo in the notorious Fresnes prison. On 15 August 1944 George was one of 168 Allied airmen transferred to the infamous Buchenwald Concentration Camp, with an explicit instruction that they were not to go to any other prison camp. Fortunately, the Luftwaffe heard of this and had them transferred to POW camps in October 1944. George was eventually liberated from Stalag Luft 4B.

Thus the entire crew of 'S for Sugar' survived the war. This survival is all the more remarkable given that at the time, only one in eight Bomber Command airmen survived being shot down. Of these, only one per cent managed to evade capture and return home safely.

Crew reunion in the Isle of Man, 1979 (with a piece of S for Sugar):
Left to right:
George Thomas (standing), Denys Teare, Bill Milburn, Bob Parkinson, Bob Cant (standing)